1990

This book is an attempt to answer the question, 'What is a person?' Although the answer is given in largely theoretical terms, the primary concern of the book is with practice: what does it mean to live as a human person in community with others? What personal, social and political practices are required by personal being?

Christian trinitarian theology is woven together with contemporary social thought to give an account of individuality and of the various dimensions of personal existence (the psychological, the interpersonal, the material, the institutional, the political, the spiritual) in terms of communication. We are called into personhood and become the unique persons we are through relation with others.

The call to personhood

The call to personhood

A Christian theory of the individual
in social relationships

ALISTAIR I. McFADYEN

Lecturer, Department of Theology and Religious Studies
University of Leeds

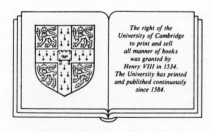

The right of the
University of Cambridge
to print and sell
all manner of books
was granted by
Henry VIII in 1534.
The University has printed
and published continuously
since 1584.

CAMBRIDGE UNIVERSITY PRESS

Cambridge
New York · Port Chester
Melbourne · Sydney

Published by the Press Syndicate of the University of Cambridge
The Pitt Building, Trumpington Street, Cambridge CB2 1RP
40 West 20th Street, New York, NY 10011, USA
10 Stamford Road, Oakleigh, Melbourne 3166, Australia

© Cambridge University Press 1990

First published 1990

Printed in Great Britain at the University Press, Cambridge

British Library cataloguing in publication data

McFadyen, Alistair I. (Alistair Iain), 1961–
   The call to personhood.
   1. Self. Christian viewpoints
   1. Title
   233

Library of Congress cataloguing in publication data

McFadyen, Alistair I.
   The call to personhood: A Christian theory of the individual in
social relationships / Alistair I. McFadyen.
      p.   cm.
   ISBN 0 521 38471 0/ISBN 0 521 40929 2 pbk
   1. Interpersonal relations – Religious aspects – Christianity.
2. Christianity – Psychology. 3. Man (Christian theology)
4. Sociology, Christian. 5. Church and social problems. 6. Self-
actualization (Psychology) – Religious aspects – Christianity.
1. Title.
BV4597.52.M4   1990
233'5 – cc20   90–32316 CIP

ISBN 0 521 38471 0 hardback

ISBN 0 521 40929 2 paperback

VN

For Patsy, my mother,
      who has taught me most about being for others in relationships;
and for Lynn, my wife,
      who knows better than anyone how little I know.

Contents

Acknowledgements

We become the people we are through our relationships with others; it is other people who enable us to become persons who, as such, may exercise a degree of autonomy in our lives and may say, think and do certain things as contributors to various discourses and fields of interaction. That is the basic premiss of this book. It is therefore no easy thing to discern the range of people who have influenced one in a specific respect, or to gauge the degree of their influence. I am painfully aware of this as I come to acknowledge publicly my indebtedness to those who have, in some way or another, contributed to the reflections contained in this book and who continue to influence me in more ways, I am sure, than I can ever hope to be aware of. Given the premiss of this work, the list of all those who have contributed to and influenced it implicitly and tangentially would probably have to extend to everyone I have ever met and include many whom I have never met but whose influence is more generally dispersed. Trying to identify all these people, even if it were possible, would be rather pointless, would be rather precious on my part and would make for incredibly tedious reading. I have therefore confined these acknowledgements to those who I know have had a significant and direct influence on this work – as well as on me whilst I have been writing it – and hope that others will understand the reasons for limiting the list in this way.

Daniel W. Hardy supervised the research and the writing of the Ph.D. thesis on which this book is based. It would certainly have been a very different and much impoverished project were it not for his interest and generosity in leading me on to new insights through our conversations. These conversations, apart from communicating specific insights, proved invaluable when I came to think through how one becomes a subject of a particular discourse, how one's autonomy may be called out by the creation of space within the relation, how coercion can be avoided.

I also owe an immense debt of gratitude to David F. Ford for his support, encouragement and advice concerning the revision of an unwieldy and too often unreadable thesis into the more accessible language of a book. His help has consistently gone way beyond anything which could reasonably be expected either of a colleague or a friend; without him I suspect that the book would simply not have appeared.

Several other people have also made comments on various parts of the work which have helped me come to a deeper understanding and appreciation of the issues than I would otherwise have achieved. Peter Scott's contribution to the finished article is hard to gauge accurately, since so much of my thinking has developed in dialogue with him; he has been a much-valued friend as well as a conversation-partner throughout the whole of the work. Haddon Willmer and Kim Knott, although more recent conversation-partners, have also been immensely supportive and generous with their comments on the text. Their own work – in particular on the influence of place on ecclesiology (Haddon) and on ethnicity, religion and identity (Kim) – helped me to see more clearly some of the implications of my views. It is also largely through them that I have come to learn what community means in an academic context.

I should also like to thank Alex Wright of Cambridge University Press for his incredible patience in dealing with such a novice at publishing, and for his many comments upon the text. Thanks are also due to Ingrid Lawrie for typing the final draft of Chapter 1 from an original which had been corrected and otherwise scribbled on to a ridiculous extent, and to Dorothy Greenwood, who assisted in this.

Perhaps most thanks must go to Lynn McFadyen, for without her support, encouragement and understanding during the six years it has taken from beginning the research to delivery of the final typescript to the publisher, nothing would have been possible.

The primary task of acknowledgements is to show that authorship is never simply and purely individual; notwithstanding this, however, authorship must remain something personal if it is to have any meaning. Whilst many different people may have contributed to a book in often decisive ways, an author has ultimately to take personal responsibility for it, not least because others may have reservations regarding its content. In particular in this respect I would like to distance those I have mentioned above from any errors in logic, understanding or judgment which may be found in the book, and from any terminological problems which may remain as evidence of the work's original incarnation as a Ph.D. thesis.

Introduction

In this book I am trying to answer some very basic questions concerning human being. What is a person? What is individual identity, and where does it come from? What makes us the people we are? The simplicity of these questions is deceptive. It is rarely as easy to give a good answer as it is to raise a good question. But simplistic answers to these questions abound and present themselves in our unanalysed common sense of what it is to be a human person, and therefore of what is good, right, normal and acceptable in personal existence. Such quick answers are both unhelpful and cheap. They are cheap because they save us from facing difficult issues, such as the origin of our views about what is good, right, normal and acceptable in personal existence, and the practical effects which these normative constructions of personhood and personal existence have. Simplistic answers which fail to account for the complex and manifold dimensions of human life are also dangerous because they will be bound to practices which are careless of the full reality of what it means to be a person. A distorted understanding of personal existence will be tied to distortions in its practice.

These questions are intensely practical. I shall explain later why my answer to them tends to operate at a rather generalised, abstract and formalistic level and why I adopt a systematic terminology. It is far from intended as a purely intellectual act of contemplation. My concern throughout is with practice and, even where my argument is at its most theoretical, I hope that it is not pure theory but functions rather as a theory of the practice of the various dimensions of personal life and of person-making. I believe, in other words, that people live and are as this theory suggests, although it may rarely come to explicit articulation in our lives.

Indeed, the reflections which resulted in this book began in my own experience of nursing in a psychiatric hospital. The questions I attempt to answer in it were first raised in the most practical ways possible, as I met people whose identities and capacities for relation appeared to be distorted in some way, those who had been injured by the networks of relation surrounding them, and those for whom society had no room because their behaviour in or perception of the world was not socially acceptable. I was not only confronted by the people, of course: I also became part of the institution of the hospital. As with all institutions there was a practical understanding of what it is to be a person operating in it, shaping the identities and relations of those of us who worked or lived within its ambit – at least while we were there. In order to comprehend the nature of psychiatric disturbance and therapy I had to try to discern and to understand how people and relations become broken, but also how the institution functioned either to heal or to exacerbate problems.

The question of what it is to be a person is raised in a particularly acute way in a context such as this, and that is one of the reasons why I think it might help the reader if I continue to use it as a source of illustration and reflection in this Introduction. However, I want to be clear before proceeding that the question does not only arise in extreme situations and in extreme ways such as this, but concerns all of us in the mundane, humdrum aspects of our lives. There is an infinite range of situations in everyday life in which people are less than persons and in which we need to think about what it means to be a human person. It may be necessary to ask the question as we are shopping, as we sit next to others on a bus, as we bicker with our partners. Even in these situations, the question may be complex and perplexing, but it cannot be avoided except by running away from ourselves, from others and from God. The benefit of using an extreme situation as an example is that it can help to clarify the issues; the danger is that it can also help to remove the recognition and discussion of those issues from the 'normal', mundane, everyday situations in which most of us confront them a good deal of the time.

The question of the person in such a place as a psychiatric hospital is urgent, necessary, complex and provocative. In it the various dimensions of personal existence which I am trying to make sense of in this book were all present together: the psychological, the social, the interpersonal, the material, the political, the institutional, the technical and the spiritual. This overlaying of the dimensions of personal life generated an array of explanations and expectations of what it means to be a person which functioned within the institution. Sometimes these were interlaced and overlaid in a way that did justice to the multidimensionality of personal existence, perhaps with different explanations (and, in this context, different interventions) appropriate at different levels or at different points. But otherwise they competed with each other, especially when a claim to exclusivity was made for a particular explanation. These different ways of conceiving the person are associated with different practices, so which ones are operating and how they interrelate can make a very significant difference to the treatment given. The following two examples may help to illustrate this point.

A conceptuality which explains everything with reference to the individual alone, for instance, will try to trace the origins of pathology within the individual and will then treat internal states without reference to the person's relationships. The most common form of this individualistic explanation attends almost exclusively to the material reality of the individual's body, explaining disorders of personal identity or behaviour in biological or chemical terms. Therapy is then a matter of physical, usually chemical, intervention. Counselling and other more personal forms of therapy will tend not to be offered. Much criticism has been made of the general biochemical medical model in the last twenty-five years, not least because this way of interpreting disease discourages carers from interacting with patients in a personal way. Patients become 'the hip in bed 3'. Interaction is with the bits of their bodies which are malfunctioning. The patient is present as body (and often only as a bit of body), not as person, for illness is not considered a personal experience but an objective, physical syndrome. Similarly, healing is entirely a matter of professional intervention in the patient's body, so she or he is not involved in that either.

Alternatively, a conceptuality of the person in which relationships are thought to determine personal identity might be operating. In this case, attention might be shifted from the individual to the network of family relationships. There may be attempts, for example, to intervene in the family structure rather than in the individual's body. The individual presenting the illness is then considered the symptom of the family's illness. Work done with the individual will tend to be of the interpretative sort. The patient may be assisted in finding new ways to understand the family dynamic and its effects on her or him and to construct new ways of interacting in that and other social contexts; to find, in other words, a new personal identity in relation to others.

The danger attending this view, if it is exclusively held or held in an extreme form, is that it can reduce the sense of responsibility and autonomy which is essential to personal being by fostering the view that one is merely the product of one's relationships – whether they be pathological or therapeutic.

There are those whom we do not count as persons, who are not included in our definition of what a person is. Our treatment of them will change for the better as they get nearer to being so counted. The assumption that the mentally ill are somehow less than persons has at times shaped psychiatric provision and treatment (our treatment of animals also seems to me to be generally related to the extent to which they approximate to 'persons'). If one's conception of personhood includes the idea that persons are autonomous and must never be interfered with against their will, then it will be almost impossible to assist the acutely ill unless one also defines mental illness as at least a reduction of personhood which permits some coercion in treatment. Consider the paternalistic way of treating the elderly and the disabled which most of us fall into without thinking ('Now, we can make a nice, big effort, can't we dear? . . . Does she take sugar? . . . Oh, no, let me do that for you – you really can't do that on your own!'). Does this, too, reflect our assumption that they are somehow less than persons? In the advanced stages of dementia there may be no sign that anything is experienced, and almost all reflexes may be suppressed or even lost. There are extremely unfortunate consequences (for us as well as for them, I think) which follow as soon as we read their state as totally lacking personal existence.

I have said rather a lot about psychiatry because that is where the present work began and it provides, I think, a helpful reference point for the discussion that follows. However, this book is not about psychiatry, or even medicine in general, but about what it means to be a person and what personal, social and political practices seem to be required by personal being. My concern in the foregoing has been merely to indicate two things: that this theoretical work has a practical origin and intention; and that the theoretical understanding we have of what persons are and should be is bound up with the way we treat people.

What does it mean to be a human person, and how can that be conceived appropriately? This is the central question which arose out of my hospital experience and is the focus of the reflections contained in this book. There were collectivist ways of answering it available, but it was striking how pervasive individualistic answers were. Even in psychiatry, which is traditionally more ready to acknowledge the place of relational and social determinants of illness than other branches of medicine, individualistic conceptions of personal being operate and are pervasive, at least as a sort of 'default value'.

Both collectivist and individualist answers (for a range of reasons which will emerge in the main body of the book) seemed ultimately to offer unsatisfactory conceptions of individuality and personal being, although each also had some helpful insights and intentions which seemed worth preserving. Individualism attempts to do full justice to personal freedom and autonomy, although these take a pathological turn as individuals are considered self-contained entities cut off from one another and God. Collectivism, on the other hand, tries to take the role of social relations and institutions in human life seriously. This too, however, creates a deficient understanding of the individual for whom autonomy, freedom and independence from social structures become impossible.

This raises the question of whether there might be a third option, steering something of a mid-course between individualism and collectivism, which can do justice to personal freedom and autonomy whilst simultaneously acknowledging the role of social relations and institutions. Can the question of what it means to be a person be answered more adequately by the construction of a different kind of conceptuality? This book is an attempt to construct such a third option. Whilst I hope that it might offer something new, both the insight that individualism and collectivism are unsatisfactory and the attempt to find a third option are hardly original. So this is really much more a contribution to a discussion already in place than the breaking of completely new ground.

Investigating the possibility of this third option has therefore involved engagement with a wide range of contributors to the conversation. Perhaps the most important of these is Martin Buber. His personalist philosophy extended Feuerbach's language of 'I and Thou' to construct a description of personal being in terms of dialogue which was at the same time something of a practical programme. His is such a pervasive presence in these pages that I am often, I am sure, quite unconscious of it, and consequently find it difficult to acknowledge adequately. Buber's terminology and conceptuality were fairly readily taken up by theology and, in particular, by two of the key Protestant theologians of this century, Karl Barth and Dietrich Bonhoeffer, both of whom shared Buber's desire to leave Idealist conceptions of the subject behind. They are also a constant presence throughout the book.

Much of the contemporary discussion is characterised by the desire to move away from the more simplistic aspects of personalism, especially its tendency to concentrate on small-scale, relatively unstructured, interpersonal relations. There is now a desire to attend to the ways in which large-scale relations and context (social, cultural, historical, political, moral, etc.) are determinative of personal being. One of the most important contemporary debates in social philosophy concerns the ways in which institutions of various sorts affect us. Jürgen Habermas, Niklas Luhmann. Hans-Georg Gadamer and Karl-Otto Apel have each been trying to explain and explore human being with reference to various aspects of social existence, and particularly its mediation through language. Their exchanges have provided a fertile range of conceptualities which illuminate the nature of human society, and the problems of conceiving it appropriately, in diverse ways. Habermas and Apel in particular have been concerned to explore how the social and political conditions of freedom, truth and justice can be conceived and secured so that a genuinely human society can be formed in which people may themselves be free and truly human. It is true to say, however, that the individual and personal aspects of human being have rarely been the explicit or central theme of these discussions.

Two of the theologians who have been most concerned to respond to this debate and to work out some of the implications for theology are Jürgen Moltmann and Wolfhart Pannenberg. Both have been important influences on my own attempt to formulate a theological contribution. Pannenberg has been more systematic in his assessment of and response to these debates, especially where they intersect with the concerns of the philosophy of the human sciences. He has been rather more concerned with the institutional; Moltmann has been more general in his discussions of community and of human being. Both understand person as a correlate of community.

I have also found Rom Harré's contribution to the conversation, a discussion of the socio-psychological aspects of identity and selfhood, extremely helpful. Chapter 3 is largely the product of engagement with his work in which he constructs a theoretical explanation of how the assumptions concerning personhood which surround us in our social, cultural and moral environment may be internalised in the construction of our own identities as we work out for ourselves what it means to be a (particular) person.

The key insight which grew out of engagement with these attempts to formulate some middle way between individualism and collectivism was the fruitfulness of understanding personal being and identity in terms of communication. Communication does not just refer to speech or to other forms of linguistic communication; it embraces every interaction in which there is change and exchange – between people, between them and their environment, them and God, or between any relatively discrete entity or system and another – and that, by definition, is every interaction. Essentially, it is the transfer of information. Information is any content of communication which has some meaning; that which is not simply 'noise', but which is coded or ordered in a way which may produce an effect on those receiving it. For the recipient to find a communication informative, its content must be sufficiently new and different from present states (say, of understanding or knowledge) to make a difference, whilst sufficiently close to those states to make contact with them, be relevant and have meaning. The communication may then be said to have informed the recipient, in so far as the recipient has been changed by it.

At the time of writing, Mrs Thatcher is the prime minister. On the face of it, that statement contains information and is meaningful but, since most readers will already know the information it contains, it is neither interesting nor informative and is unlikely to make any difference to them – although it may, admittedly, prompt some reaction depending upon readers' feelings about this fact or their understanding of why I have mentioned it. Of course, when it was spoken by a newsreader the morning after the 1979 general election, it really was news. If I say it in a certain tone of voice, then it may also convey new information concerning my political affiliation to anyone hearing me; in which case, it is communication not so much of information about a state of affairs as of my feelings. If, however, someone hears me say this who can speak English but understands nothing of English political institutions and has never heard of Mrs Thatcher, then the statement becomes meaningless and uninformative for her or him because it makes insufficient contact with what she or he presently knows and understands. Similar illustrations could, of course, be given for non-linguistic forms of communication, such as physical exchanges.

We are constantly embraced by various networks of communication and exchange and are in continual communication ourselves from the time of our conception in the womb. We become the people we are as our identities are shaped through the patterns of communication and response in which we are engaged. We carry the effects of the communication we have received and the response we have made in the past forward with us into every new situation and relationship. This happens most obviously, but by no means primarily or exclusively, through memory, and is what I later term the 'sediment' which is laid down through our communication history. It is this which makes us the people we are.

Basic problems concerning personal identity, the boundaries of the individual, freedom, subjectivity, and the distortions of communication, relation and identity surface immediately we begin to understand ourselves in this way. These problems are discussed in the course of my argument where the options which are offered by thinking in terms of communication are explored. This way of thinking does seem to offer a conceptuality which is able to incorporate the valid insights and intentions of individualism and collectivism, but which has several advantages over them. It allows an understanding of the self which is thoroughly relational but which does not sacrifice its individual integrity; it takes account of the physical boundaries and rootedness of persons, but also of their being socially formed through their histories; it overcomes the dichotomy between the personal and the institutional; and it makes possible an account of personhood which is normative and can therefore act as a touchstone for understanding distortions, but which simultaneously acknowledges the unique particularity of each person.

As the work evolved it became clear that it needed to be as coherent and systematic in its conceptuality and expression as possible. A conceptuality which is consistent and appropriate to the various elements of the discussion will help to illuminate the ways in which they are interrelated. The interweaving of central themes, treated at different levels and in different ways, throughout the different chapters makes it possible to build up a central image of this conceptuality in a gradual, but all-embracing way. This has required the use of a controlled terminology throughout the book which functions as a sort of technical language which enables more rigorous thinking.

My use of a somewhat technical language does mean that I discuss my theme at a largely theoretical level. This, however, does not imply a withdrawal, disengagement or retreat from practice, but a concentration and compression of the issues raised there. That concentration inevitably involves abstraction and generalisation, but it is only in this way that the assumptions guiding practice can be uncovered and formulated.

It also became clear that the project required a new terminology as existing ones were often inadequate to express what I wanted to say and/or were so tied to other conceptualities as to be misleading. There are no neologisms as such; all that I have done is to use some terms in a relatively novel way or redefine them so they better suit my purposes. The presuppositions of individualism are so deeply ingrained in our culture that it is impossible to carry on using our normal language for talking about personhood and individuality without slipping into its misconceptions unless we self-consciously modify it. I have tried to keep the peculiarity of this new way of speaking to a minimum, but there are still bound to be occasions when readers find the terminology a little strange. Provided it stays within certain limits, that effect can actually be positive and constructive: the individualistic way of regarding personal being is so ingrained in us that we need to be shocked somehow into a new cognition and consciously unlearn it. An unusual use of language can help in this because it stops the operation of normal presuppositions short and may also bring them into sufficient light to be examined. That is certainly the effect I wish my terminology to have. The measure of its success will be whether readers find themselves provoked into dialogue with the conceptuality I am developing, or whether it presents itself as a totalitarian imposition.

A short glossary of key terms is included at the back of the book so that readers may keep in touch with the central ideas as they move through or dip into the argument, without having to keep fingers in pages where these are first introduced and defined.

My basic conception of the person in this discussion is both dialogical (formed through social interaction, through address and response) and dialectical (never coming to rest in a final unity, if only because one is never removed from relation). In dialogue the partners are simultaneously independent (otherwise the listening and speaking of both would be unnecessary) and inseparably bound together in a search for a mutuality of understanding. The basis of a dialogical understanding of personhood is that we are what we are in ourselves only through relation to others. Persons are unique centres or subjects of communication, but they are so only through their intrinsic relation to other persons. So they are centred beings, but they become centred in a personal way only through relation with other personal centres, through commitment to others, and so on. I do not want to anticipate my later argument by laying this out clearly here, but to indicate how this conception of the central theme of the book required a specific method so that the discussion would take a form appropriate to its content.

Conceiving of persons in this dialogical and dialectical way makes it impossible to think of us as having a clearly defined 'centre' or 'foundation'. Likewise, the method has no straightforward centre or foundation, but brings two worlds of discourse into dialogue and dialectical interaction: a theology most affected by Barth, Bonhoeffer and Moltmann; and contemporary social thought, especially that of Habermas, Luhmann and Harré. Both are subject to interpretation and, where necessary, to criticism. Bringing them into contact with one another has allowed them to cross-fertilise and be mutually informative as well as mutually critical. I hope that readers will find the fruits of that interaction as creative as I have done, although I recognise that there are bound to be suspicions, on the part of those who normally work within one or other of these worlds, that setting up this sort of interaction is illegitimate and is sure to sacrifice the integrity of distinct disciplines. The danger that integrity and identity might be sacrificed attends any dialogue, but dialogue itself actually depends upon maintaining the distinct identities of the partners. So everything depends upon the interaction being structured in such a way that it remains a real dialogue. There are dangers attending the isolation of worlds of thought too, of course, as these turn into either totalitarian or artificially separated and partialised forms of explanation.

This separation and partialisation is what worries me most as a Christian theologian. Talk of human being in our society has been so completely secularised that we find it increasingly difficult to talk of humanity with reference to God in a way which is meaningful in our contemporary human situation. It is my belief that this missing dimension makes a real and important difference to our theoretical understanding and to our practice. Non-Christian readers will understandably be reluctant to accept talk of God where I build it into the argument; I would invite them to take the argument as a whole and judge whether it has added anything at the end. I am not trying to impose a Christian perspective on anyone, but I am asking that the ability of Christian theology to be a fruitful dialogue-partner with secular thought be taken seriously for the mutual enrichment of both partners in their search for the good, the true and the right.

Christians and some Christian theologians might also have their suspicions and reservations concerning the kind of relationship with secular thought on which this book is based. The theological task, in my understanding of it, has two poles: to understand and critically reflect upon Christian doctrine, tradition and history on the one hand, and the social, cultural and intellectual world in which we are living on the other. Christian reality is always bound up with its social world, and that is one very important reason why, even when the theologian is attending to the

Gadamer's conversation model

understanding of faith through its past, theology should always involve critical reflection on the worlds of which the Church is and has been a part. These are not two tasks but dual elements of a single task. Critical engagement with the world as a whole is an essential element of the theological task of formulating an understanding of Christian tradition and of the contemporary situation which illuminates Christian faith together with the world and thereby clarifies what responsible existence in it might mean.

Bultmann (existentialism

Maintaining oneself in conversation with secular thought in this task does not necessarily lead to a demythologisation of Christian faith until there is nothing distinctive or distinctively religious or theological left, but this is a risk which must be taken if Christian faith and tradition are to be meaningful. If the contact is to be a genuine dialogue, then the religious and theological dimension will be maintained so that it can speak and be spoken to; it is maintained, that is, in a situational way. Because this involves taking secular thought seriously as a dialogue-partner, the understanding of faith and theology may change in response to it. The measure of how seriously and helpfully this book engages in this dialogue will be whether those from both 'sides' think it deserves to be taken up into their own discussions.

I am particularly concerned that non-Christian readers should not be put off by the fact that the opening chapters are explicitly theological in content. I am simply trying there to clarify the kind of theology which I am bringing to bear on the field and to show that it might have an important contribution to make. I am not so much dogmatically establishing the theological grounding for what follows, as inviting readers to consider the fruitfulness of thinking about personal being from a theological point of view, and of reflecting on Christian doctrine by relating it immediately to this theme. Furthermore, the more explicitly theological Part I does not operate as a given upon which the subsequent argument is grounded. The whole argument is interrelated, and Part I is what it is by virtue of those later parts. The theology and the social thought develop in intrinsic interrelation and have been mutually informative. So Parts II, III and IV are also intrinsically theological; they contain subsequent development and clarification of the theological position prefigured in Part I and depend upon it. Similarly, Part I depends upon and prefigures the position on personal and social issues taken in later chapters which clearly depends upon non-theological and non-Christian contributions.

What I intend, therefore, is not simply a new recourse to traditional

Christian apologetics, and much less is it a simple recourse to a Barthian form of Dogmatic theology. I am more willing to take the risks of a meaningful and open dialogue with non-Christian thought than the latter would allow. As regards the former, I am not seeking to justify to non-Christians conclusions reached within the circle of faith through independent theological reflection by dressing them up in the language of secular thought. That kind of theology tries to be trendy but always ends up ephemeral, doing justice to neither Christian faith nor the secular school of thought which is this year's thing and which is simply made use of and treated in a less than serious way. Neither, however, am I uncritically accepting positions arrived at independently from faith and theology on certain aspects of reality. That is most often done where articulate Christian faith cannot find anything significant to say on its own resources about matters it thinks it should speak about. It can then only adopt, bless and regurgitate the conclusions arrived at elsewhere.

What I have attempted to do is to operate two rules of theological discourse which are normally considered antithetical. The first represents the Barthian understanding of the primacy of God in theological method which has somehow to reflect and to retain the fact that God comes first and transcends all human reality. The second is the understanding that, notwithstanding the primary orientation of theology on God alone, theology and theologians are informed by their determinate situation which constitutes, in part, a culturally specific way of going about and of perceiving things. It is my belief and hope that accepting the socially determinate character of Christian faith and theology, and bringing their insights into open dialogue with secular thought, will lead to a mutually enriching encounter in which the perspectives of the participants, whilst never ceasing to be distinctively their own, are transformed and are brought into ever closer engagement with one another as we consider how we and our world are best to be understood and responsibly transformed.

I am all too aware of the momentous nature of the subjects I am trying to deal with and of my own limitations in so doing. In particular, I have found it extremely difficult to address myself to so many large matters – each of which could have had a book to itself – and to keep the argument within reasonable and manageable bounds without some loss of rigour in argumentation. Some of my flanks are left uncovered, and I have not been able to lay out all the relevant arguments. It is also likely that some readers will want to construe major elements in the argument differently. In relation to the doctrines of creation and the Trinity, for example, there is a great deal of controversy which I have simply not had space to recount here to show why I prefer the interpretation I opt for (not that that would be likely to or should eliminate any disagreement in the minds of readers, of course). What I am trying to do is lay out what I consider to be the optimum solution to the problems posed by this book; and that solution involves both doctrines. I hope that both doctrines are illuminated by the discussion in such a way that those who do not hold them will at least be inspired to reconsider them. But, to reiterate my earlier comments concerning the dialogical method and intention of this work, it is also my hope that readers who differ profoundly with me will be enabled to engage fruitfully with this discussion. The communicational concept of the self outlined later in the book could be adapted to many other ways of understanding reality; indeed, one of its advantages is that it might enable opposing positions to enter into dialogue using this common conceptuality as a medium through which both their concerns might be expressed.

Finally, I would like to return to the genesis of this book in a practical situation. The issue of how we live together as human persons was raised for me by the constant experience of coming up against the limitations in practice of the main operative conceptions of humanity and personhood in our culture. That drove me back to reconsider my whole framework for understanding, evaluating and acting, and led to the investigations which are recorded in this book. I hope that the result of this journey through some rather abstract systematic thinking will prove as liberating for the reader as it has for the author, and that the Epilogue will help lead the reader back out into the practice of everyday life.

Part I

Persons in relation to God

I

The creation of individuality in God's image: Trinity, persons, gender and dialogue

The two major theological components in my argument are human existence in the image of the trinitarian God and the call of Christ. In this chapter I shall discuss the first of these. In doing so, I shall not attempt to develop afresh the Christian doctrines of the Trinity, creation, fall and redemption which are woven into the argument. That would be far beyond the scope of this book. Instead, I shall take a mainstream, orthodox position on them, as represented by various modern theologians (to whom I refer in the notes), and shall redescribe and reinterpret this orthodox position in relation to the subject of the book. Basic Christian conceptions, and their distortions, have in fact deeply influenced modern understanding of personhood. It should therefore be no surprise that bringing a contemporary interpretation of these Christian doctrines into dialogue with modern thought and its dilemmas concerning personhood is a fruitful exercise.

I describe the image first of all in its 'vertical' dimension as the constitution of human beings through relation to God, with grateful and praise-giving response as the normative form of this relation. I then turn to the 'horizontal' dimension of the image in the sphere of human relations. This produces a fundamental understanding of the person in social categories in which the relations between the sexes are of primary importance. The reconception of 'the fall' which concludes the chapter points to a way of conceiving the radical distortions of human existence which are a part of our mundane reality. In the process of all this, key ideas developed in later chapters are introduced, such as dialogue, sedimentation, autonomy, excentricity, and the determination of personal identity through relation in general. Overall, my aim is to introduce some basic concepts of the book in their theological setting, and to suggest that this is the most adequate way of doing justice to the reality of personhood.

My basic position throughout the book is that persons have to be understood in social terms – if only because they are somehow the product of their relations. Individuality, personhood and selfhood do not, I shall argue, refer to some internal and independent source of identity, but to the way one is and has been in relation. If it is the case that our personal identities are moulded through our relationships, then there must be some connection between the quality of those relationships and that of our personhood. And so the ontological statement concerning the way our personal being is structured (through relation) must give way immediately to ethical and political questions concerning the 'right' forms of individuality and relation.

The Christian doctrines of creation and redemption provide a rich framework for discussing the nature of personal existence in this way. The Genesis creation narratives speak of human creation together in God's image in a way that should make impossible any Christian talk of individuals as isolated, individual entities. Human persons, it affirms, are intrinsically related to one another and to God. God's creative and sustaining activity generates the ontological structures of human and personal existence – a sort of base-line which is simply given – which also indicates in outline the ideal form of and norm for personal and social life. The assertion that we are created in the divine image operates both as an assertion of the way things are – an ontological given – and as an ideal regulating personal and social conduct. It is both an 'is' and an 'ought'. Although it is a given of our existence, it is given in such a way that it requires and invites something more from us. For its fulfilment and its distortion are both possible since it is an ethical as well as an ontological structure. God's redemptive activity is a further attempt to entice and empower us towards full responsible existence in God's image,[1] under the impact of which there is a repatterning and restructuring of one's identity and relations.

The vertical image

The biblical theme of creation is not ultimately concerned with cosmogeny or cosmology but with the relationship between God and God's creatures. In the human case, this relationship has a special significance and status in its personal character. A personal relationship is essentially an encounter between two or more partners who are different, who have some independence and autonomy in the relation and who may therefore engage with each other on the basis of freedom rather than coercion. They may therefore place one another in question, and each may freely give to the other. What they say and do in the relation is thereby genuinely of themselves and not merely the response required by the stimulus of the interaction. All that is to say that a personal relation is one characterised by the call and response, the gift and return of dialogue. What is distinctive about the human relation to God in creation is that God's creative and sustaining activity elicits, enables and deserves a free and thankful response.

This is found particularly in the Psalms (e.g. 24, 33, 104, 136, 148) where thanks and praise are given to Yahweh as the Israelites' understanding deepens not only of Yahweh's responsibility for creation but also of their status before Yahweh as a covenant people. For the response of thanks and praise in the Old Testament is given not only in recognition of God as the originator and sustainer of creation; it is also given in response to the perception of God as intervening to transform Israel's historical situation, which is spoken of in terms of liberation or redemption. Thanks and praise were thought the rightful responses to Yahweh's redemptive as well as creative acts. The understanding of their relation with God as personal evolved primarily within the Israelites' experience of history as a salvific process in which they were personally addressed as a responsible community. The essential and unifying feature of God's address to them in creation–redemption was the space provided in the expectation of autonomous human response. It was this understanding of the character of their relation with God which required the corresponding conception of Israel as a community responsible before God.

In the provision of space for free human response to the divine address, the divine–human relationship is structured from God's side as a dialogue.[2] For human being is intended in this communication to be God's dialogue-partner. Human being is therefore to be described as a being-in-partnership with God, a being addressed as Thou by God's I.[3] Human being in God's image signifies the human entrance into this relationship of active partnership by answering God's Word. Human being is not a static, unrelated substance, but a response to an external address.

Because God's communication takes dialogical form, it should be conceived of in terms of grace. Dialogue here means that, on God's side at least, there is respect for freedom and independence and an absence of overdetermination. In the mystery of God's grace human beings are addressed as God's dialogue-partners. They are therefore free to make what response they will, and all that they do and make of themselves is in fact a response to God – though that may take the form of conscious or unconscious rejection. The human autonomy of free responsibility which is recognised in God's form of address is not something already in existence. The recognition is not simply an acknowledgement: autonomy and free responsibility are actually created by God in this recognition. It is the divine intention that human beings shall be free in relation to Godself as God's dialogue-partners. God's address has no precondition save the divine intention of human being as free in relation to God and is strictly undeserved. As dialogical in form, God's Word expects a free response. The power of this expectation, in creating the possibility of an appropriate response of thankfulness which is free (i.e. neither strictly necessary nor overdetermined), must simultaneously contain the possibilities of misunderstanding, wrong orientation, disobedience and unbelief. The structural freedom of human being may therefore be corrupted, but such corruption, as a 'free' though distorted response, is grounded in the power of this Word to let humanity be, even if it means being frustrated itself in the process. Paradoxically, the corruption is grounded in the structure of freedom given in the divine intention of dialogue-partnership, which is not simply a reflection of but is itself the divine image. The misuse of freedom is parasitic on that which makes such freedom possible. The image may therefore be corrupted but not lost, and for this reason we should think of it as an ontological structure of human being.

In Christian doctrine, creation begins with a primal letting-be, and it is this which gives creation the autonomy in which it can now stand over against God as an independent order of being. This lends it the character of grace deserving a thankful response, since in the form of creative expectation it brings to humanity possibilities which would have been unavailable to us otherwise, and does so without strictly and immediately demanding anything in return. The Word of creation precedes any demand; the 'Let us make' precedes the 'be fruitful'. Human responsibility before God

is not first of all a task, but a gift; it is not first of all a demand, but life; not law, but grace. The word which – requiring an answer – calls man, is not a 'Thou shalt' but a 'thou mayst be.' The primal word is not an imperative, but it is the indicative of the divine love, 'thou art mine'.[4]

Even where the Word has the character of call or obligation, it has to be understood within the context of this primary letting-be of the divinely chosen dialogue-partnership. God's choice is *for* humanity; that is, for humanity to be what it truly is, God's dialogue-partner.

The intention of dialogue-partnership contained in and guiding

God's communication establishes an ontological structure of freedom which, as such, is the precondition for any human response. It is a necessary yet insufficient condition for the fulfilment of that intention. For as a structure of freedom it is also a structure of responsibility. The freedom is precisely a freedom in, for and of response. For the relationship as a whole to take dialogical form the intention informing God's address would have to be reciprocated so that, in the form and content of the human response, we co-intend ourselves as free in creaturely dialogue-partnership with God. When grace (the determination of the relation from God's side) is met with thanksgiving (the responding acceptance of this determination on the human side), then human life has an undistorted structure. *practice gratitude*

This suggests that human being is determined by the relational form proper to it, which may be materially defined as being-in-gratitude.[5] This in turn implies that the relational structure of human being is one of openness to and for God's Word. For this being-in-gratitude involves a recognition of the incapacity to live from individual or communal human resources alone, a turning towards God in the understanding that that which is accomplished for humanity open to God's Word is decisively different from that which could happen for a humanity closed in upon itself in a process of circumlocution, and therefore locked exclusively into its own power. In this understanding of the human creature, the proper human stance in the dialogical relation with God is therefore openness. As soon as an attempt is made at grasping or possessing the Word, the dialogue is distorted. The human stance in the relation ceases then to be a grateful openness as it is grounded in the assumption that the relation can be established through human power or on the basis of a previously coordinated understanding. It therefore has need neither to be grateful nor open because God's communication would bring nothing new and could not therefore be informative. *opening to God Banner*

Being-in-gratitude as an answer, a reversed repetition of God's communication, constitutes the vertical image which is primary. Human openness to and for God in thankfulness images God's Word by returning to it as an accepting response. It is a repetition from the human side of God's movement towards us which is informed by the creative intention of God's communication (it could therefore be conceived in explicitly Christological terms, as the image of Christ). The intention which informs this response is carried in the dialogical form and content of God's communication which is structured in a way which expects and respects human freedom in response. The image is a returning to God which reduplicates the motion of grace by reciprocally acknowledging the true nature of divine and human being. Letting God be God is the reciprocation of God's letting-be of humanity.

What I am suggesting is that the form of God's address determines the structure of human being as response without determining the form or content of that response. That is, it constitutes the ontological structure of human being as relational and responsible. There is freedom within this structure as relations and identities may be either distorted or fulfilled in a rejection or an acceptance of dialogue-partnership. Strictly speaking, human being is always in the image of God because it is constituted by God's prevenient, creative communication as a being-in-response. But whilst there is freedom as to the form and content of this response, there is no freedom *not* to respond. We cannot abdicate our responsibility. For we are permanently set before God and, whether this ontological fact be acknowledged or not, all that we are, do and say is a response to, an act of responsibility or irresponsibility before God. We live and breathe within the parameters set by the divine intention in communication of dialogue-partnership with God as a more or less distorted image of and response to God. We can refuse to enter into dialogue: we cannot, however, avoid being in relation with God. Our freedom is limited to determining what form that relationship, our response, is to take. That means we have the freedom of a creature in relation – we can determine our own stance in the relation, but not that of the other. We can neither destroy God nor distort God's intention towards us.

The image cannot, therefore, be lost, but it can be distorted by a refusal to reciprocate the intention of God's communication in response. That refusal too is a response, and so the ontological structure of freedom as being-in-response remains intact even when the intention of dialogue-partnership is maintained only on God's side and there is a distortion of the image on the human side.

The implication of all this is that human beings cannot stand fully in the image of God by resting in themselves, but only by turning themselves outwards and upwards towards God. For the divine image, and the freedom associated with it, are not qualities or attributes which we can possess in ourselves; rather, they designate a way of being in relation which is made possible only because we have been addressed in a way which intends our free response. We are addressed as the Thou corresponding to God's I. We are called thereby to become, in our turn, Is in response, to enter a personal relationship – a relationship in which our distinct identities are a requirement: a dialogue. It is through dialogue that we become true subjects and share a personal existence. A person is a subject of communication and as such makes responses which are more than mechanical responses to external stimuli, and which rest on the uniqueness of personal identity. For subjectivity is neither the product of any private, internal process (for instance of thought or reflection) nor the designation of some individually held capacity; rather it is a way of being and relating as an I which is 'called out' in which one is intended as a dialogue-partner, an I in ones own right. We learn to be subjects, persons, from the expectations of our being and communication which surround us and which are mediated to us through others' intentions of us contained in their communication (see Chapter 3). Since God's communication is the overarching determining and ever-present context within which all personal communication takes place, it is primarily through participation in the history of God's dealing with us, in which we are intended as freely responding subjects, that we learn what it means to be a person and subject (although this might be mediated to us through others and be entirely unconscious).⁶ This relationship is not a once-for-all event that happened at creation and is now over. Just as creation itself is not a single act but a continuing and sustaining relationship, so the creative communication of God which intends us as free dialogue-partners is repeated, reinterpreted and recreated within a concrete process of communication and exchange through time. The depositing of subjectivity through the dialogical intention is a continuing and concrete process and must therefore be understood as a dynamic and diachronic interaction.

The notion of subjectivity as a form of response sedimented from a history of communication represents a decisive reorientation in the understanding of individuality. Individuality refers to the capacity to be an autonomous centre of action and communication, to be a separate and independent individual. The suggestion I am making is that this capacity is not relationally pure but is sedimented through relations in which one is intended and addressed as an autonomous subject of communication by God and others. The independence of individual persons as originating subjects of communication can only be partial, since their subjectivities have ultimately been sedimented in response to the extended address of God and others.

The horizontal image

The vertical image is a human response which reflects the intention of God's creative communication in either a distorted or undistorted fashion. The personal structure deposited in this history of response undergoes a social refraction, and this second reflection is what I have termed the horizontal image.

There is always a danger that theological anthropology will slip into anthropocentric ways of talking about human beings and God. This can be minimised by conceiving of human beings as intrinsically related to God, as that makes it less likely that talk of humanity can replace that of God or that humanity can be talked of in isolation. This is especially true where the direction of the revelatory process is repeated and talk of God is placed before talk of humanity. Then theology would be theocentric even when being anthropological. That is why my discussion of the vertical image has preceded that of the horizontal. But even in the horizontal dimension, in speaking of what pertains between people, it is crucial that the discussion should begin with talk of God, for the divine image is even here first and foremost a theological term and only secondarily an anthropological one.[7] If we are to understand what form of personal and social being images God, then it makes sense to enquire about the God who is reflected in human form. For surely knowledge of the *analogatum* can only come through knowledge of the *analogans*. It is something of a theological axiom that we cannot know God in Godself, but only through the divine communication and relation with humankind. But the form and content of that relation and communication, constitutive for human identity, yields information about humankind as well as about God. At the heart of the Christian tradition is a witness to the trinitarian nature of God's internal being and externally directed communication. The trinitarian nature of God's being and self-communication is determinative for a Christian understanding of human being in God's image as I unfold it here.

Trinity

Orthodox trinitarianism depends upon the maintenance of a balance between the indivisibility of God and the distinct identities of the three divine Persons. I will be arguing that a theory of human nature analogously informed by the nature of God as Trinity will lead to a specific understanding of individuality as a sedimentation of interpersonal relations which is intrinsically open to others as to God. I will begin by describing briefly the pathological ideal-types of absolute monotheism and tritheism. Since these depend upon a pathological notion of individuality, this will help to clarify the genuine nature of individuality as it exists in the Trinity and is imaged in human being.

Pathology

Paradoxically, the opposite pathological extremes of absolute monotheism and tritheism involve an identical mistaken assumption about the nature of individuality. Both take individual identity to be something pre-social removed from the sphere of relation as such. They are therefore bound to regard dialogical relations with others which make a difference to individual identity (inform it) as the fracture of an integrated personality or the alienation of identity. The two extremes are the inevitable result of pressing for hard and exclusive definitions (closed boundaries) of personal identity.

The desire to preserve monotheism at all costs becomes pathological when the supposed exclusivity of individuality invites the affirmation of a single, unrelated and undifferentiated divine subject of whom alone may all divine communication be predicated. Consequently, God is understood to be self-generating and self-enclosed: the unmoved mover, the first and only cause whose relations cannot be informative for the divine being or will in any way, as that would seem to destroy self-consistency and constancy. God becomes, then, the archetypal individual: impassible and apathetic. Relations and communication must be a one-way (monological) exercise of determinating, manipulative and dominating power, which may affect others but which leave God untouched.

In the understanding of hard monotheism, a person is taken to be a source or subject of communication, and the Godhead to be the sole divine subject. The Trinity cannot then consist of a plurality of Persons, so defined, if the singularity of the divine subjectivity is to be maintained. As non-persons the members of the Trinity have no individual (i.e. separable) identity or consciousness. They cannot therefore be internally differentiated but related members of the Godhead constituted as a community: they can only be external modes of relation of the one individual and not individual identities themselves. The three Persons are reduced to distinct *Modalism* modes of being and relation through which a single, transcendent subject acts.[8] If individual personhood is taken to indicate a subjectivity centred in an exclusive manner, then centring the divine subjectivity in the highest organisational level (the Godhead) and reducing the status of the lower levels (the Persons) is the only available means of securing monotheism.

Similarly, a commitment informed by the same asocial conception of individual personhood but committed to the distinct identities of the *Arianism* Persons can only destroy the unity in the Godhead. Each Person has the status of full individuality which, as asocial, jeopardises their interrelationship and creates three gods, each of whose subjectivity is exclusive of the *Tritheism* others and of their interrelationship. Divine activity may be predicated of only one of these at any one time. They cannot therefore act through, in, with or from one another. Tritheism subsumes relations into Persons totally distinct from all relations and hence from one another. The unity and oneness of the Trinity is completely abandoned to the along-sidedness of the three distinct personal centres who have only themselves and not each other at their own disposal.

The human image of the one or three divine individuals whose identities remain pure from the taints of relation is the isolated, solitary human individual who, as intrinsically unrelated (i.e. only accidentally or incidentally related in a way which is not determinative of identity and being) is both the sole source and object of his or her communication. The anthropology which corresponds to pathological models of the Trinity is an individualism in which the person is a closed circle of communication engaged in a cyclic orientation on oneself through oneself for oneself. Such relations as do exist are not only non-determinative but internalised, so that external reality (including others) is subsumed into forms of self-reference, which reduces its reality as other. What is other is perceivable only as self-confirmatory and in terms of self-interest. Communication may intend the other only as an object, rather than autonomous subject, of communication.[9] Otherness is reduced to a self-relation, real only as it appears in the subject's consciousness, as a repetition of a previously privately coordinated understanding: others cannot confront one as other, with their own reality and interests independent of one's own which establish both limits and claims on one.

As an anthropology, of course, individualism confirms the individual nature and relationally irreducible reality of all persons, not just one. Yet because it may only affirm the universal reality of individuals as that identical in each, its apparently irreducible pluralism collapses into a sort of monism. In monism proper there is a single, undifferentiated reality. In this individualistic pluralism individuals are bearers of a universal substance (individuality or subjectivity) which is identical in each person. Knowledge of another is then tantamount to knowing oneself, and what may be known by one of another is only that which confirms the knower's individual perspective.[10] Individualist epistemology and anthropology may only know others as bearers of an identical abstract identity. What is truly other, different and individual can be neither informative for others nor a matter of public knowledge, interest or communication.

The primary problem with this understanding of individuality as self-contained and independent from the sphere of relation as such is that it posits individuals as self-constituting. The self-enclosure of individuals isolates them from a formative relation with God as well as others. The divine–human relation must be taken to be non-constitutive for human being or else reduced to a primal originative determination, but one which did not endure beyond that creative act and which is no longer determinatively effective in human existence. The most that is possible here is a form of deism, the affirmation of the existence of God such that it makes no difference. Individualism can only lead to an internalisation of God according to human predicates which effectively prevents God from appearing as other within the relation to humankind as a whole or to separate individuals.[11] An orthodox trinitarianism, however, yields a definition of individuality which, in anthropological application, remains open to a continuing formative relation with God (and others).

Person and relation. In what I take to be an orthodox understanding, I propose a model of the Trinity as a unique community of Persons in which Person and relation are interdependent moments in a process of mutuality. Each Person is a social unity with specific characteristics unique to Him or Her but whose uniqueness is not an asocial principle of being. The terms of personal identity within the Trinity identify not just unique individuals but the form of relation peculiar to them. Father, for instance, denotes both a specific individual and the form of relation existing between Him and the other Persons. Or, rather, it identifies that specific individual through an implicit (metaphorical) reference to His unique relational form (Fatherhood or origin) and, thereby, to the other Persons. The Father, Son and Spirit are neither simply modes of relation nor absolutely discrete and independent individuals, but Persons in relation and Persons only through relation. Persons exist only as they exist for others, not merely as they exist in and for themselves. Personal identity refers to the communicative form (the stance in relation; the form taken in call and response) which a person habitually takes and which endures through a plurality of relations within which personal being is both given and received. As the Persons are what they are only through their relations with the others, it must also be the case that their identities are formed through the others and the ways in which the others relate to them.

The three divine Persons are united by sharing uniquely in a common nature. By sharing in this common nature they are all equally divine; by doing so in an asymmetrical manner, each is uniquely divine.

When this understanding is combined with the interrelationship represented by the Trinity, it is possible to arrive at an appreciation of their uniqueness in terms of Personal identity:

> since the trinitarian Persons are unique, they cannot merely be defined by their relationship to their common nature. The limitation to three would then be incomprehensible. The personality which represents their untransferable, individual being with respect to their common nature, means, on the other hand, the character of relation with respect to the other Persons. They have the divine nature in common; but their particular individual nature is determined in their relationship to one another. In respect of the divine nature the Father has to be called '*individua substantia*', but in respect of the Son we have to call him 'Father'. The position is no different in the case of the Son and the Spirit. The three divine persons exist in their particular, unique natures as Father, Son and Spirit in their relationships to one another, and are determined through these relationships. It is in these relationships that they are persons. Being a person in this respect means existing-in-relationship.[12]

Both Personal identity and relation depend upon the Persons' incommunicable Personalities. An incommunicable Personality designates the character of the relations one has with the others but is not reducible to them. It is the unique pattern of communication and effective silence, or incommunicability, which establishes the individual and non-exchangeable nature of each Person. But whilst Personal identity as such is unique and incommunicable, it is reciprocally derived from and present only in communication and relation. The Persons share the divine nature, but their particular Personal natures are determined only in relation to one another. Being a person means existing in relation. Personal identity or discreteness is not asocial, but the form of punctuation which both separates and links one to others. The Persons are three individuals of a common divine nature in which they each share in a unique and asymmetrical manner (the Son and Spirit receiving it from the Father). The unique nature of each is derived from their asymmetrical subsistence in the divine nature (substance), together with the different relational form in which each has His or Her existence.[13]

They are Persons only in so far as they are related in these particular ways, and they may be related only in so far as they are discrete, as Persons, both from one another and from any one or the totality of their relations. Person and relation are inseparable but not the same thing. There is no logical or historical priority, but a dialectical genetic connection between them. The substantial individuality of a Person and His or Her manifestation in an appropriate form of relation are two moments of the same dialogical history in which the Persons become what they are through mutually interpenetrative relations with the others, wherein they exist through, in and for one another. The individuality of the trinitarian Persons is not achieved through a private discreteness from relation, but through this trinitarian process of existing in and for the others.

In this unique community everything is shared except Personal characteristics, but even these cannot be said to be independent of the relations in which this sharing takes place. Personal existence means living beyond one's borders in an orientation on others, to be in the other and to understand oneself and the other from the perspective of the other.[14] The triune life is marked by the most profound interpenetration.[15] Yet it is precisely in this interpenetration that the Persons have their distinct being, and it is only through their unique individual identities that this inter-penetration is possible. The unique subjectivities of each Person are formed through the unique form of intersubjectivity which pertains to them. Like all living things they are neither fully open nor fully closed systems. It is their radical openness to and for one another (in which Personal closure still retains a place) which constitutes their existence in this unique community decisive for all life in God's name.

This discussion of the triune being of God has yielded a way of conceiving persons in relation which is central to later chapters and which will be further developed in them. The essential element of this is that personal identity and individuality are neither asocial nor presocial, but arise out of one's relations and community with others. Those relations and that community require individual uniqueness and incommunicability – that which cannot be fully shared or communicated. Yet even this is derived from relation and is best construed as the form of punctuation operating between oneself and others; the way one exists 'in', with and for others.

Triune creation

The structure of the Trinity is open in respect of its external as well as its internal relations. The quality of life within the triune being of God, which is given and created in the Persons' dialogical interrelationship, overflows as God's externally directed communication in creation-redemption. In this external communication God relates with what is other in a way which guarantees its independence, but which calls it into free relation with God; calls it to join in the fullness of divine life in a manner appropriate to its own creaturely existence. Through this trinitarian history of creation–redemption human being is invited and drawn into a form of life which is a creaturely reflection of the trinitarian being of God. God's creative–redemptive activity involves the three divine Persons' dialogical interrelation and interpenetration. For if the interpenetrative intersubjectivity of the Trinity is formative for the Persons' identities, then it must also inform their external communication. The interrelations of the Trinity and therefore the identity of the other Persons is carried implicitly in the communication of each. Creation–redemption may then be understood as a continuing process of external self-communication involving the unique subjectivity of each Person, but also the unique intersubjectivity of their triune being, in which creation itself may join.

Creative (originating and sustaining) communication may be described in this way as primarily the work of the Father, but as involving the other Persons in such a way that it cannot be predicated purely of the Father. Each Person is a subject of creation in a unique way in tri-unity with the others.

In other words, creation may only fully be predicated of a tri-une intersubjectivity. In traditional Christian terms, we may say that the Father creates through His love for the Son (whose nature is a complete response to the Father's self-communicating love), and therefore it is also creation through the Son. Creation itself is destined for fellowship with the Son, and so may conjoin in a repetition of their love for one another. The distinctive contribution of the Son is made through His subjective identity as Word, providing structured form as response. The Holy Spirit contributes the creative energy and power through which the Father creates something other than Himself, in contradistinction to the begetting of the Son who, like the Spirit, shares in the same essence. The Spirit's Personal identity is as life-giver, and the social consequence of Her life-giving activity is organisation, and organisation which is orientated towards life in its fullness. Through the out-pouring of the organisational energies of the Spirit created beings achieve an independent and integrated structure; She breathes their own life into them.[16]

The human creature created by this outpouring and overflowing of the divine being and interrelationship has a special status and significance. Human creatures are said in the Bible and Christian tradition to be in the image of God; human being corresponds in some special way to God's Being. I have already suggested that this correspondence, or image, should be interpreted in relational and dynamic terms, that we image God by 'returning' to God in a movement of thanks and praise. But what is the significance of the Christian understanding that the God in whose image we stand is internally differentiated and related? Is it significant that Genesis places talk of human being as male and female in close proximity to talk of the image?

There has been a strong tradition in Christian thought that the image is an internal attribute (reason or consciousness, for instance). Every human is then in God's image merely by being a human individual. This kind of interpretation may well translate into a basis for treating others with respect, but it leaves the image as something static and internal which does not relate one intrinsically to others. If, however, the God whom human being images is not a simple, single individual with certain internal attributes, but is more like a community of Persons, then it would seem more adequate to conceive of the image in relational terms.

The analogy between God and human existence in the image is then properly not one of individual substance but of relation. Just as the Persons of the Trinity receive and maintain their identities through relation, and relations of a certain quality, then so would human persons only receive and maintain their identities through relation with others and would stand fully in God's image whenever these identities and relations achieved a certain quality.

The image as male and female

The fullness of the image consists, then, in the fact that the structures of divine and human being both contain a dialogical encounter between separate but intrinsically related beings. Whilst the Bible does not directly equate the image with human existence as male and female, it places the latter in such close proximity to the former that they should be thought of together. If we are to unravel the meaning and structure of human life in God's image we should therefore focus on our gender differentiation.

Dialogue is a bipolar process involving both distance (individual discreteness from the relation) and relation. Distinct identity is impossible except through relation, and relation possible only through the distance which separates the partners. Dialogical relations require structured distinction as well as relatedness. Gender difference and relation is the paradigmatic case of structural distance and relation in human being. Although it is socially instantiated in a variety of ways, to exist as man *or* woman and as man *and* woman is the concrete and necessary form of all human existence,[17] and it is the biblical paradigm for human life as co-humanity or community. Using sexual differentiation as a paradigm for humanity points to the fact that what is intended by existence in God's image is not only distinction (individual or communal discreteness) but relation. God created us 'male *and* female'; that is, in sexual encounter rather than simple opposition. Both creation accounts affirm that it is only through this encounter, through the *and* which unites the different, that life may be called human, an image of God.

In the Jahwist's account, humanity is considered incomplete prior to the creation of Eve. The lone Adam is not truly human; life becomes human only when he greets and accepts Eve. Humanity is therefore equated with neither lone individuality nor masculinity. Adam and Eve become human only in relation to each other. Humanity is fully in the image of God only where it is a lived dialogical encounter. It was not good for Adam to be alone,[18] or at least only with the animals; in relation to them, to an animal Thou he could affirm only an animal I. Alone with the animals, Adam was unable to enter dialogical relations. He was therefore a single being in need of an appropriate dialogue-partner.

> What is sought from him is a being resembling man but different from him. If it were only like him, a repetition, a numerical multiplication, his solitariness would not be eliminated for it would not confront him as another but he would merely recognise himself in it. Again if it were only different from him, a being of a wholly different order, his solitariness would not be eliminated, for it would confront him as another, yet not as another that actually belongs to him...[19]

The encounter is dialogical and is therefore a reciprocal mutuality. This means that it involves equality in the reciprocal occupation of dialogue roles, or that the partners may become alternately I and Thou, creating space for the independent communication, or communicative autonomy, of each. The essence of dialogue is that it is an encounter based on the independence, freedom and uniqueness of the partners. The partners are really and always other, but this is not a basis for their exclusivity and separation, but for their orientation on one another. Precisely because they remain other, unknowable in any total sense by another, their relation requires the independent communication of each, their participation as autonomous subjects of communication (Is). Because they are different, they cannot be adequately understood by the other unless they actively participate in the relation as an I as well as a Thou (speak, for instance, as well as be spoken to): the communication of the different makes a difference (is informative). They cannot therefore achieve a real mutuality of understanding or be properly orientated on one another if one is always only making direct response to the other and is therefore only ever a Thou and never an I for and before the other. Such a relationship would be monological because the one is determined by the other and has no independent existence apart from the other. The communication is effectively one-way because the otherness and difference of one has been silenced and does not appear in communication.

The presentation of the Jahwist's creation account from Adam's side is a narrative device and cannot be taken as an exclusion of Eve's active participation. For if Eve only belonged to Adam without his also belonging to her, his isolation would not be broken. He would have then only another animal being and not one for whom he may also become a Thou. Adam can only say 'I' in the recognition that Eve is a human Thou before him and therefore an I for herself. The relationship between them involves the recognition of both her independence and that he becomes what he is only in relation to her; only, that is, through their mutual recognition or co-intention of each other as related but distinct Thou-Is. Their relation is a continuing communication process in which their identities are formed together as distinct though related (see below). It must therefore be regarded as diachronic (proceeding through time rather than momentary or synchronic) and dialectical as well as dialogical. It is dialectical because their orientation on one another makes a difference to and changes the partners as they move towards an increased mutuality of understanding, but this does not overcome their difference, so further dialogue and change are always necessary because the creative 'tension' between the partners is never abolished.

Eve's designation as Adam's 'helpmeet' must be understood in terms of this dialogical relationship. A helpmeet is not a subordinate assistant, but a help-corresponding-to-him, denoting the closest physical and spiritual mutuality of 'help and understanding, joy and contentment in each other'.[20] Eve's designation as helpmeet represents, from her side, the existence of a personal community of reciprocal assistance in the necessities, art and joy of being human together. The natural state of a human being, then, is to be in need of community with another. The individual is created in need, incomplete in him or herself. The structural openness of human being for another is a social refraction of the openness to God.

Human being is distorted unless there is recognition of individual and communal incompleteness and inadequacy which leads to acceptance of the help prescribed by God (which may be socially mediated by others). Human insistence on going it alone, to be one's own help, fractures both human community and our relation to God. Openness to the help of human other is the social practice and consequence of the humility operative in openness to God.

Adam and Eve's mutual acceptance, as the conjoining of distance and relation, symbolises the basis for all human life in God's image.

> Man is directed to woman and woman to man, each [is] before the other a horizon and focus ... man proceeds from woman and woman from man, each before the other a horizon and focus.[21]

Our gender distinction is derived precisely from the radical mutuality of our being, the direction of each gender towards the other as gender related. Yet this relation is not a synthetic union but one which retains the real and insuperable differences between men and women and therefore the basis for a continuing dialogical relation between us. Because the distinct being of male and female are human only together we are internally directed towards one another. The distinct natures of men and women are indispensable to one another because they share in human nature only as they share in one another, such that 'we cannot say man [*Mensch*] without having to say male or female and also male and female'.[22]

This dialogical encounter has a structure of open question and answer. The open consideration of one another in their difference, otherness and mystery leads to an open questioning of each by the other. Such ontological proximity-in-distinction, or identity-in-difference, automatically places each in question from the perspective of the other in a process of making responsible answers to one another.[23] Our identity-in-difference means that men and women become a norm and criterion for one another, a challenge to live in gender distinction/gender relatedness. In this gender interdependence, then, there is a fidelity to one's own being coupled with an openness to the other which is respectful of the other's difference and mystery.

Although this process of mutuality involves the closest form of proximity (for which interpermeation would be an appropriate metaphor), the identities of the partners are strictly inexchangeable. In this mutuality otherness is neither subjugated nor negated but honoured. By entering together into a relation of mutuality they are each set, and set each other, in a space peculiarly their own. This space as well as the distinct identities of male and female will change through the course of the relation so no permanently valid definition may be given to them, and particularly not one which has been arrived at outside of this dialogue in which men communicate what women are for them and in which women also communicate their identities themselves, and vice versa. The existence of difference seems to present an almost irresistible temptation for it to be inscribed in a hierarchical pattern of domination;[24] the Genesis creation accounts speak not of domination, however, but of mutuality.

Control

Woman's creation out of man in the second creation story does not signify her subordination but her equality with man as his fitting co-human partner. That Eve's creation takes place whilst Adam is made to sleep is surely a sign that it is God's and not Adam's work. Her creation from one of his ribs is a sign of their common nature, of their interdependence, and not of her subordination:

> he contributes no more to her creation than to his own creation; the mystery of her being is the same mystery as his own being. Her being is as unmistakably her own as his is his own; he cannot put her in his debt. Not that her being is alien to his, competing with his, for she is bone of his bone and flesh of his flesh; but her being is hers even as his being is his.[25]

If the paradigm for human existence in the image is male–female relatedness, then the specific, undistorted character of that relatedness will have a bearing on the character of human relation in general. The divine image represents an ideal codification of relations, which, as ideal, is universal and socially abstract. Yet it also requires realisation in concrete form within determinate social situations. Under concrete, determinate conditions the ideal undergoes transformation so that its concreted form is a socially relative mixture of approximation to and distortion of it (the distortion is not identical with the social relativity). The attempt to formulate and realise the regulative ideal of the image and, in particular, its paradigmatic case of gender difference and relatedness within a concrete situation is necessarily socially relative. Such attempts should not therefore be given the character of a universal or absolute formulation. The interpretation of gender distinction/gender relatedness apart from the concrete forms in which we already know, understand, recognise and criticise it is impossible.[26] That is not to say that the revelation of Genesis cannot stand over the socially and temporally relative structure of relations in judgment. But the critique of the given situation which it enables is already bound to it, through contradiction. This is to say nothing more or less than that God addresses us in our concrete situations. If God's communication is to be informative and transformative of our identities and relations, then it cannot exist in a vacuum but must have some form of contact with the concrete and determinate situations and structures within which these identities and relations are formed. That contact cannot be entirely in the form of negation – even judgment is a more dialectical relation than that involving affirmation as well as judgment. (This point will be elaborated further in Chapters 7 and 9.)

If male–female relatedness is a structural paradigm of human life in the image, then there must be more to their distinction and relatedness than their physical sexuality. In which case, it would be a tragic oversimplification to reduce either their gender distinctiveness to their specific sexual organs or their relatedness to forms of bodily sexual union. The image is connected with the form of their relation rather than with any specific medium or content of it. That notwithstanding, the relation between male and female does have an essential physical component which it cannot be understood apart from. Whilst the status of sexuality ought not to be overemphasised, it also ought not to be isolated out from male–female (and, indeed, all human) relation. Male and female community is not a mystical union of disembodied subjectivities but a shared bodiliness. This includes the whole range of bodily contact, both sexual and non-sexual (no particular relation need include the whole range!), though it can never be simply reduced to it. The form of the related bodiliness is as important as the bodiliness of the relation.

The specific nature of men and women is partly, but not exclusively, bodily. The relation of mutuality pertaining between them will therefore have its bodily aspects. This bodiliness is partly, but not exclusively, sexual. Where it becomes explicitly sexual (this might range from attraction to intercourse), sexuality becomes an active expression, as well as an active deepening and determination, of the form of relationship pertaining to the partners. It is not sexuality and sexual relations per se which should be considered questionable, but only those whose context (for example the extended personal commitments of the partners), form or content is non-dialogical. The most enduring form of distorted sexuality is its decontextualisation from other aspects of life, and hence from the wholeness of personal responsibility, so that it ceases to be a part of an encounter between two whole human persons and therefore to be anything really personal at all. A purely sexual encounter is lived as though the genitals have a life independent from the rest of the person, capable of making their own peculiar commitments and of ignoring those made by the rest of the person. Rather, sexual relations should conform to the dialogical pattern of mutual whole-personal orientation, in which case they would take place 'only in the totality and context of the life of each of the partners including the whole sphere of their encounter and co-existence'.[27]

This would mean that a man is called to be a man, not simply a penis, in relation to the woman, who is similarly in part, but never primarily or completely, a vagina. In order to be whole, sexual relations should take place within the general dialogical orientation on the other which is unreservedly affirmative of him or her in the totality and integrity of their personal being in a sexual encounter which, in turn, deepens that orientation.

The biblical creation narratives closely relate human existence as male and female and God's image without equating them. For that reason I have suggested that the former should be considered as a paradigm of the latter. Reflecting on the gender differentiation in human being as it appears in Genesis 1–3 has produced an understanding of the image in terms of dialogical relation. It is this form of relation as such and in general which constitutes the image regardless of whether those so related happen to be respectively male and female. It would undoubtedly be a distortion of the image if men and women were never or only rarely to enter into dialogue. That their relationship is paradigmatic for human being as such suggests that this will be a crucial dimension of life in which to work out what it means to be human beings together before God. The image is not limited in its reference to relations between men and women, and those relations are not limited to the explicitly sexual. Similarly the use of male–female relatedness as a paradigm for human life does not imply a limitation of sexuality to the relationships between men and women. Neither heterosexual relations nor the form of enduring dialogical commitment (monogamous marriage) which is mentioned in the creation narratives constitutes the image and therefore cannot be taken to be the prescription of a universal for human life. Marriage is clearly closely related to the paradigmatic form of humanity at creation (Gen. 2:24), but they are not equated. The narrative is concerned with a primal event rather than with the foundation of an institution such as monogamous marriage. Further, becoming 'one flesh' denotes neither sexual intercourse nor its product (Seth), but human existence as a whole under the aspect of corporality.[28] It is the dialogical form of relatedness which is normative for marriage, as for all relations and so for all sexuality, not marriage and heterosexuality which are normative for our understanding and practice of dialogue.

Marriage and sexual intercourse are not equivalent terms for the paradigm of 'male and female'. If they were, then the corresponding understanding of human nature would be exclusivist. It would place those male–female relations in which neither marriage nor coitus is a part into a subordinate position and the humanity of all those unable or choosing not to enter such relations in question. The elderly, the impotent, the widowed, the celibate, the hermaphrodite, the transsexual, the deformed and handicapped, and the homosexual would have their humanity and the humanity of their interrelationships denied them. The creation narratives do afford some special status to procreative, and therefore potent, heterosexual relations; however, procreation is construed as a blessing which is bestowed not primarily on individuals but on the species so that it can continue through generation. In short, this way of understanding the image provides no basis for the exclusion of the homosexual, the single and the variously infertile from the image.

Procreation is described as a blessing since it secures the distribution of the image through time as well as space. The family is not the exclusive location of the image (as Gregory of Nazianzus held), but an indication of its temporal character. The family is a paradigm of the image as temporally as well as spatially distributed. The anthropological triangle in which one lives as male and/or female and as child and/or parent has its significance as the paradigmatic case of spatio-temporal human community and is not a universally valid criterion of human life as such. It is here that the ever-present distinctions (those between the sexes and the generations) are brought together in a single community. Existence as man and woman, child and parent signifies the relational structure of humanity through space, whilst existence as parent and child does so through time.[29]

The importance of the connection between human existence in God's image and gender distinction/gender relatedness cannot crudely be exhausted by any understanding of sexuality, marriage or family life. The paradigm's importance lies in the structure of distinction and relation in dialogical encounter which it contains. It says nothing concrete about the distinct nature of sexual differentiation except that it exists and that every practical and theoretical formulation of it is to be conformed to the dialogical pattern of relatedness. Further, it neither supports nor itself promulgates a rigid differentiation between men and women, a complete equation between (supposed) feminine or masculine gender characteristics and physical sexual distinctions. That would only anchor differentiation and hence relation in physical sexuality. The firmness of gender stereotypes is destabilised in the relational process in which distinct identities are formed only through one another.

> One cannot occupy [one's sexual distinction], nor fulfil the requirement of fidelity to one's sex, without being aware of woman if one is a man or of man if one is a woman. And openness to the opposite is not an incidental and dispensible attribute of this position; it constitutes its very essence. All the other conditions of masculine and feminine may be disputable, but it is inviolable, and can be turned at once into an imperative and taken with the utmost seriousness, that man is directed towards the woman and woman to man, each before the other a horizon and focus, and that man proceeds from woman and woman from man, each before the other a centre and source... It does not mean a denial of one's own sex or an open or secret exchange with its opposite. On the contrary, it means a firm adherence to this polarity and therefore to one's sex, but only in so far as such adherence is not self-centred but expansive, not closed but open, not concentric but eccentric. Relation to woman in this sense makes man a man, and her relation to man makes the woman a woman.[30]

Understanding human life in the image of God as paradigmatically male and female, then, does not produce gender or sex definitions. Instead, it suggests the dialogical nature of human life as the orientation of the different upon one another in a complete bodily and spiritual community. It is

> a clear indication that the image and likeness of the being created by God signifies existence in confrontation ... in the juxtaposition and conjunction of man [*Mensch*] and man [*Mensch*] which is that of male [*Mann*] and female [*Frau*].[31]

Human relatedness at creation and fall

The image in its vertical and horizontal dimensions refers to human being as a structure of address and response, of responsibility before God and others (the latter being a social mediation of the former) which, when properly enacted, takes dialogical form. The image, in that case, even in its undistorted form, does not signify an essence or a static substance, but a form of relation pertaining to both vertical and horizontal dimensions. In and through the history of this relational form humanity has its being not as something created and established once for all, but as that which is renewed and reorientated constantly in the open history of address and response. Humanity is something an individual shares in with others rather than being the product of or consisting in acts of separation, such as individual and individualising acts of freedom or reason.

If the image is construed in relational terms, then the structure of human and personal being may be seen to be ex-centric. By this I mean that persons are orientated upon themselves (centred) by moving towards the reality of others. Where this ex-centricity, or orientation on others, takes a dialogical form, there is recognition of the otherness of others, an intention of them as centred in themselves, and therefore as constituting a limit to as well as a claim on oneself. In dialogue, then, one is directed towards other personal centres, and it is through such interaction that one and others become centred (this will be described more fully in subsequent chapters). The form which one's relations takes determines the form which one's personal centring and hence personal identity takes. This can be expressed simply through the dictum that persons are what they are for others or, rather, the way in which they are for others. Human being is a relational structure (ontological aspect), and we are defined by the form our relationships, and thereby our individualities, take (ethical aspect). Personal identities are not fundamentally structures of internal, private, personal attributes, but the form taken in communication, the way in which relations are entered and one exists for others. In Chapter 3 I will argue that this personal form is partially generated by the structures of public communication through which persons come to an understanding of the sort of subjects they and others are and the understanding others have of their and one's own subjectivity.

Persons are a manifestation of their relations, formed through though not simply reducible to them. The Persons of the Trinity, for example, are identified by terms which indicate their most significant relations. Yet they appear in many more relations in a formally identical but materially different way. Hence the Father is identified principally in terms of the relation with the Son but has other relations less significant for, but consistent with, His relational identity and being. He is properly referred to as Father because His communicative identity remains one of generative source and the relation with the Son remains constitutive for His being even in relations where the Son has no direct involvement. The Father is not identical with any one of His relations, but is a sedimentation of His significant history of relations. The effects of a significant history of relation 'fall out', settle and then accumulate around distinct personal centres gradually building up specific personal identities.

Persons, as I will argue in more detail later, are structures of response sedimented from past relations in which they have been addressed, have been responded to and have communicated themselves in particular forms. The image exists in its fullness where undistorted, dialogical address meets a formally reciprocal response; where the invitation to enter dialogue is accepted. It is through the experience of being called into dialogue that a structure of personal responsibility before and for others may be sedimented, in which one becomes a true subject in the divine image. Human being as response is an intrinsically moral structure, since it is a matter not of private subjectivity but of ex-centric orientation. One can come to oneself only through intersubjective processes of mutual recognition. The process through which one's own identity as a dialogical communicative subject is received is simultaneously one in which it is uniquely borne for others. For one's identity as an I is inextricably linked to the reality of the I of other people: an I only for an I!

As stated at the beginning of this chapter, I take the image to be an ontological structure of freedom in response. As ontological, it is a permanent and indestructible structure establishing the parameters of homo sapiens as a being-in-relation. Yet, as a structure of freedom, it has to be understood in terms of potential, as a structure of relatedness in which relations may take a variety of forms. Dialogue, as the undistorted form of the image, is its normative ideal, intended as the fulfilment of human being. The image is capable of both distorted and undistorted realisation; if, however, the image is to become actual in its full, undistorted form, it requires enactment in confirming and conforming response. It is therefore both an ontological and an ethical structure capable of distortion in any and perhaps even all particular situations, but never of destruction as an ontological structure of possibility and responsibility. As ontological, it is a universal structure of human being to which all human persons correspond without exception as defined by their relations and as potential dialogue-partners. The image denotes the creation of all human beings for a life of dialogue-partnership with God and others.

Interpersonal relations do not, however, take place in a vacuum. They are transacted in and through the overarching structures of social relation which make up the general and more localised social contexts within which the partners live (see Chapter 3). Only an absurdly optimistic portrait of the social and societal dimensions of human life would paint them as completely and totally free from distortion. All intelligent analysis and mature reflection regards the overarching social structures which regulate our life together as distorted to a greater or lesser extent and in more or less permanent degree. If it is the case that social structures tend towards distortion, then the possibilities for enacting undistorted interpersonal relations through their mediation would appear to be severely limited. Consequently the chances of an undistorted personal identity being sedimented from these relations are similarly restricted. The Christian doctrines of fall and original sin provide a way of talking about such distortions and the way their effects accumulate in subsequent generations. It is my understanding that the doctrines of fall and original sin describe the distortion of human being through the fracture of relations with God and one another. This distortion of being through fractured relations endures and is passed on through individualising socialisation processes. These entrench the already distorted sedimentation process to the extent that undistorted persons and relations become humanly impossible to create. The fall represents human beings' choice of themselves as a species over against God and as individuals over against one another. Individually and communally humans make themselves the sole basis of value as they enact and constitute their identities in isolation from and in opposition to others and God.

The choice posed by the Serpent in the story of the fall (Gen. 3) was between the constitution of human being either in obedience and faithfulness on the one hand, or in the making and giving of laws on the other. The choice is between orientating oneself through faithfulness to values transcending oneself (otherness), or to oneself and one's own values alone and without limit. Constitution in fidelity and obedience denotes an ex-centric orientation in the free recognition of values external to but with claims upon the self. In the free (*voluntas*) response there is a recognition of an extrinsic law with an intrinsic claim. Law-giving, in contradistinction, represents a self-constitution which, in a purely individual act of freedom (*arbitrarium*), recognises as binding only that which is self-chosen.[32] (In the following chapters I will have to show that ex-centric constitution in an orientation upon the extrinsic claims of God and other is an autonomous, and therefore personal, response and not heteronomic subservience.) This represents a reversal of creation since it is a rejection of the reality of God and the other as intrinsically related to oneself; their rejection, more precisely, as claim and limit. Instead of accepting the other as other in dialogue, as a transcendent limit and claim who can never be assimilated by oneself, there is here the desire to overcome, deny or possess one's limit.[33] The fall represents the desire to be a self-constituting and isolated being rather than a limited creature.

The fracture of relations with one another and with God is the immediate result of the decision to transgress the limits placed on humanity by God to eat the fruit of the tree of knowledge and become like God. The narrative offers a powerful image of this disruption in terms of shame: Adam and Eve can no longer stand before one another openly, in their nakedness, neither can they stand before God and admit what they have done – first they hide, then Adam blames Eve and Eve the Serpent (3: 7–14).

The Christian doctrine of the fall is an attempt to recognise and bring to expression the distortion of human being in the image. The image is a norm for communication which is not presently realised. It exists therefore only as a norm or ideal and has a future aspect. It is both an ontological structure of freedom and a project towards its future reconstitution. The Christian understanding of fall implies that that reconstitution cannot come through human activity alone because, first, the concrete conditions of human communication have become overbearingly distorted and, second, the attempt at reconstitution in isolation from God would only be a repetition of the fall and so a further accumulation of its effects. The future orientation of the image is to be understood in terms of the active co-inherence of the three trinitarian Persons who were similarly working together in its creation. In the future enlivening power of the Spirit the image is directed towards God's future communication in creation–redemption, a future in which all three Persons are involved but in which the Spirit and Son/Word have particular significance.[34] Communication cannot be redeemed by our acting alone, but only in partnership with God and one another as we make autonomous responses to God's address as it continues through history. In Christian tradition there is a witness to the mode of this continuance through history as the call of Christ. This is the subject of the next chapter.

The doctrine of the fall means that the question of the right practice of relations (ethics) has to be relocated. The ethical question cannot be equated with possession of the knowledge of the difference between good and evil, for that is precisely the form of self-possession which led to the fall. Adam and Eve thought they could dispute what God's Word really meant, get behind it to judge both it and God.[35] The assumption that we have the capacity to know the difference between right and wrong and to act upon it is in itself and on its own already a corruption of the image. It isolates one from God and others because what is right for one and others is assumed to be already known. The assumption that one already knows what is right stops communication because no new information or external agency is necessary. In what follows I will describe the image and its redemption as a relational process of seeking what is right in openness to others and God and thereby to the fact that one's understanding and capacity are fundamentally in question.

> The choice between good and evil implies that people are already in touch with reality and their only task is its administration ... The choice between good and evil calls elements within our environment into question: the real ethical question calls us into question.[36]

Consequently the focus on our own possibilities is replaced by an emphasis on our need of, and thereby our relations with, God and others.

In this chapter I have been trying to lay out the basis for a theological understanding of human being in relational terms using traditional Christian doctrine. Central to my elaboration of the assertion in Genesis that humankind is created in God's image has been the notion that both human being as such and individual persons are structures of response. Human being is defined by the form of its response to God's offer of dialogue-partnership – that we be orientated on ourselves and free through our orientation on and binding to God. The Christian understanding that humanity is in a fallen state refers to the rejection of this offer. Instead of entering into a free and thankful relation with God we have become closed in upon and orientated on ourselves. We are still related to God and in God's image, but we are so in a distorted way. Consequently, we are also related to ourselves and to one another in a distorted way.

I have also been indicating that personal identity is linked with the reality of others and the way in which one relates to them, although I have done little more so far than suggest the way in which the determination of identity might take place through relations. I will do this more fully in later chapters. I have already made some initial reference to the fact that dialogue is the preferred form of relationship since it is based upon the mutual recognition of the partners' unique identities. The partners to a dialogue recognise themselves and one another as autonomous subjects of communication – as those who have something unique and independent to contribute to their relation and one another. It is in dialogue therefore that one can be a person in the true sense and it is therefore persons-in-dialogue who are the image of God.

2

The re-creation of individuality: the call of Christ

Basic to the conceptuality I introduced in the first chapter is the under-standing of human being in terms of response to God's address. God intends us as free dialogue-partners. Accepting this invitation means turning ourselves outwards towards God and echoing God's intention of ourselves, God and our relation. Our intentions in communication, the way we relate to ourselves and to God, and the form we expect ourselves and God to take in this relation then reflect or image the intentions and expectations God has. This happens when the prime informant of our communication and being is God's communication towards us and we respond to it in thanks and praise. This openness to God whereby we find our proper human identity by moving beyond ourselves is carried forward in our relationships with one another. In our social relationships, we become fully centred personal identities through moving beyond ourselves in dialogue with others. Living out the fullness of God's image involves relation in both dimensions.

However, even the corruption of the image, the turning away from God and the reality of others, is enabled by the divine intention of dialogue which requires and so creates the possibility of freedom in relation. So even the rejection of God reflects and images God's communicated intention, but it does so in a distorted way. In this sense, human being is always a response to God. The Christian doctrines of fall and original sin are representations of the fact that we are all born into networks of communication and relation in which distortions have become so embedded that it is not humanly possible to avoid them and conduct undistorted relations. That, of course, makes the learning, securing and maintenance of undistorted personal identities similarly impossible.

Christian tradition speaks not only of fall and sin, however, but also of redemption. Redemption refers to God's communication which gives new possibilities of responsibly living in God's image, properly orientated on oneself through dialogical relation with God and others (and so through a proper orientation on them). In redemption, God maintains the intention of humankind in creation as free dialogue-partners, but does so in a way which makes this possible within the limits of a distorted situation, and which is directed towards the fulfilment of what was given in creation. Redemption restores the conditions of creation but, in doing so, also exceeds them. God's redemption of fallen persons and relations does not restore Eden but gives people, where they appropriately respond, a transformed orientation within a world which remains fallen. This is not a return to innocence, then, but a new way of being together in the fallen world – in traditional Christian terms, it is being forgiven and justified by (made right with) God.

God's communication in creation–redemption, the right human response to God and the proper orientation of oneself towards others ought, in a Christian framework, to be formulated in explicitly Christological terms. The second Person of the Trinity, who Christians believe became incarnate in the historical person of Jesus of Nazareth, is also named as God's Word as well as the Son. In Greek thought 'word' (*logos*) did not only mean something spoken, but incorporated much wider reference to anything which is rational or logically ordered, and could refer to this ordering itself. The involvement of God's Word in creation–redemption may therefore be understood as the agency which produces logical and rational structure in, for instance, the created order, redeemed individual identities and their community.

In redemption, a Christological formula is also required by the Christian belief that Christ is not simply the mediator of God's redemptive address to humankind; he actually is that address himself: he is not simply a human vehicle carrying and conveying God's Word; Christ is the Word. Christ is the content, not simply the conveyor, of the communication. Christ, merely in his Person, is God's call to us.

Furthermore, for Christians, Christ is not only the second Person of the Trinity, but divinity and humanity together, a human as well as a divine person. From the divine side, Christ is God's address to us; but from the human side, he is the perfect human response to that address. Christ is therefore the place where divine address and undistorted human response coincide, the place where God's call and proper human response meet. Christ is therefore the enacting of the image in its fullness. Jesus is the human person properly for God and others, and therefore properly for

Himself – both his relations and his identity are undistorted. To be fully in God's image, to make a right response to God and others, is therefore to be conformed to Christ.

This conformity cannot be the establishment of a static substance or state of being, since it denotes living in dialogue and therefore in continual movement beyond oneself. It is not so much something one is in oneself as a way of being towards and with God and others in a variety of situations. Conformity to Christ has the dynamic and open form of following a person. Christ's call to follow Him (which is mediated consciously in the present through scripture, proclamation, sacraments and other forms of witness, and unconsciously through any call to meet the genuine needs of others) is for Christians the paradigmatic form of God's redemptive address which intends humankind in the fullness of the image. Christ himself is God's call to proper forms of personal identity and of relation with God and others, to proper forms of responsibility. But Christ Himself is also the paradigm of the intended form of response. Christ is in Himself a call to responsibility before God and others whose presence patterns and structures identities and relations in dialogical form.

There is a danger of becoming abstract in working all of this out, which must be resisted. Christological formulations cannot properly be abstract or speculative, but must be rooted in the concreteness of a specific historical existence. (This does not mean that the redemptive activity of Christ is limited to the space and time of Jesus' historical existence – it may become personally present among people at any time and in any place.) The historical Jesus, proclaimed in Christian faith as the perfect meeting of God's Word with human response, is normative for Christian understanding of the nature of both call and responding personal orientation: conformity to the presence and call of Christ is the redeemed form of individuality and of relatedness.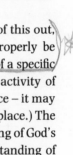

Whilst the Person of Christ is in Himself God's redemptive call – so, strictly speaking, an understanding of Christology and redemption should be based upon an examination of His life, ministry and Person as a whole – there is some benefit in focussing on the particular aspect of His ministry which I shall explore here. My chief concern is to describe individual identity in terms of response. A discussion of Christ's calling of the disciples should throw light on the nature of Christ's call more generally and on the form of individuality and relatedness which are repatterned in response.

The calls to discipleship may easily be individualistically misconstrued as the constitution of isolated individuals in correspondence to the individual Person of Christ, rather than as creating an intrinsically relational and communicative form of individuality. It is easy to see how the calls to discipleship might seem to require such an individualistic interpretation. It is therefore quite crucial to show how and why that would be mistaken, and to defend a relational understanding of individuality here, since it would undermine the theological dimension of my entire argument. For the call of Christ would then be a matter of being true to oneself rather than to God and others and being fully oneself only in giving oneself to God and others.

The call to discipleship
Call, individuality and context

The call to follow Jesus comes to the first disciples in the form of an immediate and uncompromising demand to 'leave everything and follow me'.

> And passing along by the Sea of Galilee, he saw Simon and Andrew the brother of Simon casting a net in the sea; for they were fishermen. And Jesus said to them, 'Follow me and I will make you become fishers of men.' And immediately they left their nets and followed him. And going on a little farther, he saw James the son of Zebedee and John his brother, who were in their boat mending their nets. And immediately he called them; and they left their father Zebedee in the boat with the hired servants, and followed him. (Mark 1:16–20)

The call to the first disciples individualises them by forcing them to stand out in sharp relief from their surroundings and present context.[1] Individual existence (*ex histēmi*, literally 'standing out'), by definition, involves some form of contrast with and independence from context. As a minimum requirement, an individual has to be an internally centred, indivisible whole (although the self-centredness need be neither absolute nor exclusive).[2] The decontextualisation which occurs here, however, seems to be extreme and therefore to contradict the communicative understanding of individuals developed in the preceding chapter.

The disciples' response to the call of Christ is definitive for the nature of individual conformity to Christ. But if what happens to them in responding to Christ's call is a removal from their relations and social (relational) context, then they would appear to be reconstituted in their response to the redemptive call as asocial individuals. I would then be compelled to adopt an individualistic notion of the person as devoid of context and relation or at least only incidentally contextualised and related. Any umbilical cord between individual and possibly formative relations would then seem to be cut by the sword which separates a disciple from his or her family.[3] Does this not, after all, show that responsibility and destiny are individual, that authentic individuality is formed by leaving the inauthentic public mass behind, in going one's way alone?[4]

The individuality recreated in response to Christ's redemptive address could be construed in asocial terms if it were taken as a decision to forsake all relational contexts, to turn away from relation as such and to be centred on oneself in an isolated existential decision and act. This individualistic interpretation is, however, a misconstrual of what is taking place here. The decision and act which reconstitute the individual are not a withdrawal from relatedness as such; it can only be understood in terms of response, as the incorporation into a different relation and relational context. It is not so much a decontextualising act of self-constitution as a recontextualisation in response to an external address. The call brings a possibility which could not be present otherwise in the internality of the called person. The possibility of redemptive reconstitution of the individual is externally and not internally generated. It is not an act of self-constitution through an internally generated and self-directed decision, but a response to an external address.

The individuality reformed in response is dependent upon the creativity of the call; the call is not dependent as such on the pre-existent formations and possibilities of the persons called. It is through the call of Jesus alone, and not through the linear development of their previous identities, that these men are properly reconstituted as individuals. As I shall argue below, this does not mean that their previous identities play no part in the transformation, but that the transformation is wrought in the creative power of the call. The call comes to individuals in their particularity, but this particularity, whilst significant in determining the transformed identity, is not a presupposition of the call. Indeed, this creative Word has no presuppositions whatsoever. A striking feature of the synoptic accounts is the lack of explanation for the disciples' immediate obedience: we are told nothing of their personal histories or psychological dispositions. The Word of God addressed to these particular concrete persons has no presupposition but itself.

There is a great reluctance to accept this. D. E. Nineham, for instance, takes the position that these men must have had some knowledge of Jesus, otherwise their obedience 'would have been inexplicable and irresponsible, and they would not have known what was meant by becoming *fishers of men*'.[5] But what does this really indicate? That the call is not really something transcendent and external? Or is it simply that the call took place within a certain context and history, and addressed certain concrete men within that context (this will be discussed below)? And this need not mean that this history, this context and these men form the presupposition for obedience to or recognition of this Word. What Nineham goes on to call the 'moral' of the story as presented in Mark is, in fact, the reality of the situation. Indeed, if the 'moral' is in any sense true, then God's Word in Christ must, at least sometimes, have this character in reality.

> The call of God in Christ comes with a divine power which does not need to wait upon accidental human circumstances; it can create the response it demands. And that response must be one of unconditional obedience, even to the point of sacrificing the means of livelihood and the closest natural ties...[6]

The call of Levi[7] underscores the fact that this command is without presuppositions. As a tax-farming publican, Levi was considered unclean, and therefore outcast from both decent Jewish society and normal religious practice. It is immediately obvious that the Word's address to this man can hardly have been connected with either his own merit or the status of outcast proscribed in the larger social (communication) context (i.e. the co-intention of him in intersubjectively valid communication as outcast). It can only be grace, grounded in neither this man's history nor that of the covenant between God and Israel, which is its wider context.[8] The graceful call to obedient discipleship happens *to* rather than *in* Levi's human nature and its possibilities, *to* rather than *in* his own history and its development.[9] The graceful call is its own basis and introduces truly revolutionary possibilities which were not and could not have been there before and which are not, in any case, internally held.

Transformation and autonomy

The Gospel accounts focus on the power of Jesus' call to command obedience in and of itself, on Jesus and his emphatic invitation.[10] This does not mean, however, that the individual identities (sedimented from significant histories of relations) of those called are abnegated at this point. On the contrary, the call comes to and transforms concrete persons. As *creative* it must be understood as introducing new possibilities and inviting a transformation of the old identity which could not have been made developmentally. That is, it could not have come as the isolated development of an internally held identity, but only by being set in this new relationship with God through Christ. As *transformation* the old identity has to be involved and somehow recognisable in the transform. There is not a completely new beginning but a transformed orientation, a reconstituted identity empowered by an extrinsic address, the nature of which overshadows the determination of and orientation upon other relations. For some of the first disciples this actually meant abandoning their significant communication context of proximate relations in order to follow Christ. It did not, however, mean totally abandoning the identities sedimented from these significant relations by becoming *completely* different persons. Personality remains recognisable, though it endures in a transformed way and, in these cases, in a new situation.

The obedience of the disciples has no antecedent – not even faith, which becomes possible only through this obedience. Faith and obedience are mutually generating, each becoming possible through the other.[11] The first disciples are called to physically follow Jesus, to take a first literal step whereby faith becomes possible. Whilst it cannot really be said that they understand what this first step entails, it none the less involves a personal moment of decision in which their understanding is somehow engaged. That is to say, it is not a purely external act of overdetermination but an invitation requiring an internally motivated response, an act of personal responsibility which, as free, may be refused. The call is directed towards concrete persons whose possibilities and freedom are therefore contingent and determinate.[12] It destroys neither this contingency and determinacy nor personal responsibility; rather, it awakens the disciples to their responsibilities before God and others in their determinate, historical (but not necessarily proximate) situation.

The disciples are faced with a stark choice, to obey or to disobey, which they make through their own freedom; but, as a choice resting on their own freedom, it does not in itself bring about their transformation. It neither secures their salvation nor makes faith inevitable. The transformed individuality created here is not a product of the exercise of individual freedom. Individual freedom is an external requisite rather than the internal precondition for faith and grace;[13] if it were otherwise, grace would be reduced to a work, representing a binding to the self rather than to the Word of God in Christ. It is just this binding to the self which the disciples are called to leave.[14]

This is the answer which the rich young man who questions Jesus receives but is too self-concerned to accept.[15] Instead of affirming God, he affirms himself in a distorted form of individuality (isolation and self-interest). The narrative shows that his interest is primarily in himself, first of all in his own destiny and then in justifying himself through his answers and questioning of Jesus. He is able to understand the commandments only in relation to himself and his own moral problems.[16] In John's Gospel Jesus' first words to disciples are 'What do you seek?',[17] indicating an either/or choice between self and God, a choice which the rich young man made incorrectly because he supposed that his own destiny and present self-understanding were absolute.

The decision is the individual's active contribution to the transition from the old situation to the new. To be sure, God is involved in this internal moment as well through the indwelling of the Spirit (see below), but that does not depersonalise the contribution of the individual. It is the person who responds, not the indwelling Spirit. But the individual's contribution is still response, a second and therefore dependent moment, following rather than taking the lead. It has to follow God's initiative in Christ because the transformation it offers could not begin with a self-empowered decision. If the accounts of the calls to discipleship were focussed on the power of individuals to constitute themselves through their decisions, then discipleship would be an offer based on an individual's own resources. It would be a self-interested exercise in which nothing would have to be given up for the sake of the Gospel because the cause of the Gospel would be identified with the power of each individual believer to achieve heaven on her or his own resources and therefore for her or himself. Grace would then be entirely domesticated and cheapened.

This interpretation of the narratives implies that discipleship is not an offer one makes in confidence of one's own power and resources; and grace is not the reward for labouring in one's own power. It is just this isolation with one's own possibilities which the Gospel of Christ destroys. The disciples are not called to build up their own individual merits so that they may earn the kingdom for themselves. Hence the obedient response, whilst a necessary requisite of faith, is not identical with it, and justification is through grace alone. Claims made against God based upon the illusion of one's own competence and righteousness can deserve only punishment, for individual power is never sufficient and never more sinful than when exercised as though it were. The illusion isolates one from both God and others. Discipleship, on the other hand, does not mean following oneself, but Christ. The individuality transformed in response is not therefore of an isolated form; it does not signify an internal orientation on oneself, but an ex-centric one.

The man who says to Jesus, 'I will follow you wherever you go' (Matt. 8:19/Luke 9:57) does not fully understand what discipleship entails. For discipleship does not begin with this 'I will', still infatuated with oneself and one's power; instead, it involves its renunciation in an act of obedient response open to the realities of God and others and to one's own insufficiency. This 'I will' shows that the man holds the capacities he possesses at his own disposal and is now ready to lend them to Jesus. Holding himself entirely at his own command, he finds difficulty in understanding what it means to subject himself to the command of God. He is quite prepared to see his capacities used by Jesus, but he is not prepared to renounce this 'I will', to be at anyone's disposal but his own. Jesus' reply indicates, however, that discipleship means joining 'the ranks of the dispossessed, and [being] prepared to serve God under those conditions'.[18]

Self-renunciation

The obedient response frees one from an enclosed and absolute self-binding. Nothing of what Christ's call offers is possible if there is concern only with the response 'I will' make. Grace is domesticated as an individual work where openness to God, indeed anything other than oneself, is impossible:

> this [first] step is, and can never be more than, a purely external act and a dead work of the law, which can never of itself bring a man to Christ. As an external act the new existence is no better than the old... If a drunkard signs the pledge, or a rich man gives all his money away, they are both of them freeing themselves from their slavery to alcohol or riches, but not from their bondage to themselves... If we take the first step with the deliberate intention of placing ourselves in the situation where faith is possible, even this possibility of faith will be nothing but a work. The new life it opens to us is still a life within the limits of our old existence...
> ...[This] means that we can only take this step aright if we fix our eyes not on the work we do, but on the word with which Jesus calls us to do it.[19]

Allegiance to Christ displaces (by transforming it) that to self. The command is to 'follow me', not to choose a way of life for oneself.

Looking, like the rich young man, for some unique and extraordinary demand applicable only to oneself is an attempt to establish one's independence and special nature apart from others, to claim for oneself the ability to judge between good and evil (by rejecting the real command as insufficiently concrete for one's own situation).[20] Faith is empowered by its object, Jesus Christ, whose claim reconstitutes (in a transformed orientation) the individualities of those he calls. The call does not abandon the disciples to their own resources but empowers them through the Holy Spirit. Christian mission and discipleship did not begin with the planned deployment of resources already at the disposal of individuals either alone or together, but with the command to wait for the Holy Spirit.[21] The attitude that 'it all depends on me' 'is precisely what Jesus forbade at the start of it all. They must *not* go it alone. They must *not* think that the mission is their responsibility.'[22] The marching orders for the apostolic mission were given through the empowering of the Spirit. Similarly, the baptism of Jesus in the Spirit immediately preceded his mission, of which the calling of the disciples was an integral part. The disciples were called to share in his ministry and therefore in the power of the Spirit also. Jesus' mission, and therefore that of his disciples, is established not through any power of his, and even less their, own, but through the annunciation of the Spirit.[23]

The response of the first disciples to Christ's call was an act of renunciation of all that gave them security. Through the call of Christ a situation was created, in these first instances, where the irrevocable decision between the old life of self-orientation and the new orientation of obedience and service was obvious. Discipleship is not an addition to the old life. In these first instances that is clearly evidenced by the demand to yield every previous attachment and renounce all that one has. The kingdom is near, the decision must be made whether to follow self-interest or give up everything to follow Jesus.[24]

The call to discipleship is therefore what Bonhoeffer terms costly grace as it shatters all claims to independence and self-orientation. In those first instances this was explicit and immediately obvious. The disciples entered a style of life where such claims could not possibly be sustained; a situation of radical dependence on God's gracious Word it most certainly was, but it also meant a dependence on the material charity of others. For the invitation to share in Jesus' ministry and destiny was also an invitation to share in his poverty and suffering. Christ's call to repentance meant abandoning any absurd notion of isolated self-sufficiency and acknowledging instead one's poverty, one's need of God and others. Those Christ called had, like children, to be incapable of living alone and unaided in order to enter the kingdom.[25]

This may be why the poor are called blessed, since for them there *give up your right to yourself*

can be no illusion of independent self-sufficiency. In the Beatitudes Jesus blesses those who exercise no independent rights because they are not allowed any, those whose lot is so miserable that they can only look to God for its relief. He blesses all those who either cannot or who do not stand upon their own rights and resources through acts of self-assertion. Similarly, discipleship confers no additional rights but strips one bare of every self-assertion which may stand in the way of communion with God and others. It may even mean undergoing the way of suffering rather than establishing one's rights. It may even mean physical death. But whatever discipleship means in any concrete instance, it will always demand a concentration upon him who calls, rather than the respondent. Concentrating on the person called or the response made might build up again the illusion that discipleship is undergone in one's own power, that it establishes a claim on God, and is therefore just another form of self-orientation. The fact that self-renunciation, even to the point of death, is entailed makes it clear that the integrity of an individual is not an absolute or something which occurs in isolation (see Chapter 4), but an ex-centric orientation. The rights which are to be surrendered are those which an individual may grasp as the basis for one's individual identity, but only at the expense of fellowship.

Recontextualisation

The decontextualisation of the first disciples should not be directly equated with the individuality which is recreated by the call. Individuality is not essentially an isolation from relational context. The removal from context made explicit what was involved in obediently following Jesus, but it is not essential in form or content to discipleship as such, as the example of Legion shows.[26] The response of faith effects a transformation such that nothing may ever be quite the same again. On these first occasions it meant a decisive break with the present context and system of relations. Even here, however, both before and after, those concerned are contextualised individuals living within systems of relation and communication. In the first instances the context changed along with the mode of interaction. It is the transformed mode of interaction (what I later term the spirit of communication) which is the essential aspect of individuality formed in response to the call. The decontextualisation which attended it in these first instances was required of these people there and then, but is not a permanently necessary feature.

The decontextualisation is not a moment of supreme individual isolation: it is itself a relation between the called person and Christ – a simpler one than those surrounding the person both before and after, but a relation none the less. The individuality recreated by Jesus' call reorientates the called person in his or her future relations, and it is this which is its essential feature. That it means being at Christ's disposal rather than at that of 'the things of this world', however, must not be individualistically misunderstood. This transformed individuality is not an ascetic retreat from the world, still less from every reality except the disciples' own. The transformation propels them either back into the social context from whence they emerged or else into some other. In either case disciples are firmly contextualised in 'this world', though it can never be the same for them again. This is so, not because they have a reconstituted individuality which is quite independent of overarching social context and significant relations, but because, in the encounter with God's Word in Christ, the determination of both context and self are relativised. Individuality is reconstituted in this response through a recontextualisation in which the relation with God (the God context) becomes absolutely determinative. It is a recontextualisation in a double sense, then: as one is placed in the context of God's redemptive communication one receives a new orientation in one's social context, and so a new form of communicative subjectivity, a new way of being in relations.

The God context in which these called persons now find themselves is not, however, primarily individual. Such individual confrontations take place within a history of salvation which in the Bible is not principally individual but corporate. Whilst events of grace do not happen *in* (i.e. are not contingent upon), they none the less happen *to* individual and corporate history, which are already in place. They therefore take contingent form. They are a part of God's history with God's People and do not destroy the past but transform its interpretation and therefore the way in which it is present.[27] The call to discipleship through which a person's individuality may be recreated is part of a divine–human communication context much larger than the individual. It is only as part of a larger, enduring communication context that the call was comprehensible (in at least its immediate implications) to the called and may be understandable to those outside it.

The address is made in recognisable forms of communication dependent upon, though not completely constrained by, the intersubjectively valid structures of meaning which belong to the social context in which it takes place.[28] Through a prevailing social communication code (language), the content of Christ's call may be understood. Yet such understanding remains only partial. For the call may also transform and overrun contemporary codes and meaning-structures in such a mysterious way that only an indirect or incomplete appreciation of its form or specifiable content is possible.

Christ's call recontextualises persons into a new meaning-frame. It is not the provision of a new world but a new way of being in the old one, a transformation of the old world by giving it new meaning. In the consciousnesses of properly responding persons, the world is recontextualised in an overarching framework of relation to God. As a result they are recontextualised in a world which has remained objectively the same but which is transformed in their subjectivities and which is therefore intended by them in a different way in communication which may, in turn, lead them to transform it. This means a new way of having space and time which, while never ceasing to be personal and therefore marked by the life of a distinct identity, is not absolutely individualised but is ex-centrically orientated. The intention of oneself and one's own space–time is de-absolutised in redemption by the co-intention of others with their own equally valid space–time. For ultimate meaning can no longer be found in one's own space–time, which has henceforth to be related to that of others and God; that is, recontextualised and hence relativised.[29]

The disciples were not called into a one-to-one confrontation with Jesus in order to advance their self-understanding, but into a public form of existence and ministry for others. Jesus did not establish a school, but a ministry which tried to wake people up to the fact that their primary context was God. The first disciples, who were told that they might leave their present proximate contexts for the sake of their special task,[30] immediately entered into a new community with Jesus and one another. They did not enter it for any purpose of their own and so form a closed community, but existed in an open fellowship directed towards God and others.

The disciples were sent out (*apostellō*), and only in this sending out did discipleship achieve its proper orientation and meaning. Luke's Gospel clearly and unambiguously equates the twelve disciples with the twelve apostles. Whatever historical basis that identification has, it is clear from the New Testament as a whole that discipleship and apostolic mission stand in the closest proximity. The 'Follow me' cannot be separated from the 'and I will make you become fishers of men'.

> When Jesus calls them to Him, He does not promise that He will make them Christians and then as such apostles; but He immediately promises that He will make them fishers of men – that is, apostles, bearers to men of a commission that will be given to them, the commission to seek and gather men as a fisherman seeks and gathers fish in his net.

> If from this moment and on the basis of this calling they are called His
> [*mathētai*], what He has to teach them and they have to learn from
> Him is not to be understood as being from the outset a kind of private
> route to their own salvation and blessedness, but as the message
> which they are to proclaim to men in order, through this message, to
> seek and to gather men. What is involved is calling in the fullest
> meaning of the term. Jesus takes them from their previous calling, or
> more precisely He transforms their previous calling, so that they now
> have their new calling in this seeking and gathering.[31]

Discipleship, then, in itself means this orientation out of oneself in the
service of others.[32] The individuality recreated by the call is an ex-centric
orientation towards the call of God and service of others.

Conformity to Christ

In Christian tradition Christ is the concrete history wherein God's
call and human response are present together. His individual identity
(individuality, or form taken in communication) together with the content
of his communication therefore has a normative status for Christian
understanding. A properly orientated individuality and a genuinely
responding relation must be thought of in Christian terms as conformity to,
and the presence of, Christ. Christ is present among us only in so far as our
relatedness conforms to Him; that is, inasmuch as we are genuinely
orientated on God and on one another. Our relationships are properly
structured only where Christ takes form within them. Thus the Christian
ethical norm for relations is not a code of practice as such but something
much more open: conformity to a person whose individuality and
relatedness have a non-distorted character and who represents not just an
ethical model but a demand, a call.

As call it requires explication in terms of general truth, but such
explication must always be for the purpose of making the call of Christ and
of others concrete in the here and now. For the Word does not come to us

through speculation but through the concrete demands and addresses of
others in concrete situations.[33] Abstract ethical formalism is irresponsible
precisely because it constitutes a withdrawal from the concrete situations in
which one is called to responsibility by and before God and others. Genuine
ethical reflection and discourse are always conducted within a concrete
situation of responsibility.[34]

The position I have been taking up in this and the previous chapter
amounts to this: the structure of God's relatedness to human beings

establishes and maintains their individuality by having the specific structure of the call of God who in communication and essence is 'for us'. This may then enter every other relation as a formative principle so that ethics becomes, in Christian terms, a concrete conformation to Christ (see Part III). In this conformation one's communicational form is established and called out in a directedness out of oneself towards God 'for us' in Christ and therefore (because God is 'for us' and not just 'for me') towards others.

Individual Christians are often denoted by their 'being in Christ' or by 'Christ being in them' in such a way that the indwelling indicates the special form of individuality proper to faith apart from any relation in which it might occur. If, however, my argument is correct that a genuine individuality emerges only through properly structured relations, then this might seem to leave the dwelling-in and the indwelling of Christ in an awkward position. Tradition seems to warrant that Christ's presence is individual; my argument, that it is relational and therefore also socially determinate (i.e. the presence of Christ, God's Word to humankind, is heard and responded to within the limitations of specific and concrete social structures of communication such that there is some intrinsic relation between divine and human words). In the rest of this section I will be trying to unite the individuality of Christ's presence in separate persons with his presence between them in their relation together.

Conformity to Christ concerns both of the dual moments of individuality and relation. Indeed, it is only in this conformity that the two moments achieve their true connection and are thereby properly established. For conformation can be neither an autonomous self-constitution nor an heteronomous imposition. It can only be a call and response, a non-identical coincidence of relation and individuality, of the between and the within. Christ is present in both the call and response of one to another as they are conformed to Him.

The terms call and response, however, indicate the dialogical form of the relation as the partners alternately become the active subjects of communication ('speaking' and 'listening' in turn). They only implicitly identify the calling and responding individuals (communicative subjects, or persons) themselves. Christ is therefore present in the dialogical form of the relation, and His presence should always be conceived primarily in relational terms. Yet His presence is not exclusively confined to the relation. He is not only between but also within the partners to a dialogical relation. In the communicative understanding I have been developing, person and relation are reciprocally dependent terms, having a dialectical genetic interconnection. It is not therefore possible to separate them and to predicate Christ's presence only of one to the exclusion of the other.

A relation is conformed to Christ, and He is present in it, when it tends towards an undistorted dialogical structure of call and response. In their dialogical relatedness the partners are also properly structured and conform to Christ. Christ is present in a genuine individuality, but by its very definition as an external orientation, this individual conformation is best understood from its relatedness rather than from its isolation. The genuine presence of Christ in the individuality of each human partner is what establishes the transcendence of each from the other and from the relation. But this individual transcendence does not denote a lone individuality, for Christ's presence directs the individual beyond his or her own borders. 'Being in Christ' or 'Christ in me' indicates not an isolated individuality but an individual's ex-centric constitution in answer to an extrinsic call, an orientation on that which is individually transcendent. The presence of Christ is not an indication of an essence but a movement with others towards 'Christ between us'. Only in this movement is it proper and meaningful to speak, in faith, of Christ's presence in or between persons.

In Christian faith, Christ is the meeting point between God and humanity, the person in whom God's Word and obedient human response are conjoined. In this He is an individual but at once more than an individual, the mediating point between all humankind and God. As such He is turned towards all humankind, becoming the mediation not only of our relation to God but of our relations to one another. In His humanity Jesus is the Person for others, the place where a person is genuinely present in, for, and with others. By being *for* and *with* us He is differentiated from us (this is the maintenance of distance in His relation with us, not a withdrawal from it), but by being *in* us He becomes the principle for the identification of our individualities (this indwelling is based on His differentiation from us and therefore can imply no more than our conformation to, rather than our identity with, Him). Christ is beyond us. From this transcendent position He comes to us, calls us to Him and so calls us to become what we truly are. In other words, Christ is in us as the formative ground of the dynamic movement in which we transcend ourselves and, in this transcendence, come to ourselves; we come to be the persons we are.

By being beyond us He establishes the pattern of transcendence and therefore grounds the very possibility of dialogue (individual discreteness and relation). Yet Christ is not simply a beyond but a boundary, a

[handwritten: faith is not simply belief; faith is response — response to a call that comes through concrete situations + relations.]

related transcendence, a field through which all dialogical communication and relation must flow. Christ is the mediation of the transcendence of God and of others, and therefore a mediation of their claims on us. We are called by Christ into dialogue with the transcendent reality of others and of God. Through dialogue we ourselves are transformed through the processes of sedimentation (see Chapters 3 and 4) and so transcend ourselves through the dialectical spiral of dialogue. Christ is therefore 'in' us as the ground of this self-transcendence, as a centre within us pushing us outwards, and as a centre beyond us pulling us towards God and others. Bonhoeffer is right, therefore, to conceive of Christ existing as the centre beyond us and as the mediation of all genuine transcendence.[35] Because He stands on the boundaries of our individual existences 'for us', He calls us into movement beyond ourselves towards the realities of God and others and to new forms of self-identity. In this movement our individuality and our relatedness become conformed to Him.

Christ's presence in relations safeguards the transcendence and individuality of the partners. The person in Christ can be subsumed by neither the relation nor a partner. If a relation is conformed to Christ then it has something of the character of a buffer which protects the individuality of each from untoward incursion. The protection of the partners from one another must only be understood, however, in the context of their full and undistorted relation. Christ's presence between people should be understood as a properly bound and binding relationship and not as a guarantee of unrelated individualism or of unrestrained self-interest. Bonhoeffer's dictum that 'Christ stands between us, and we can only get into touch with our neighbours through him'[36] stands because in any genuine relation there must be respect for the transcendence of the other, as an orientation upon or response to him or her, and that can only be mediated through Christ. The presence of Christ within and between individuates only as it binds together.[37] *[handwritten: Christ within mediates movement toward the transcendent other.]*

The presence of Christ in the Church

This Christology has immediate ecclesiological implications which can only be hinted at here. If faith is understood in terms of responsibility, then it both establishes faithful individualities (redeemed communicational forms of personhood) and binds them together into a corporate body of Christ (redeemed communication community). These two realities are coincident and normative for each other. 'The Church' is any place where properly structured individualities and relations are co-present. In this community there is genuine response in answer to genuine call. In the empirical Church Christ is consciously and explicitly present in the communal communicative activities of proclamation and sacrament and therefore as community.[38] This is an ideal for the Church as well as the means of its identification. It is only in so far as Christ is truly present, in response as well as call, that the Church is identical with itself as it is conformed to Christ, thereby becoming His body. (An understanding of body in social and communication, rather than just physical, terms is necessary here.) In the Church the address and claim of Christ are mediated (primarily through proclamation and sacrament) and responded to in the concreteness of a particular situation. As a pattern of address and response it shapes concrete spiritual and material community around the person of Christ who, in this concrete community, is the Truth. The Truth is Christ shaping concrete relations between people as a community in His name.[39] The presence of 'Christ between' is Truth and fidelity.

The presence of Christ as Word is community because the communication, and therefore reality, of that presence through proclamation and sacrament are themselves forms of communication which build up community in and of themselves. The Word is not something individually possessible, but the subject of communication within community. That is why the Church is not simply the place where Truth can be heard, where the presence of Christ is witnessed to; it actually is the presence of Christ for us, 'Christ existing as community'.[40]

The Church, then, has its identity as a pattern of communication. There is listening and response to both divine Word and human words (this can, of course, happen beyond the empirical boundaries of Church in unconscious ways). The reality and presence of individuality is denoted by the ordering of communication in a particular form which, because this form must be concrete, is partly socially relative (see Chapter 7). Christ's personhood or individuality is Word-present in the Church and is therefore a real presence, structuring and ordering identity and relation. The nature of the Church is to be 'wherever two or three are gathered in my name'. Christ is really present in the communicational form (redeemed intersubjectivity) of this gathering. The sociality of the Church makes ethics ecclesiological as it provides a principle of concretion for what might otherwise slip into abstraction.

The redemption of individuals opens them to transcendent realities. On being opened to and by God, one is automatically opened to the transcendent reality of others.[41] Sociality and community are created with the response of faith. The communicational form which the Word takes creatively assumes and intends the status of a freely responding (autonomous) subject of communication.[42] Formed through God's gracious address, it is not a freedom from relation but a freedom only in and for relation. This individuality transcends the determination of particular relations by having the status of a free response. But as free response it is grounded in the address and not in some form of autonomous self-sufficiency. Faithful individuality is free response to address and is therefore inseparable from faith in others. This incorporates the acknowledgement and respect of their otherness, but also of the fact that this otherness is precisely what calls one to responsibility before, and therefore in dialogue with, them. These issues will be taken up in the following chapters.

The power of the Holy Spirit

If the Church is constituted by the presence of Christ, whose history was a co-inherence of the Son with the empowerment of the Spirit, then the Spirit must also be expected to co-inhere with Christ's presence in the Church. Individual identity is attributable to a person's spirit of communication, the communicative form in which he or she enters relations which, in turn, is derived from previous relations. An individual's spirit organises his or her communication and relatedness which, through communication, becomes formed and structured into an individual identity. Yet the forming and structuring do not happen directly through spirit but through concrete communication. Individual spirit is life-giving energy, the social consequence of which is the organisation of communication which then ossifies into structured form. As an individual's spirit is itself formed through relational processes of sedimentation, it is a manifestation of the person's relationships. But, being in itself formless energy, it is only manifested in those relationships in the consequences of its organisational activity – in the production of ordered communication and, consequently, of a structured individual.

The Holy Spirit may then be conceived as the organisational energy of communication open to others and to self-transformation which, through co-inherence with the Word, the ordering *logos*, produces open forms of individual and communal life. The Spirit is neg-entropic energy (i.e. energy which produces ordered openness in systems, as opposed to the disorder of closed systems, which is entropic), which is the organisational life-force; Word is the form-giver to organised life. Where Spirit and Word co-inhere, they create undistorted forms of individuality and relatedness which, whilst structured, are open and, whilst open, are structured.

The Spirit operates in creation–redemption in both the social and natural spheres of life. Creation begins when the Spirit is breathed into the formless mass. The infinite energy and potentialities of the Spirit do not create a simple series of entities but a world in which individuation is a punctuation in a system of relations (environment or context). In this punctuated cosmos individuation and integration, closure and communication are bipolarities of the one life process. The name of complete separation is death. The name given to a partial separation, of a boundary where both closure and openness begin, is life in all its varied forms. If a living being is cut off from its environment, if it is unrelated, if it is not integrated into its cosmos, then it disintegrates and dies. The structure of biological open systems tells us that life cannot be lived merely from a centre as an internal and private process.[43] It is only through communication and exchange whereby a centred existence transcends, returns to, and, on the basis of this movement, adapts itself, that beings can live. The stability of a living structure is derived neither from inflexibility (closure towards the future or change) nor incommunicability (closure from relatedness) but from self-transcending movement.

Recent physics and biology have provided a compelling model of a universe in which relations are primary, and in which it is proper only to speak of relations between relations rather than of entities in themselves. This provides an interesting and most useful analogy for social life,[44] but care must be taken not to overestimate the degree to which the analogy applies and on what basis it may be made. There has been a tendency to romanticise this rediscovered relatedness of nature in which everything has its reality only through its relations with and 'in' other things.[45] The switch from mechanistic to organic language which has accompanied this changed perception can cloud the fact that these relations are self-interested structures of response to external stimuli. They are ultimately more complex and open forms of mechanism, but they approximate to mechanisms none the less. Stimulus and response do not provide any scope for ethics because they cannot be subjected to external criteria of justice. Were social relations to be based on the principles of biophysical relatedness, the results would be disastrous. There would be no means of securing the continued independence and opposition of the other, merely an injunction for self-preservation through self-transcendence; and that transcendence could take on any form whatever, as the form required in nature is bare of content.

In the social world, however, the Spirit's activity is normative for communication and does, therefore, inform a social and personal ethic. In social terms the power of the Spirit is operative in breaking open hard structures of distorted communication in order to establish dialogue and community and therefore the redeemed form of individuality. The social consequences of the life-giving Spirit are simultaneously self-preservation and self-transcendence. But here the form of transcendence indicated is dialogical and therefore radically open to others. The movement beyond one's own borders is not only towards but for others. The activity of the Spirit in the social world is therefore primarily an orientation on others and only secondarily, and by this means, an orientation on oneself. This is something of a reversal of the priorities of communication and exchange in the natural world. In the social world under the impact of redemption both self-preservation and self-transcendence are for the other.

In this and the previous chapter, I have been trying to show that an orthodox understanding of humanity created in the image of the triune God and redeemed through God's address in Christ seems to require a relational understanding of human being. The principal features of the account of created and redeemed humanity are:

- the identities of humankind and of individual persons are to be construed in terms of their response to God and others;
- individual identity denotes the way one enters relations and is for others;
- this identity is derived from one's previous relations – the way one has previously been addressed by and has responded to others;
- a person, in the technical sense in which I use the term, is a subject of communication, an I before the I of others;
- personhood is fostered through being addressed, intended and expected as a person by others; that is, through relations which take dialogical form.

These elements are all crucial features in the discussion which follows. I have also alluded to the Christian doctrines of original sin and fall, which assert that the structures of human being and relation have fallen into distortion. In the context of the relational determination of personal identity and communication, this clearly raises the question whether and how the possibilities of dialogue and undistorted identity may be recovered. The question of what the practice of dialogue might mean and what its wider implications might be in terms of personal, social and political structures is taken up in Chapters 4–9. Before that can be adequately addressed, however, it will be necessary to describe in more detail how people might be formed through their relations: this is the theme of the next and, to a lesser extent, of the subsequent chapter. In the following chapter I shall describe the normal social processes through which our identities are formed. It is only through an understanding of these processes that there can be an appreciation of the way in which God may use and work through them to achieve the redemptive transformation of persons and relations.

Part II

Social relations

3

The social formation of persons

I am concerned in this book to explore the possibility of conceiving individuality and personhood in social and communication terms. The major and critical issue in this is how persons are formed and may be transformed. The issues and conceptions relating to this question which are the most crucial for the thesis I am advancing are dealt with in this and the following chapter. Together they therefore stand at the very heart of my argument. The basis of the position I shall be taking on these issues is the understanding of persons as individuals whose consciousness, experience of and interaction with the world are internally centred. Conducting oneself from a personal centre of being and communication is what makes self-direction – that is, personal control of and intervention in oneself and one's interactions – possible. In other words, personal centring enables performance as a subject in communication, being an I for and before others and for oneself (through self-reflection and consciousness). As a person one understands oneself as a unified source of interaction, consciousness and experience who has continuity through different times and places. All one's consciousness, experience and action in different times and places are centred on oneself and therefore form a continuous point of identity.

But how does such personal centring come about? Does everybody have some internal organ of unity, a personal centre or self, simply by virtue of his or her natural constitution as a human being? If that were the case, then it would be difficult to account for cultural variations in the ways persons centre themselves and for the way in which different communities seem to yield different senses of personal identity. Individualistic conceptions of persons and their centres of personhood (generally termed 'selves' in Western tradition) as essentially asocial, or at least presocial, would also seem to be unavoidable were this the case. For personhood would then be something entirely individual, a result of internal, individual processes. A number of consequences would seem to follow from this. Individuals would come to social interaction with the form and content of their personhood already acquired. Social and societal life cannot make any significant difference to an identity which is intrinsically private and individual. One would not enter social life in order more fully to understand and become oneself in relation to others if self-understanding and the manufacture of personal identity were internal. One would not realise oneself through relations with others; one could only bring an already realised identity to public expression. One would enter relations with individually predetermined interests, and it is hard to see how one would wish to meet any other interests in interaction unless they directly or indirectly assisted one's own, given that persons are centred in such an exclusive way: orientated upon their own rather than others' personal centres.

Against this individualistic conception of persons, relations and society, I shall be arguing that the sense of oneself as a subject, a person, is not individually but socially acquired. The way others have related to, regarded and intended one as a subject is individually appropriated as a distinct personal identity. This history of personal interaction is in turn governed by social codes, the socially relative expectations attaching to persons in general and particular which pattern relations in a given society. The general social context therefore determines the ways in which people may be routinely recognised and addressed and enter communication, and so orders the pattern of relations around each individual from which a unique personal identity is sedimented, along with the understanding that one is a person, a subject of communication, by virtue of the socially recognised fact that one is a single, continuous centre of interaction. In other words, what one learns to recognise from others' recognition of one is that one is a subject who organises one's experience, consciousness and interaction in a centred way.

One very important consequence of this way of thinking is a reconception of the 'self' as linked to others and to more general social structures. A 'self' is not some internal organ of identity, but is understood in communication terms as a way of organising one's life and communication in a centred way. It is not something one has so much as something one does, which is learned in social interaction.

Clearly, if personhood and identity are linked to the concrete form of relating one is habitually a part of, then many of the distortions of personhood and identity (i.e. people regarding themselves as less than subjects or as totalitarian subjects) will be traceable to distorted patterns of relation. Similarly, since personal identity will undergo modification with incorporation into new forms of community, distortions in identity might be overcome through new patterns of relating. In the following chapter I discuss how such transformations (in theological terms, redemption) might come about through interpersonal relations, and explore the qualities those relations must have if they are to remain (relatively) undistorted. How I may genuinely seek, relate to and call the other; and how I may be for the other are the concern of the following three chapters. Given my conception that we become subjects only through relation to other subjects, the question is not only about how I can secure the genuine identities of others, but my own as well.

Natural theology?

The processes through which persons are formed are neutral, in that through them both distorted and undistorted relations and individualities may occur. My primary concern in this chapter is to indicate the neutral structures through which both fallen and redeemed forms of personhood may be sedimented. In doing so, however, I will be preparing the ground for subsequent chapters, where my concern is primarily with the redemptive transformations which occur through the processes of person formation when one is brought into relationship with God and others through Christ. The 'neutrality' of the processes constitutes them as an ontological structure, something like an 'order of creation', in which the minimum (i.e. necessary but insufficient) requirements of personhood are retained.

But if God uses the relational processes through which we are formed as persons for our redemptive reconstitution, does this not bind God's redemptive communication to an arbitrary and independent 'natural' social reality? Or, if their reality is not arbitrary, does God's use of these processes show them to be above 'natural' reality, to have a special and non-neutral status? Both questions must be answered in the negative as soon as God is understood to be the creator of an independent world which is structured as free in relation to its creator. God's creative communication takes dialogical form and thereby gives reality its freedom over against God. If God's redemptive communication is seen as a re-creation, rather than as a doing away with things followed by a completely new *creatio ex nihilo*, then it will respect the reality of that which is to be redeemed. If God did not use and respect the realities of personal existence, including its distortion, then redemption as the re-creation and reconstitution of the *same* person *as* a person (i.e. free and responsible subject) would not be possible.

Notwithstanding God's use of 'natural' communication processes they are still, apart from God's direct use of them in redemption, fallen into distortion. But even these distortions owe their reality to God's creative communication which, taking dialogical form, structures the world in freedom. So there is a continuity between original creation, fall and redemption in the form and intention of God's communication. Redemption is rooted in God and, whilst it happens to natural reality, it is not a natural process which could have taken place without God's active engagement. Further, the fact that God is redeeming the world in a way which does not corrupt the world's nature cannot be taken as an indication that that nature has not been corrupted, or that God is tied to some arbitrary and continuing reality. The continuities between fallen and redeemed reality are attributable to the continuity and faithfulness of God throughout creation–redemption.

A natural theology in which redemption is somehow rooted in and dependent on either the fallen or the original form of creation would therefore be quite illegitimate. Either option would give creation an absolute form of independence over against God, binding God to an arbitrary reality, 'nature'. Even if it could be shown that the distortions of reality were parasitic upon, and therefore presupposed, the primacy of undistorted reality, there would still be no basis for placing undistorted 'nature' over against God as the precondition for redemption.[1] The distorted residues of pre-fallen processes do not constitute the necessary and sufficient conditions for redemption; it is, rather, the continuity of God's communication in creation–redemption which is the necessary and sufficient condition for the continuities between original, fallen and redeemed reality.

Personal formation through social relations

In order to understand how it is that persons may be constituted anew by incorporation into redeemed forms of relationship and community, it is necessary to comprehend how personal identity is socially formed prior to such redemptive contact. What I shall be trying to show is that individuality is socially structured. My position is that individuals are formed through social processes, their identities sedimented from histories of significant relation. The form which a person's significant relations have taken is determinative for that person's identity.

This understanding intimately binds personal identity to the identities of others and to the relations one has with others. But because relations never take place in a social vacuum, only within a determinate social context, personal identity is also bound to the social and societal structures which constitute the larger environment of both persons and smaller-scale personal relations.

Interpersonal relations take place within a given social context. They are therefore interpersonal exchanges conducted within a communication code (social 'language') given with that context. The communication code is a semantic system regulating exchange values within a moral order (social orders may be considered moral orders because they regulate values in this way). It routinely structures (codifies) communication and relations according to the system of values operating in a given social context and governs the way distinct groups and individuals may be recognised and addressed and may enter into relation with others.

The process of call and response must therefore be considered a moral discourse, since it is carried on and structured within the moral order of a particular social context which attaches different values to certain identities and communications. So the call and response of one to another is loaded with moral content and implication. Interpersonal communication in which one responds to the call of another is a reciprocal process of the taking of moral responsibility before the other in which the partners paradigmatically ask for and give help in situations of practical difficulty. An individual identity is both expressed in and derived from the moments in which one responds to others within the framework of a given moral order. Individuality may thus be termed a sedimentation of moments of moral responsibility within concrete relations.

Individuality, it must be understood, however, is not purely momentary, but is a structured, continuous identity sedimented from significant 'moments'. (These 'moments' are not as isolated as the word might be taken to imply from its use in other philosophical and theological contexts. The 'moment' is isolated neither from the individual's history nor from the more general social context.) For if individual identities were to be equated with the moments of their particular responses, then they would have no reality beyond their active engagement in particular relations. The partners to a relation would then be nothing more than 'turns' within it. There could be no sense of continuity to account for the way in which the same individual may be a 'turn' in not one but many relations, or for a person's discreteness from relation evidenced by, say, the privacy of individual psyches and the private or 'internal' presence of a person to him or herself. Individuals do not simply arise out of a present moment of response only to fall away again afterwards (which would make each moment of response absolute, yet only while it lasted), but endure 'between' as well as in relations.

The 'moments' we have to do with here are ethical and refer to the time of decision in which a whole person is faced with a concrete call to moral responsibility. Because they concern the concrete demands of a concrete situation to be met by a concrete person, they cannot be absolute, nor can the decisions made in them be universal. This is not, then, a Bultmannian eschatological moment which lifts one out of a concrete historical, social and moral context into 'the fullness of time' and value. For such a moment would be one of irresponsibility (or would at least be morally arbitrary), because it decontextualises from any 'objective' system of moral evaluation in which the relative value of concrete times and places can be judged (doing this, here and now, against, say, doing it later or elsewhere; or, again, against being somewhere else to meet other demands). The moments are, in fact, more like Bonhoeffer's, in which the person remains whole (is not a bare subjectivity, mind, or whatever), particular, and in concrete context (rather than being an abstract, universal subject placed in eternity). The moment, the decision, the responsibility and the person are all of relative value because they are all set concretely in relation to God; set, that is, in an overarching communication context.[2]

If individuals are called into being by others, then it is impossible to think of individuality as isolated, for the existence of one and other is inextricably linked. I hope to show that they are linked by concrete moral (or immoral) community. Individuals are not linked through an abstract metaphysical principle but through concrete relations in which one's individuality is addressed and called into being as a communicative, and therefore moral, subject of a certain form. The individual character of a person is dependent on the form of recognition afforded her or him, the manner in which she or he is addressed by others, within a moral system (society) which regulates such interaction through locally valid communication codes.

Each call or address contains certain assumptions regarding the called person's capacities, abilities, disposition, etc., and these partly determine the form and flow of the relation and of the individuals who take part in it. In a particular way (described below), this is a mediation not only of what is being expected of one by another but also of the general definition of what it is to be a person in that particular society, and of what form of personhood (communicative identity) is expected from particular individuals in particular social situations. It is through such generalised and more specific mediations of what personhood in a wider community of persons is about that a distinctive variation, or unique personal identity, is built up. (A full discussion of this follows in subsequent sections of this chapter.)

It is impossible, then, to abstract individuals either from others or from the wider social context of which they are all members. It is similarly impossible to abstract the relationships from the individual persons or from this wider context and so imbue them with absolute reality. Neither persons nor relations nor societies may claim to be absolute and determinative in an unrestricted (i.e. unrelated) sense. For all are intimately intertwined.[3] The basis for such a claim should become clearer later in this chapter.

Physical and social embodiment

Embodiment as source of identity

A person is a singular subject of communication, an individual who can enter and initiate communication more or less autonomously (i.e. in a way which is not overdetermined). Communicative subjectivity and its correlate, autonomy, do not denote an essential or absolute discreteness from relation, but the power to persist as a distinct person in relation; and this power of personal agency is obtainable only through relation. In order to organise oneself and one's communication as a subject, a person must regard her or himself as a unified, continuous source of communication capable of self-directed and controlled interaction in various fields, and therefore as a subject who may recognise, 'own' and take responsibility for one's communication. But how and why does one come to regard oneself in this way? If it were by some private and discrete intuition of oneself as the possessor of certain internal psychical attributes, then an individualistic account would be sufficient and necessary. In the following, however, I shall be arguing that this sense of one's subjectivity is socially acquired, that it is given through participation in social processes of communication and relation, rather than being something individually innate which develops in isolation from others. In this argument, I will be drawing heavily on the groundbreaking work in psychology and the philosophy of science of Rom Harré.[4]

A person recognises him or herself as a singular, unified and

continuous subject responsible for the consequences of his or her communication. This self-recognition, however, is secondary and is derived from the
recognition afforded the person in the structures and processes of public
communication. The public recognition of persons is primary; their
recognition of themselves as persons, secondary and derivative. In the
public structures and processes of communication, a matrix of persons is
recognised in which persons are potential sources of communication. Here
a person is a simple, publicly identifiable location from whence communication may emanate and to which it may be directed. A person must be
publicly recognisable as a distinct and continuous location and will
therefore be afforded a distinct public identity evidenced by the form and
degree of distinction in public recognition.

The source of the public identity of persons as non-complex
locations is the simple and empirically observable fact of their embodiment
in the physical and social dimensions of the public sphere as distinct and
continuous individuals. The body is the strongest source of the recognition
of a person as the same: if we can recognise this body as the 'same' body (i.e.
notwithstanding developmental and other changes, there is a recognisable
continuity between then and now) which we saw five years ago, then we
would need very persuasive and extraordinary counter-information before
we would be prepared to recognise this location as a different person (a twin,
say).[5] If we knew someone to have died, then if we saw an identical body in
the future, we would be more likely to call this an uncanny resemblance
than the same some*body*, because we know physical continuity to have
been broken.

If we doubt the physical continuity and identity of a person, then
we may look for evidence of continuity in his or her social embodiment in,
for instance, habitual forms of speech or behaviour, the display of publicly
verifiable memory content, or the retention of artefacts connected with his
or her claimed social location (for example birth certificate, heirloom, badge
of office). There are many published, filmed and dramatised accounts, not
all of them fictional, of people who have been asked to prove their identities
in this sort of way, usually before claiming an inheritance, a title of honour,
or both.

Public embodiment and public recognition of the simple fact of
personal identity as a locus of communication are the primary sources of
the sense of identity necessary to regard, and consequently conduct, oneself
as a distinct, continuous and integrated subject of communication: that is, a
person. The fact that one is taken to be a distinct, integrated and continuous

subject of communication deposits an understanding of oneself as a distinct, integrated and continuous subject. It is this and not some innate, asocial sense of self, or the possession of certain asocial, innate psychological capacities, which is the primary source for personal identity and which makes personal existence possible.

Individuals are distinct locations in both the physical and the social dimensions of human life. Individuality is derived from the fact of one's embodiment as a distinct spacio-temporal location in both the physical and social worlds. Because each person is distinctly located, we all hold unique perspectives of experience and interaction (points of view and action), which provide us with unique experiences, fields of interaction and possibilities of communication (where, when and how we may undertake communication). The fact of this embodiment in both dimensions of the public world as a unique point location, and its consequent recognition by others in communication and relation with one, together constitute the source of the understanding of one's identity as distinct and personal, and for the particular and unique character of that identity. I hope that the reasoning behind this assertion will become clearer as the argument of this chapter develops.

Is a person a physical or a social 'thing'?

Social life and communication are founded on bodiliness, and interpersonal communication is both a social and a bodily activity. The specifiable meaning of communication is anchored firmly in existence in an objective (i.e. intersubjectively valid) *social* world. But the possibilities of communication and of social organisation as such are derived from embodiment in an objective *physical* world. The body has a language of its own, but even speech and hearing are physical events which become possible only through a specific form of bodily organisation and functioning. The possibilities of community and of communication are rooted first in the physical organisation of the human organism, and second in the social organisation of human beings and of public meaning. This leads to a specific conception of individuality in terms of embodied communication, and therefore of the body as a communicative form rather than a point of closure.

The body is an important element in the public recognition of personal identity; it is, indeed, our first and best tool in the identification of persons. But it is not our only tool, and that fact is crucially important; important, because it introduces a resistance to the reduction of persons to the status of physical 'things'.[6] Whilst it is vital to take physical embodiment with the utmost seriousness, and to resist the artificial separation of the physical from the social, the reality of persons is, none the less, primarily social. Social and personal life are founded upon embodiment in and interaction with the physical world, but individuals are constituted as *persons* through processes of social, rather than physical, communication and exchange (see below).

In what follows, I shall be trying to take physical embodiment with appropriate seriousness, but to steer away from a reduction of the person to the body and from a conception of the body in terms of static substance, towards an understanding of both person and body in terms of organised communication. A person is formed through communication and relation; personal identity denotes the way in which one enters communication and relates to others. In which case, individuality is a punctuation, not a separation, and a person is to be thought of primarily as a pattern and organiser of communication.

Making it clear that I am not thinking of person primarily as body and of neither as a static, physical 'thing' ought to remove any suspicion that my argument for the social formation and determination of persons leads to a strict determinism. That kind of determinism could only result if the communication processes through which persons are formed were described in terms approximating to the physical, conceived in mechanistic terms, as a process of simple stimulus and response. If, however, personal and social realities are described in moral and dynamic terms, as structures of response and responsibility, then social determination need not denote the strict causality of the world of engineering. Persons are not component parts, things, entities or mechanical devices, just as the processes which form them and in which they participate are not mechanical. As a subject of public communication, a person is more like a 'place' (a location of communication) than a 'thing' or an object.

Locations in social space and time

As bodies-in-motion, individuals and their physical activity can be located using physical space and time as a locating grid laid over the totality of all physical objects and interactions. Their location and activity could then be expressed in relation to, and coordinated with, other physical bodies, events, places and times. Persons and their communication, whilst founded on physical embodiment, are primarily social. Whilst they always exist in physical space–time, the physical locating grid is insufficient to coordinate them as social realities, as contributors and contributions to a social discourse. Social space–time is the appropriate grid for the location and coordination of persons and the content of their communication as social realities. The physical and the social are distinct but interdependent dimensions of human life. They should not therefore be thought of as competing and mutually exclusive, but as interrelated. Social space–time is distinct from physical space–time, but not absolutely so. The two grids should be deployed alongside one another because social and psychical communication and exchange are physical as well as social interactions. There is only one world, which, for humankind, is doubly dimensioned.

By using the appropriate grid, communication can be located in the physical dimension and coordinates given to the time and place of its occurrence, as well as to its subject, object and referent, all as physical realities. The coordinates given to the point locations in physical space–time which these realities occupy can be indexed by expressions such as 'here', 'there', 'then', 'now' and 'next'. The physical space–time grid is not made up of all possible physical objects and events, but of all possible locations at which objects and events may be and may take place. It is therefore possible to track physical interactions and exchanges as the relative location of objects changes. In this grid, of course, individuals appear merely as physical bodies.

Such a grid is inappropriate for referring to and tracking the constituents of the social 'world'. To engage in social communication it is necessary to be able to locate other persons and their communication relative to oneself, to understand what others mean by their communication, and to anticipate how one's own will be interpreted. That is to say, one must know where one stands in the matrix of persons, which is a structure of interpersonal commitments, and thereby understand the relative significance of different persons and their communications. To refer adequately to the dynamics characteristic of personal and social life, 'the location and tracking of thoughts, feelings, intentions and commitments and so on' is necessary.[7] The social space–time grid will therefore function to coordinate such socio-psychological phenomena (i.e. psychological dispositions, states, and so on, which appear in communication as socially significant commitments) which are the constituents of personal and social life.

Communication and the socio-psychological phenomena embedded within it are like the interactions and objects which may be located through the physical grid. In the social grid persons are not like physical objects, but like the places where phenomena may be located at particular times, and to and from which they may move:

> thoughts, feelings, intended actions and so on are indexically located at persons, at the time of their utterance, just as things are located at places at times... Things can be at some places and not at others, and they can move from place to place. In parallel ways, thoughts can be entertained by some persons and not by others, and they can be communicated from person to person.[8]

The array of all physical locations, together with the spread of all possible times, constitutes the physical grid through which distinct point locations in space–time may be identified. Similarly in the social sphere, the spread of all possible times together with the matrix of persons constitutes the social grid through which social and psychological 'objects' and communication may be located at distinct point locations (i.e. at a particular person at a particular time).

The personal pronouns mark the point of origin or destination of a communication or the psychological state, activity, disposition, etc. behind it. In the social 'world' personal pronouns and verbal tense replace the adverbs which refer to the relativity of place (here, there, etc.) and time (now, then, etc.) in the physical world. A pronoun indicates a *relative* point location in social space–time, the 'here' and 'now' of social communication. When I index an object by saying, 'it is over there now', you will have no idea of what and where it is unless you understand where I am in relation to you and it. This understanding will make it possible for you (perhaps only through imagination) to occupy my position and look along my index finger to see what I am looking at and referring to. Precisely the same is true when I index a person by using a personal pronoun. To know whom I am indexing you must know my, their and your relative positions in social space–time. 'Here' and 'now', 'I' and 'you', as expressions of relation, are quite meaningless unless related to a definite point. The abstract locating grids have some anchor in reality, as it is for 'me', in order to be used appropriately. That is to say, the grids must be anchored in the particular location in the physical or social dimensions which 'I' occupy, so that all locations are related to the points of view/experience and of action 'I' have.[9] The pronoun it is appropriate to index a person with in a particular communication situation may vary according to the relative position of the user.

Pronouns are not proper names and need to be distinguished from them, just as indexical adverbs are to be distinguished from place names. Proper names identify a member of the matrix of persons by public criteria which do not relate that person to communication, to oneself or to others as personal pronouns do. This act of indexing could therefore be carried out from any location in the matrix.[10] Whereas proper names always index the same person within the context of the whole matrix of persons, a personal pronoun can mark several persons as the points of origin or termination of communication. We know that the 'she' I am indexing now is not the same as the one I indexed in the previous sentence, or the one you indexed yesterday, if the contexts within which we are speaking, and our relative positions in the matrix, have altered significantly.

Personal pronouns function to identify 'where' speech, for example, is coming from and to relate the time at which 'I' am speaking (and therefore the content of what 'I' am saying) to, for instance, psychological states I have had at other times, to those others have or have had, to previous times at which I have spoken, to the times at which others have spoken, are speaking or will speak. Personal pronouns mark the contribution and engagement of people in a particular network of communication; they show who speaks or acts and when (in what order), in relation to the speaking and acting of the others. This makes it possible to track social communication and exchange, as meanings are shared, understandings reached, and so on, through social space–time.

Through the social locating grid, persons can index themselves and others as the communicating subjects of particular moments through appropriate use of pronouns and verb tense. That is, they can relate themselves and others to the contours and contents of public communication. To use a proper name competently, it is necessary only to be competent in the procedures for public identification of persons. But competent pronoun deployment indicates a more generalised communicative competence, the ability to contribute to and participate in social communication. This is so, because it represents the ability to relate 'me' as a spacio-temporal social location to other persons and their intercommunication, and so the capacity to be a potential contributor to that intercommunication. For, in using 'I', I am not referring to a thing (e.g. my 'self'), but to my position as a point location relative to others, and referring to that point as the location from whence communication may originate and with which communication may be conducted. 'I' does not indicate an internal entity or a static substance, but might be considered a portable means for contextualising oneself (a 'shifter'),[11] a means for engaging in communication in various contexts, and constructing local personal (relational) identities.

The ability to index oneself as, and therefore the ability to become, a subject of communication (an I) represents the achievement of competence in certain aspects of the system of public communication. The understanding of oneself as an I can then be the product neither of some internal experience nor of the possession of a static state or substance (e.g. 'self'); it can only be the product of engaging in processes of social communication in which others experience 'me' as 'you' and address and treat me as such. The 'I' is abstracted from experiencing membership of a communication community in which one's status as a person (an I) is assumed. It is derived from being treated as a person within a given social (i.e. moral) order in which socially relative expectations are attached to the assumption that persons are continuous points of experience and of action and locations responsible for communication:

> the acquisition of the idea of personal identity for oneself, through which one develops a sense of identity, is at least in part a consequence of social practices which derive from the fact of identity as it is conceived in a culture. Our first preliminary conclusion must be, then, that a person learns that he or she is a person from others and in discovering a sphere of action as the source of which he or she is treated by others as the very person they identify as having spatio-temporal identity.[12]

Personhood is a social gift given in processes of social communication in which one is addressed by and responds to others. Personhood and participation in communication are therefore coincident, for person indicates a subject of communication rather than a private subjectivity.

Person and social structure

Communication is not an abstract, but a concrete process conducted through a determinate social code. There are different possibilities of communication for different people in different communication contexts. For the contents and contours of public communication are structured by moral and political considerations; structured, that is, by rules governing access to social space–time. A relatively benign example of such rules would be those governing polite conversation in any particular relationship. These convey rights to interruption which may be unequally distributed among the members of a relational context. These rights indicate which people and what topics of conversation may take priority over others and under what circumstances.

Social space–time is not uniform, but morally and politically relative. So, alongside the meaning encoded in the content of a communication, there is the social meaning attached to a given person making this communication at this point in the exchange (i.e. relative to that of others). Not all persons in the matrix will be simultaneously recognised as potentially valid contributors to a given exchange, just as not all potential contributions will be equally valid. To enter a particular communication at a particular point in a given exchange is to make an implicit claim concerning the social validity of such a contribution.

If a person is a location in a communication context, rather than a static substance, then the nature of the context in which the person is a location will be determinative for identity.[13] This applies both to the general systems and structures which govern relations in a given society and to the localised networks of relation in which an individual may be indexed at any particular time. That is not at all to suggest that there are no continuities of personal identity or no identity apart from relation. It is, rather, an assertion of the relational nature of a person and of the way in which the person 'I' am, the way 'I' enter communication, changes with relational context – such change will, however, be limited to parameters set by the identity 'I' have (itself the sediment of a history of relation conducted within a given communication code). It would not, for example, be appropriate to communicate with my wife, my students, my colleagues, my bank manager, shop assistants and the people I meet in the pub in the same way, because the ground rules of each communication context are different. These ground rules structure (codify) the relation by indicating the socially recognised and valid ways in which 'I' may be indexed; that is, when it is appropriate for 'me' to be the subject, object or referent of communication and what the appropriate content of communication (what is said or done) may be. The person 'I' am for the various others of these different relations is different in each case because the appropriate form and content of my presence before, for and with others varies with context. The social space and time it is appropriate for 'me' to occupy in each case is different.

Each local context of relation will have different rules regulating access to social space–time. It might therefore be inappropriate for me to: ring my bank manager at 2.00 a.m.; continually interrupt a student presenting a seminar paper; arrange a dinner party when my wife should be leading a Brownie meeting, expecting my plans to take priority. There are, in addition, rules for communication which belong to the overarching context in which these localised patterns of relation take place. These operate in like manner in both the physical and social dimensions as restrictions on rights and practicabilities of access. Certain forms of communication are prohibited by the 'laws of nature'. These render it impossible, for example, to: be in two places at once; for a body to fit into a smaller hole; to go backwards in time; to occupy the same space as another physical object; to see with no eyes; to walk without legs. These are 'rules' governing our communication and exchange in the practicalities of physical life, although some of them can be circumvented through social practices and/or an adequate level of technology.

Personal life in the social dimension adds another range of socially relative rules regarding access to social space and time, usually relating to status, and to physical space and time, where this has social significance. These social codes determine when, where and how, in relation to others and to their communication, a person may be recognised and expected as a contributor to social interaction. These might include such rules, codes and 'facts' of social life as: ladies go first; blacks may not own land; women know nothing about politics; it is impolite to interrupt one's elders; thieves cannot be trusted; adults only; mad people and children cannot make rational judgments; hours of business – 9.00–5.00; entrance fee £50; only literate and numerate English speakers may apply. These rules determine how appropriate it is for people occupying a social location with a certain status to be given social space or time in certain situations. This sort of rule can also regulate access to physical goods and services through rules of distribution. The meaning of these 'rules' also changes with context. 'Whites only' means something different in South Africa, at the Henley Boating Regatta or a tennis club and in a cookery recipe – although in each case it operates as a rule of exclusion.[14]

Effective communication must therefore depend upon an understanding of the overarching codes of society at large and of their locally valid variants in particular proximate relations, of the structure of each context which regulates exchange values and the relative value and significance of different locations in social space–time for particular persons.

The social 'world' is primarily structured through interpersonal communication.[15] Social codes and structures are not arbitrary but are ossified from an expansive history of interpersonal communication within a given society. So the social codes and structures which are simply 'given' for persons are not arbitrary realities antithetical to the personal, but ossifications of previous personal communication; they are not so much objective as intersubjective realities. The matrix of persons and the networks of their intercommunication structures a social 'world' through which persons may be formed; so persons and the social structures and processes through which they are formed must be considered as co-determining and ontologically coincident realities: chicken and egg. (This point will be further elaborated in the final section of this chapter.)

Secondary to this primary structure, there are social structures regulating the distribution and organisation of labour and of social status, and internal psychological structures which give a means for patterning and ordering psychic activity and so the means for ordering and regulating a person's communication.[16] The secondary social structures give the abstract and universal primary structure concrete reality and form; they constitute the specific ways in which a particular society is structured. In the primary structure persons are simple locations but, through the concrete processes of social communication, they acquire secondary psychological structures (in Western culture, some form of 'self') which reflect the way in which the social 'world' is structured and which enable competent personal interaction in it. These secondary structures constitute the ground over which the locating grid of social space–time may be laid and which relativise the value of different point locations in it. Secondary social structures codify all relations by regulating exchange values between persons.

The distance between persons in the matrix is not equal, just as particular locations are not of equal value, because the distribution of persons and of social space–time is morally and politically structured. The particularity of one's location and the nature of the society within which one is located are prime informants of personal identity. As a unique social location each individual person is a unique locus of communication, a point about which communication uniquely revolves and which is incorporated into social communication processes in a unique way. A person is a distinct point from which communication may originate (person as point of action/sender or subject of communication), to which it may be directed (person as point of view or experience/receiver of communication) and to which communication may refer (person as (grammatical) object of communication) in unique ways. A unique personal identity may be thought of as deposited or sedimented at a point around which communication has flowed and at which information has gathered in a unique way.

Persons are dynamic realities whose location is not permanent, but the result of their histories of communication. Personal identity is not the simple result of the static particularities of permanent social and physical location or embodiment, but a line of continuity which endures (although often in changed form) through changes in location and embodiment. Present location and embodiment are the result of a history of communication and exchange. Persons are therefore unique histories of interaction through which they have come to occupy these point locations through a process of learning, growth and behaviour modification. Individuality is a compounded sedimentation of this biography of interaction with significant elements of the physical and social environments. In order to understand the relativity of one's location and thereby to engage effectively in communication via the social code, it is necessary to anchor the social locating grid at oneself. As a point location the individual experiences the world as centred around and related to that point. Communication may then be directed into that world as the person is linked to it through the relevant rules for and possibilities of communication. It is through understanding oneself as a unique point of action and experience within a particular society, and therefore as having a particular field of communication, that a personal identity becomes an *auto*biography, because communication and therefore personal life may now be consciously steered.

The uniqueness of location and of the history of communication around that point are co-determinants of personal identity (the way one patterns and tends routinely to enter communication). One's history of communication and present location constrict the possibilities and practicalities of communication to a certain form and range. It is this limitation which gives the life-trajectory the features of continuity. This does not annihilate freedom but indicates the way in which previous selections of communication options and the results of communication restrict choice in future interaction. This happens either through their direct results (for instance producing a relational incapacity, either physical or social) or by their being built up into well-rehearsed modes of practice which establish an individual character of receiving ('listening') and responding which has been found efficacious in the past.

Body
The argument of the preceding sections may be clarified through an extensive consideration of the body, of its place and significance in all of this. The processes of sedimentation which restrict the possible and practical form and range of communication apply equally to physical as to

social interaction. Using the body as an illustration of sedimentation should also serve to clarify the links between the social and the physical dimensions of personal life.

An individual body is conceived as the result of a series of physical, organic interactions. The bodily form, together with a range of psychological dispositions, is first determined by genetic coding, an unpredictable outcome from an almost infinite number of possibilities derived from the original relation of egg and sperm, which is itself the result of a social as well as physical relationship between the parents. The child's later understanding of the nature of that relationship can influence his or her psychological disposition (this is most obviously the case where the relationship has some pathological aspect, but may be more extensively the case than the following examples indicate), for example where the child is unplanned, as in incidents of rape or casual affairs which leave the mother a single parent, or where the child was planned as the missing 'cement' of the parents' relationship.

The foetal relationship with the mother is a second stage of physical development. Although this is chiefly a physical process, it is determined by factors such as the mother's health and the supply of an adequate and balanced diet, which can hardly be divorced from social conditions governing the mother's life. The psychological atmosphere of the parental relation might also affect the mother's inputs to, and therefore the development of, the foetus. It is, in any case, an indisputable fact that matters such as social and economic status, the provision of pre-natal care and education, and the general status and expectations surrounding pregnant women will have a direct effect on the mother's physical input and therefore on foetal development. Bodily form is determined in part through these and subsequent physical interactions, coupled with the nature and availability of contemporary medical practice.

As a punctuated open system, the body is in a continuous process of internal and external communication and exchange whereby it adapts itself to sustainable patterns of existence by 'listening' to its environment through systems of feedback loops.[17] Some of these adaptations to environmental demands might be irreversible, especially in the short term, and will restrict the range of possible future communication or adaptation. Bodily form, then, is determined through previous environmental relations by a process of sedimentation which narrows the available options for further sustainable communication and exchange.

Alongside the physical fact of a bodily form there is a social meaning which can hardly be separated from it. In the meaning-frame of any given social world some bodily forms have an ascribed status. This is observable in, for example, the operation of a caste system or in the provision of social systems assisting the handicapped (economic assistance, easy access to buildings, etc.). Bodily form may also influence the form of personal interaction without necessarily being enshrined in social beliefs regarding status, but in a 'common-sense' perception of a body's physical possibilities. Bodies of certain shapes and sizes are more easily perceived as, and more easily convey the messages of, say, intimidation or compliance. Systems of social expectation, which may or may not be rooted in such a common-sense perception, can also determine bodily form and the way in which it is displayed.

By this I mean to indicate two things. First, that a person who is expected to behave in a certain manner (for example to be physically intimidating) learns this as an appropriate form of relation. If it is accepted and practised as such, then the body begins to bear the marks of this as the result of previous exchanges – say, by scarring, flattening of the knuckles, deliberate muscular development. Similarly, a person expected to be good-humoured, perhaps on the basis of previous experience, might develop creasing around the mouth from smiling and laughing so much. These bodily signs will be an unconscious display open to interpretation by others and their own subsequent bodily and social responses.

Second, there is the learned form of display required to produce or enhance a message by reproducing or enhancing a bodily form. Intimidation is compounded where an appropriate body assumes an appropriate posture. A person's experience of the way others react to his or her body will influence the way that body makes subsequent social appearances, either to negate or to confirm previous perceptions and present structures of expectation particular to her or him in particular relations. Shame or pride in bodily form and appearance, for instance, becomes a social statement about the way a person wishes or expects his or her body to be received through, say, the manner of dress and deportment. A body may be presented in a way designed to elicit a certain response. The body becomes, then, a public social display of such diverse things as, for example, sexual availability or interest and the need for assistance (e.g. by assuming a posture highlighting a physical difficulty or incapacity). By presenting the body in a particular way, a person may attempt to elicit a response from the same system of public meaning as that in which the physical communication was encoded. That is to say, the body is rarely a simple, brute physical fact, but can be a message appearing in a social code. The body is a social as well as a physical means of embodiment.

There can be, then, no strict separation between the physical and the social dimensions of life. The body is the base-line of individual and social existence. Our presence with, for and 'in' others is primarily our physical, or at least our physically mediated, presence.[18] Personal and social life cannot be physically disembodied, not even conceptually. The body may be a social communication, and communication is always embedded in the physical. The particularities of the body must therefore be significant in the formation of personal identity and social relationships.

The body is essentially communication, rather than the stationary fencing closing off an asocial personal identity. It is engaged in dynamic processes of exchange and cannot therefore be a static substance. As an organised system of communicational openness it may be considered a language for spirit (the organisational energy of personal life). At times it is the medium of communication, at others it is the communication itself. Similarly, there is no static organ of identity (e.g. self or soul) made up of some other kind of substance over and above the body. Personal identity is a sedimented history of response, that which endures through time; it is not a static substance but an entire historical corpus of response which includes the body, for it is only as a body that such a history has taken place. The body is essential to this history, but it is this history of communication rooted in and happening through the body, rather than the body itself, which is important. The body's importance is as a medium for communication and as communication itself, as the root of a process through which a unique individual comes into being through embodied communication.

The body is not, then, a closed boundary between exclusively private and public life, but a field of communication, a point of punctuation, or an organised space in which the personal existence of an individual is rooted. It is therefore a boundary, but it is a semi-permeable one which demarcates physical space as having a particular ethical significance as the peculiar space of a particular life. As a particular life-project, space beyond the body (both social and physical) will also be entered and organised and consequently imbued with particular ethical significance relating to this person. The space beyond the body which may be personally organised is not a vacuum, however, but is already organised naturally and/or socially. It is not neutral but already overflowing with ethical content. Everything depends, then, on how this space is entered and organised, how life on this frontier is lived, for 'it is on this frontier that forms of life acquire their definition'.[19] Individuals are defined by the form of their communication.

The body can become a social barrier; it is not so naturally, however. It may be deployed as such by those whose sedimented form of identity tends towards isolation. The body is therefore a communication transmitting the sort of person one takes oneself and others to be, and consequently the sort of relationships expected, sought and desired. In this sense, it is true to say that the form of bodily closure is an ethical act rather than an ontological fact. It is a social performance, rather than a naturally given form; hence the constitution of embodied individuals must perforce be a moral project open to distortion.

Self
Self as a public structure

I have been arguing that the social 'world' in which individuals are indexed as subjects of communication in particular ways is a prime determinant of personal identity. The secondary social structures regulate the ways in which one is indexed by others in various communication contexts. And the way in which one is indexed or addressed informs personal identity, the understanding of the sort of subject one is in relation to others. This, in turn, determines the way in which one enters and understands communication. I will now go on to argue, again following Harré, that the internal structure of persons (a psychological complex or 'self') which organises a person's communication is primarily a public structure which is only secondarily appropriated by individuals as a private psychological complex. This reverses the individualistic assumption that persons are constituted by the possession of an innate, internal psychological structure by means of which they then organise communication, and enter and structure a public world.

My argument, however, is that individuals are internally structured as persons through their membership of and engagement in a primary public world. In the matrix of persons a person is a point location, a 'place' where psychical phenomena may be located and from which they may be communicated. Psychological activity, states, dispositions, and so on are embedded in a communication, whether they are its explicit (grammatical) subject or not. Communication contains information. This information is, strictly speaking, psychological in character. If I tell you about a tree, I do not communicate the tree itself to you, but my thoughts, feelings, perceptions, intentions and so on regarding the tree. The communication therefore has an implicit subjective referent (me) as well as an objective one (the tree).

Psychological phenomena have a public exchange value which is primary over their private reality. Having a public exchange value, they aid interpretation in a social (intersubjective) 'world' which is structured by the patterns of commitments and the taking and exercising of responsibility in communication. In particular, the intention behind a communication, the attachment between it and the person communicating, is a crucial element in public interpretation. But for others, this is ordinarily significant as a social rather than a private fact. Intentionality 'is interpreted within a social framework of interpersonal commitments rather than as the outward expression of some inner state'.[20] Nevertheless, it must be construed as the product of an organised psychical unity.

It is important that psychological phenomena can be accurately located in social space–time as they appear in communication. In order to trace the origin, direct and plot the movement of these phenomena, it is necessary to index individual persons and to assume that these phenomena are the property of an internal point of personal unity at a particular point in a relation. The suggestion here is that the processes of social communication, in which psychical phenomena are essentially what are being communicated, require the supposition of the existence of a structure within individuals which is responsible for them. Persons then appear as psychological as well as social beings.

In the primary structure, persons appear as simple locations. But the simple, public aspect of their being is insufficient to account for their personal unity and continuity as subjects of communication which is evident in public communication. To regard communication as personal, as having a responsible subject who may be appropriately indexed, is to consider it to be the product of intentional organisation. Certain public suppositions must be made as to what sort of 'place' a person must be in order to organise communication in a unified and continuous manner.

The assumption that persons contain a secondary structure of internal complexity operates as a causal explanation for organised communication. It makes it possible to track communication back to a person's intentions, mentation, etc. The secondary psychological structure (self-hood, in our philosophical tradition) is a public assumption of internal unity corresponding to and responsible for that which is external and publicly observable. If communication is to be taken as intended (has a subject) and rational (non-arbitrary), then it must also be taken to be centred in some way. There is consequently a pressure within the processes of social communication for the deployment of a collective assumption concerning the internal organisation of persons, so that communication may be interpreted, commitments made and acknowledged, and so on.

This is a universal requirement of social interaction. Every society deploys an assumption concerning the internal organisation and unity of persons as embodied subjects of communication. The form which that organisation is supposed to take and the internal structure responsible for it are, however, relative to the moral orders in which they are deployed.[21] In Western culture, personal communication and psychological activity are centred on a distinctive notion of selfhood which is the result of centuries of discussion and debate in practical and theoretical disciplines which have marked the cultural history of the West.

The public deployment of an understanding of 'selfhood' is a universal which takes socially relative form. That there is such diversity in what the organ of personal identity is taken to be is an indication that it has theoretical rather than ontological status. It is more like a social belief or theory than an objective description. The content of individual selves (whom individuals take themselves to be) within a society will, of course, be immensely varied, but the form of selfhood deployed by them will accord to a public standardisation. It is through deploying a theory of 'self' that an individual is able to centre and organise communication from within a social location. As this theory is socially relative, the internal, subjective possibilities and priorities of persons should be expected to vary relative to the societies of which they are members. People of different societies should therefore be expected to think and organise their experiences differently, and to operate different value systems concerning psychological dispositions, etc.

Private appropriation of the public structure

The simple fact of personal identity, the public identification of a person as one and the same, is rooted in the physical and social embodiment of individuals in the way I have already indicated, and refers to their unity and continuity, which would be experienced by any potential third party. This is clearly significantly different from a person's own sense of his or her identity as a unique and singular being, an identity which is similarly a continuity through changes in time and place. The uniqueness of personal identity is derived from occupation of a unique social location around which a unique history of communication has taken place. The personal sense of identity is of oneself as a singular subject of communication whose being is internally centred. It is this internal centring which makes subjectivity in communication and acts of privacy possible as personal existence is organised from a uniquely located centre (and therefore in a unique way). But what makes such centring possible? Is there some internal, substantial inner core of unity?

I shall be arguing that there is no substantial personal core, but that personal centring is enabled by holding a belief or a theory about oneself, without which personal life in the network of responsibilities which constitute a morally structured world would be impossible. Through centring one's experience and communication, self-control, and therefore the taking of responsibility, become possible. It is consequently an achievement which has crucial personal and social consequences. If the personal core is a belief, rather than a pre-social substance internal to individuals, then we have to ask where such a belief comes from and why it comes about. I shall be arguing that such a belief is socially acquired and is a social as well as a personal necessity.

Social structures are ossifications of personal intercommunication. In the processes of social communication which these structures regulate, it is necessary to assume that communication is personal; that, in other words, it is centred on an internal, organising psychological complex, and may consequently be considered to be the product of the intentions and commitments of a subject who is responsible for it. This assumption is necessary for the tracking of social responsibility in a moral order. But how is such a public theory appropriated by individuals, and what difference does it make to them?

Through the deployment of an individually valid transform of a social theory of personal centredness, an individual is able to live as a unity subject to central control through self-reflection and intervention; enabled, that is, to be a person. This theory is socially generated and learned through personal interaction in which the operation of communication codes plays a vital part. In interpersonal communication one learns to become a particular type of person through the network of expectations of being a person which surround one in significant communication contexts. These expectations may be either deficient or relatively undistorted.

Perhaps the most easily recognisable example of such learning is the development of personal identity in children. For a child to develop a sense of autonomy (subjectivity) in interaction, she or he must deploy an understanding of her or himself as an internally centred unity. As centred on 'self', the child is subject to self-control rather than external direction and determination and may maintain a stable identity in a gradually expanding range of relationships and relational contexts. This self-centring will be acquired primarily in a parental relation in which the child is encouraged to take appropriate responsibilities. An essential element of this parental relation is the recognition of inappropriate exercises of responsibility which would lead to continual disappointment, frustration and distrust of 'self', and when and where it is appropriate or otherwise to compensate for the child's deficiencies (e.g. by providing interpretations on his or her behalf, or of what the child wants or means when this is not clear to others, or by speaking or acting for the child where understanding, emotional life, cognitive faculty or mode of interaction are insufficiently developed).[22]

This process of supplementing the psychological and social attributes of others can confer a deficient form of selfhood and identity if an unrealistically pessimistic assessment of the person's possibilities is routinely made.[23] Parents, for example, who routinely act and speak for their children in inappropriate situations deny them the chance to develop adult ways of taking responsibility for themselves, of constructing adult personal identities and therefore living responsibly as adult persons. The personal identity sedimented from this form of relation will tend to be deficient and to require the same supplementation of deficiencies in a wide range of relationships.

I discuss the distortions which can occur through small-scale personal relations in Part III. For the moment, however, I want to concentrate on the way in which an understanding of selfhood and personhood is mediated by the social communication codes through which relations are conducted.

It is primarily through the acquisition of language (for example through learning the rules for pronoun use in language games as a child) that the socially valid theory of selfhood may be appropriated. Through language games we learn, from others' assumptions of our centred personal unity and its consequent obligations within the moral order, the three unities essential to personhood in a socially relative form: point of view/experience, point of action, and life continuum/trajectory through time. We learn, that is, to regard ourselves as specific social locations of and for communication who have arrived here through our personal histories. On this basis, we can develop a sense of ourselves and a capacity for self-distance. This represents the ability to distinguish between the indexical and self-referential use of 'I'; between the 'self' as indexed as the subject and object of communication, as in the statement, 'I [indexical] know what I [self-referential] did was wrong.' This capacity coincides with the acquisition of the social theory of 'self' current in the society. Then the three unities of personal being become tools for autonomous organisation as a centred *subject* of communication in the form of self-consciousness, self-intervention and autobiography.[24]

The understanding of oneself as a continuous point of identity ('me') in an extensive range of relations, evidenced in self-referential and self-indexical use of 'I', is not the result of some private, inward experience of one's 'self'. It is, rather, the result of others indexing and referring to 'you' in this way. This is a communication of their experience and expectation of 'you' as a unified and continuous subject of communication, a 'self'. Persons are therefore literally called into personhood and selfhood by others in the language games in which they treat one as a point of unity and continuity organising communication; that is, as a unitary locus of responsibility for communication.

The individual identities of unique and autonomous persons (subjects of communication) are sedimented from interpersonal communication in a way which analogously corresponds to the formation of their physical bodies through physical interaction. As it is in the social sphere that persons appropriate a theory concerning their self-identity, then it is here that they acquire the means for subjective (autonomous) interaction. Subjectivity is a sediment from participation in processes of intersubjectivity. But persons are subjects in physical as well as social interaction. Intersubjectivity must therefore be the source of all centred and controlled communication and exchange, in non-social as well as social contexts.[25] The basis of all subjective (personally centred) interaction is other subjects' interaction with oneself in which one is assumed to be a personally centred subject of communication. Correspondingly, a history of significant social relations in which one has routinely been regarded as an object (passive recipient, a thing rather than a 'self') of communication will tend to sediment an incapacity for centred interaction in other contexts.

Becoming a person involves, above all else, acquiring competence in the system of social communication. To be sure, it can and does involve the ability to think and to act. But thoughts and actions are dependent on language and therefore on social structure, without which they, and the intentions behind them, are incomprehensible.[26] Thinking and acting are not purely private operations but displays of competence in the social code, even if undertaken privately. For even the apparently most private psychological activity draws upon the codification of public meaning. Every interpretation, and every communication seeking interpretation, presupposes a competence in the linguistic mediation of a moral order which can in some sense be said to have formed (i.e. informed) the minds displaying and interpreting. The structure of communal intentions, meanings and perceptions mediated by and constructed in a particular communication code is the prime informant for the possible contents of individual consciousnesses. Meaning is never purely subjective. The 'objectivity' (intersubjective validity) of meaning is present in individuals at a pre-conscious or pre-reflective level. Whilst it may be idiosyncratically transformed by them, meaning is none the less determined by the structures of the social 'world' and, in particular, the nature of its enduring corporate intentions.

The form and structure, and therefore the possible contents, of consciousness are socially determinate according to the specific accumulations of corporate experience. These accumulations are carried in institutional and other social structures. They predispose the perceptions and apprehensions of that society's members towards a certain shape and range. The accumulated structure of corporate experience is exhibited in the gradations of importance, relevance and interest accorded in a society to different contents of experience, consciousness and communication which function communally to structure consciousness. It is mediated in particular by the exchange values of the communication code. It is a prime determinant of intersubjectively valid cognitive content, of the way in which the world has meaning, is intended, and therefore of the way in which it may be apprehended. Certain elements will be pressed to the foreground in cognition, whilst others will remain on the horizon or be repressed from consciousness altogether.[27] This establishes social communication, and therefore the existence of others, rather than the fiction of a relationally pure ego, as absolutely primary for an adequate conception of personal selfhood (individuality).[28]

Full personhood is afforded those in a society whose communication counts as intersubjectively valid because its content has public meaning. Through competent communication the content of an individual consciousness may be shared, becoming the content of consciousnesses located elsewhere in the matrix of persons. For this to happen, the structure of the consciousnesses involved in the exchange may only be idiosyncratic in insignificant detail. If this were not so, then the changed location would alter meaning beyond critical limits. In other words, the subjectivities involved are intersubjectively structured. The sending and receiving subjects must also be competent in the system of communication and understand the conditions to be met if meaning is to stay within critical limits. This entails competence in the conventions by which personal meaning may be displayed and how it may be interpreted via the prevailing communication code.

It should be clear by now that the distinctive structure of a language, particularly its rules for the self-reflexive use of pronouns, facilitates the construction of self-organisation (the formation and deployment of an understanding of one's life as centred) in a distinctive way.[29] The structure of a social code, which regulates exchange values and codifies meaning, facilitates the formation of distinctive modes of internal organisation through which the elements of personal being may be centred on oneself.

Personal deployment

I have been following Harré in suggesting that the public appearance of persons as simple locations is insufficient to ground social life as interpersonal communication. In addition to the publicly observable fact of identity, there is a social need to assume some form of internal organisation of identity. This social assumption takes the form of a particular and socially relative theory regarding the nature of this internal complex. This social assumption may then be individually appropriated as a tool for private (psychological) and public (communicational) self-organisation. The precondition for such an appropriation is the individual's sense of personal unity and continuity. This is not a pure, internal element, but the simple result of being a stable location in interaction. What is sensed is that 'I' am one and self-same, a unity of consciousness, experience and communication. It is sensed that it is the same 'I' who eats the apple, knows 'I' am eating it and knows that 'I' know that 'I' am eating it; the same 'I' who eats the apple as bought a newspaper in a different town yesterday; and not the same 'I' as the person next to me saying, 'I am eating a plum.'

This sense of personal identity raises the question of how 'I' am self-same and one through changes in time, place and relational context. The raising of this question predisposes one to the acquisition of a theory concerning an internal point of personal identity as the answer to it. It is through the deployment of a belief in or theory of an inner personal core which remains constant through changing circumstances that the simple sense of identity becomes the subject of structured experience.

This theory of 'self' is, it must be remembered, a social rather than a private construction. For that reason, its deployment enables internal and external personal organisation to take socially valid and publicly meaningful form. The individual appropriation of a social theory of the self is, however, always idiosyncratic. The theory provides the formal means for structuring one's experience and communication as internally centred on and directed from a continuous point of identity. It does not provide the structure of selfhood with its specific content. That is derived from a history of communication related to a unique point location in the matrix of persons. The way in which that personal history is structured from within (subsequently guiding communication) to give a specific personal identity is socially determined; the individual nature of that identity is not.

The experience of oneself as a specific 'self' constitutes personal self-identity, the understanding of one's specific individuality. The specific experience of one's unique personal identity (unity and continuity) is structured through a socially relative understanding of an identity-giving internal complex. Understanding one's personal identity in this way is what makes personal interaction as a particularly centred, responsible subject of communication within a determinate social situation possible. It is what the deployment of a theory of 'self' makes possible that is significant, and not whether it corresponds in reality to some substantial inner organ. The 'self' should not be conceived of as an organ, but in terms of the organisation which believing in it enables. For it is not some*thing* one *has* but something one *is* and *does*, a way of being in public and private. It is not a substance but a means of organising one's experience, thought, knowledge, beliefs, action, etc. *as though* centred on a substantial inner core. That is to say, it is something like a belief or theory.

Every human culture seems to assume the existence of personal centring in some variable form and degree. This suggests that the central organisation of persons is a universal requirement of human life. The capacity for self-referential and indexical use of 'I' (or its equivalent), which is derived from understanding oneself as a uniquely centred individual, must, in fact, be a universal necessity, given that all societies operate as moral systems requiring the location and acceptance of social responsibility.[30]

Others treat us as having a *point* of view, roughly as the physical
centre of a sphere of things and events literally in space. But those
same others also treat us as the centre of an expanding set of ripples
of consequences of what we do, in making us members of a moral
order, an order of beings who take responsibility for their actions and
at least for some of their consequences. But why do we need the
theory that we are selves? Why not just continue in the reproduction
of appropriate practices? Only if a person knows or believes that he is
the author of his actions does it make sense for him to attend to the
quality of his actions and the thoughts, emotions and projects with
which they are connected as intentional objects on which he might
operate.[31]

Where persons are taken to have an internal point of unity and identity, it is
possible to interpret communication as intended and to locate the
intentional source responsible for it. By deploying a theory of 'self', persons
regard themselves as self-same and continuous identities because they
understand themselves to be centred in a particular way. The theory is then
'proved' true in practice as it enables such centring to happen. Persons may
then experience their communication history (life) as internally centred
and present themselves in.communication as more or less consistent,
centrally organised existences. They may therefore appear in public as, and
accept themselves to be, responsible for their communication as it is
centrally organised by a self-identical person.

In the processes of social communication one is treated by others as
a continuous personal identity centred in a socially specific way. Others
assume that one's active communication and experience are personally
centred on a particular understanding of 'self'; this assumption is embedded
in their communication to one and coincides with one's simple sense of
identity (probably derived from primitive interaction). The social theory of
'self' is appropriated, but filled with idiosyncratic content so no two
identities are alike (individuality is therefore a variation on a social theme).
It is through appropriation of a socially valid theory of oneself that one
becomes a centred person capable of engaging in social communication, a
subject of communication within a determinate social situation. The
acquisition of the primary tool for subjectivity and individuality is a social
achievement. It does not centre one in splendid isolation from others, but
links one's internal life and centredness to the reality of others and of social
life in one's general situation.

Centring one's experience and communication means anchoring the locating grids of physical and social space–time in oneself, referring features of the world to oneself, so that one's world-view and the possibilities for action become self-ascribed. Through the practice of self-referral the business of conducting a centred and controlled existence is embarked upon, learned and embedded. It is this practice which is constitutive of personal existence rather than the possession of some substantial internal entity, although it is the belief in such an entity which makes that practice possible. 'Self' is not a thing people have within them, but a theory which they have about themselves which facilitates personal existence:

> when we learn to organize our organically grounded experience as a structured field, and cognitively as a body of beliefs built up of self-predications, we are deploying a concept of 'self' that functions like the deep theoretical concepts of the natural sciences, which serve to organize our experience and knowledge, whether or not they have observable referents in the real world.[32]

Selfhood does not indicate a substance but an organisational process. As this process is practised in communication, an ordered structure of sedimented information is deposited unique to each particular point of experience, action and autobiography. The significance of information (the meaningful content of communication) varies according to personal identity and location, and so the structures of personal identity are idiosyncratically informed. The self, then, is not an empirical entity which is internally experienced by people who then know themselves to be centred personal existences. It is an hypothesis used to refer to the organisational properties of an underlying ordered structure of which there is and can be no direct empirical experience. This experientially transcendent concept enables one's experience and activity in diverse places and times to be unified in a central organisational structure which transcends the embodiment in any and all particular contexts. There is then a continuous point of experiential continuity enduring through and uniting the dispersed experiences and events of one's life into an autobiography.

The 'self' must transcend experience, because there is always an 'I' beyond the 'I' of present experience. Consider the sentence, 'I am aware that I am eating an apple.' It must be assumed that the subject and object of this self-awareness are somehow unified. But where is the terminating point, the source, of this unity? It cannot be the 'I' eating the apple, because there is another 'I' aware of and therefore transcending it. The 'I' which is aware of it is not being directly experienced at this time, because it is doing the experiencing. But neither can this 'I' be the 'self' in any absolute sense because it, too, and its activity can become the object of 'my' experience, as in: 'I experience myself being aware that I am eating the apple.' Clearly, 'I' will never reach a point at which 'I' cannot be attended to by 'me', becoming the object of 'my' experience. The regress of self-consciousness is potentially infinite. For in any self-referential statement 'I' make, the 'I' indexing the present speaker can be referred to by an 'I' behind it in the self-awareness that 'I' am making the statement. One cannot reflect directly on one's 'self' for, in doing so, there is an 'I' behind the 'self' doing the reflecting. The unity of self-consciousness and experience must therefore be experientially transcendent if the infinite regress of self-consciousness is to be escaped.

As the 'self' is experientially transcendent, its existence cannot be verified through empirical observation. It can, however, be indirectly verified by empirical experience of the consequences of its organisational activity. A 'self' theory enables personal centredness. The fact that such centring does take place is verifiable in experience and indicates the existence of a personal organisational structure beyond experience. The self clearly has such a strange status that it is most appropriate to consider it as a metaphysical construct, functioning very similarly to a grand theory.

Its empirical status may be compared to the hypothesis of gravitational fields.[33] The 'grand theory' of gravity generates a series of lower-level models which theoretically reconstruct the way in which it operates at various levels of reality. The 'grand theory' as such is not empirically verifiable and is distanced even from the means of indirect empirical verification. The lower-level models, however, are indirectly verifiable through the observation of effects attributed to their operation at various levels of reality. There is, then, a distance between a 'grand theory' and the context in, or level at, which it can be verified. This distance can protect the 'grand theory' from the effects of irredeemable failure of a local model to account for its supposed effects. Lower-level models can be rejected, be significantly changed, and even contradict each other, without necessarily endangering or disproving the 'grand theory' in which they have their transcendent point of unity.

The 'self' is an experientially transcendent structure of organised and continuous identity, which structures and organises all subsequent experience and communication into this continuity which is itself reworked in the light of new information.[34] The 'self' is the carrier of a continuous identity through changes in time, place and relational context. It should be clear from the preceding argument, however, that this continuous identity is not static, but dynamic. It is not a substance, but a relational reality which therefore undergoes modification with changes in relational context, as well as with the accretions of new experiences. I have already tried to show how one changes with relational context, that I am indexed differently in relation to my wife and to my bank manager. This is not merely a matter of adopting appropriate strategies of public appearance, but of having a different sense of myself in different contexts. So, although I am self-same in all my relations, there is a very real sense in which the 'I' which appears in them is variable. The different ways in which I am for others in these relations is closely related to differences in the way I am for myself. In one relation I may be assertive and self-confident; in another, unsure of myself and reticent.

This seems to indicate a distance between, on the one hand, a structure of selfhood which is deeply embedded and removed from particular relations (deep 'self') and, on the other, a model of 'self' generated by it which structures and organises communication and experience amid the practicalities of a particular context (practical or local 'self'). Deep 'self' would then be a transcendent point of unity behind a number of lower-level models.[35]

This comparison of the 'self' with a 'grand theory' may help to explain its resilience in the face of apparent difficulties, negations and defeats in particular communication contexts. Provided there is sufficient distance between a local 'self' and deep 'self', then the former may be resistant to significant negations of or tensions with the latter. It is therefore possible for a 'self' to encounter many local problems – even, perhaps, for a local 'self' to disintegrate. Provided the communication context is relatively peripheral, this need not lead to a complete disintegration of the personality. The deep 'self' offers a security reserve so that a breakdown in a peripheral context will not lead to a breakdown of the whole. Breakdown in a local context can therefore either be tolerated and left, or else dealt with on the basis of a deeper sense of security.

The relation with a life-partner is usually a sphere of communication which has been profoundly and deeply sedimented. The local 'self' structuring experience and communication here is very close to the deep 'self' – which may have largely been sedimented from communication and experience within this relation. It may be from this relation that security is drawn for functioning in other contexts. In which case, disruption of the relation (through, say, bereavement, divorce, either partner's infidelity, or even the introduction of third parties as in the birth of a child) which brings the local 'self' into question is likely to bring deep 'self' into a corresponding crisis.

Deep 'self' is therefore to be conceived of as a unity of or behind the unities represented by a plurality of local 'selves'. Personal identity in a particular relation is not a complete and exhaustive self-presence. Self-identity varies across a range of communication contexts ('I' as 'shifter') whilst maintaining itself in continuity at a level transcending any communication or relation in particular. Selfhood indicates personal organisation, a structured personal identity. Communication and personal identity can be empirically experienced as organised rather than random, but the agency behind that organisation can be neither experienced nor directly verified. In being self-conscious one is aware of this central organisation, not of some additional organ or entity, and aware of it only in a restricted field or aspect, not as such. It is by application of this 'grand theory' in practice that life may be lived as a centred and organised being among others similarly centred who expect such centring from onself.

Individual uniqueness and social determinacy

There is a predisposition in our culture to fear the worst from this sort of talk of social formation and to equate it too readily with absolute forms of social determination. The question will inevitably be asked whether this theory turns individuals into passive recipients of an objective social language, the life of which carries on somehow over their heads.[36] The unity which occurs within relations could also be similarly misunderstood by taking the personal openness involved to be a receptivity to apersonal, objective processes.[37] The question posed by both reservations is whether the individuality I allow is anything more than a location of receptivity for super-individual processes.

The question relating to interpersonal relations is adequately answered by referring to the discussion above, where relatedness was not defined in terms of an objective process received through a general principle of relational openness, but as a sedimentation of *particular* relations. An I is not born through appropriation of an objective process, but through participation in particular relations in which this process is not only received for oneself but actively and uniquely borne for others. That is to say, subjects are born through processes of intersubjectivity in which openness is not absolute, for alongside it there is a closure and discreteness from a particular relation at a particular time: there is not only the relation but the participating individuals. It is through this closure that one may be spoken of as a subject of communication, an active participant rather than the simple bearer of an objective communicative process. This does not mean that there is an asocial, individual core which is discrete from social relations as such, but that there is a person sedimented from previous relations who comes to particular relations in an incomplete openness; that is, as a structured presence.

The communication process *is* objective, in the sense that it is super-individual. But because its super-individual nature has the form of intersubjectivity, it is also subjective. To the extent that it is undistorted (dialogical, and therefore properly personal), it deposits an ethical space for the independent communication of each individual person. It is only through this 'objective' process that existence as a communicative subject becomes possible. Individuality and subjectivity hereby become inseparable from participation in an 'objective' public world.

Communication, and the code through which it is conducted, are properly personal to the extent that social space–time is allocated for the independent communication of the partners (i.e. in so far as they take dialogical form). Individuals are persons (communicative subjects) to the extent that external inputs are internally processed, becoming partly idiosyncratic information. They are therefore simply determined neither by their social relations nor by the social codification of those relations. Rather, persons emerge in a process which engages their autonomy. Intersubjective communication is not a simple stimulus–response mechanism. Communication is personally informative only when processed by the person by combining it with previous subjective content. 'Objective' social processes inform subjectivity only by being idiosyncratically transformed into personal information. Despite the intersubjective validity (public meaning) of the content of encoded information (even in individual consciousnesses), it is uniquely informative for different persons.[38]

These conditions are not inevitably met in communication, but they can only be met in communication. As a subject of communication a person may emerge, be distorted or be properly constituted, only through communication processes of structured (coded) intersubjectivity.

Further, persons are more than they are publicly recognised to be. They are exhaustively identifiable neither with any particular public appearance, whether this be momentary or more enduring, nor with the totality of such appearances. But nor are they to be overidentified with the general social role assumed by themselves or that supposed, perceived or expected of them by others. Personal identity is a self-identity and deep 'self', where identity is lodged in a semi-stable structure, and is distanced from the practicalities and possibilities of direct public appearance and therefore from a complete identification with social role or status. This clearly rules out the complete determination of persons by the contours of the social roles or ethical space–time available to them in the social 'world' as a consequence of their social role or status.[39]

None the less, social communication is indeed an objective process and an objective point of unity beyond the direct control and manipulation of individuals as individuals, and of partners in relation. It is therefore both legitimate and necessary to consider persons as already essentially related and to think of their individuality in terms of a partial closure or punctuation within the social 'world' which, at this level, is simply given as an 'objective' fact.

The independence of individuals from the overarching objective reality of their social 'world' is, perhaps, most easily seen where a lack of direction and control is apparent. If people were simply mechanical response mechanisms to social stimuli, completely determined by mechanically operating social forces, then instances of social incompetence would be difficult to explain. In instances of social incompetence, people's idiosyncrasies are painfully apparent in their limited understanding of their social situations.

I have already stated that meaning must be considered a social, rather than individual, phenomenon. For all communication and encoded information (including, therefore, private mentation) is a public enterprise undertaken in a social code which the individual must use in order to be understood and to understand. It may well be that the public meaning of a communication overruns that intended. Where the ramifications of communication outstrip those which were foreseen at its origination, it becomes possible to distinguish between the individual person and the objective social form in which both person and communication are embedded. This yields the possibility of communicative competence being idiosyncratically and imperfectly appropriated. In which case, individuals cannot be simply 'spoken' by an objective language. This also indicates that the social process is beyond the control of personal intentions at certain points, and that it displays latent as well as manifest meaning. There is a(n) incomplete) distance between persons and the social processes which formed them. This distance may become a critical one in which these very formative processes are criticised and both persons and society opened to transformation. There is therefore a distinction to be made between social formation and strict determinism.[40]

There is also the possibility of misunderstanding occurring. This must mean that at least one of the partners has been communicatively incompetent in some way (suggesting a degree of social indeterminacy), and/or that there is some kind of mismatch between individual and public meaning. In the latter case, the idiosyncrasies of individual meaning must be significant, at least at this particular point in this relation. Persons are punctuated open systems. This means that their internal content and self-identity are not transparent or directly accessible to others. Identity is discrete within a particular location in the matrix of persons which is bounded by a semi-permeable membrane (a social skin?).

Individual identity and its sedimented information content are never completely communicable. Information held internally and related to an individual identity is coded according to its meaning and significance as related to a specific social location and autobiography. Whilst appropriated from public communication, its present communication context is the individual's self-relation. It is not currently a public phenomenon. It cannot appear in public communication without transformation in coding and, potentially, in the meaning it has for others. That transformation in meaning need not, but will sometimes, be significant and lead to misunderstanding. It is because individual identity and its content are incompletely communicable that persons are inexchangeable. The fact that individuals are unique and ultimately unfathomable identities may be apprehended by others through their idiosyncrasies and obscurity or misunderstanding concerning their intentions and meaning. Although clarity concerning intention and meaning can develop through interpretation and feedback, a complete, exhaustive understanding of another's self-identity is impossible. Personal identity is not transparent. If it were, then privacy, deception or secrecy concerning real purposes would be impossible.

Notwithstanding that, it must be understood that there is no complete incommunicability. Individuality is a variation on a theme. Persons tend towards only moderate differences and to moderate or emphasise their idiosyncrasies to correct their perception (usually via others' communication) of themselves as excessively conformist or idiosyncratic. We are deeply embedded in an objective social world. This limits the range of idiosyncratic variation through the necessities of everyday social communication by providing us with a semi-stable structure of shared expectations. This does not make for complete social uniformity, however. An individual may not conform to social codes and norms, but their conveyance as a structure of expectations through the exchange values of a public language will exert a certain pressure towards conformity, if only by identifying deviance as atypical and thereby rendering it extremely visible.[41] Participation in this objective network of communication with socially defined rules of exchange and semantic contents is primary. It is not possible for a completely private language (madness or fantasy) to be sustained as the primary and permanent mode of practical life.[42]

If meanings can be privatised to the extent where they cannot be made public without being transformed beyond critical limits, then can meaning still be said to be primarily public? If what is meaningful to oneself and the way that it is so cannot be communicated to others (publicly encoded and exchanged), then is not meaning shown to be internally and privately manufactured? This is not, I believe, the case. Self-identity, and therefore a unique framework of personal meanings, derives from the uniqueness of social location, of relating to, and experiencing the world as related to, a unique point of continuity through social space–time. The relative meaning of people, events and things is reflexively derived by and for a self from the position they occupy in that self's life: i.e. through a unique point of view, point of action and life-trajectory (biography). Put simply, the whole of the world is meaningfully structured into differing patterns of significance and signification around each 'self'. This must, however, be more than a private affair because the 'self' and the structure and content of consciousness are appropriated through social communication. So even the internal symbolic mediation of meaning is public, because self-identity is sedimented from a history of relations.

> The significance that a person or thing acquires for a person in an individual life relation is thus a mere derivative of the meaning of an entire developmental history of which the subject can become aware in retrospect at any time, no matter how implicitly. This guarantees that every specific significance is integrated into a meaning structure that represents the inalienably individual (and not merely singular) unity of a world centered around an ego and a life history held together by an ego identity.
>
> On the other hand, meanings, which must be fixed in symbols, are never private in a rigorous sense. They always have intersubjective validity. Thus nothing like significance could ever constitute itself in a monadically conceived life history. Obviously an expression of life owes its semantic content as much to its place in a linguistic system valid for other subjects as it does to its place in a biographical context.[43]

There is thus a bi-dimensionality in personal meaning, of private and public. The basis, then, of apparently private personhood is in fact interpersonal communication within given public structures and codes.

There is still a further way in which the accusation of complete social determination can be refuted. This concerns the creative interplay between persons and objective social structures, which must be considered to be co-determining. For just as the structure of sociality generates a certain range of personal existence, so the range of actual personal existence can be said to determine social structures. Social structures are ossifications of social communication, and social communication is persons communicating.[44] Persons cannot exist in a vacuum, but only within a structured social 'world'. Social structures can exist, however, only where people are structuring their social life together (although always in a manner constrained by the prevalent communication structures).[45] This objective form is a solidification of previous and continuing personal intercommunication. The social 'world' is as structured by persons as they are structured by it, although not in such an immediate fashion (which is why it appears as an objective and immutable reality). Social structure, personal communication and personal identity are co-determinants of a social and personal 'world'. This means that the stability of social structures and of individual identities are inextricably intertwined. This relationship need not be static and is better thought of in terms of mutual adaptability.

But can a structure which is 'objective' change? I have termed the structures objective as they are not the immediate product of subjective wills and action but, from a practical point of view, are simply given. It is quite obvious, of course, that social structures do change through time. Changes in the possibilities of 'subjective consciousness' accompany such changes. It is apparent from history that every era contains people whose consciousness and vision are 'ahead of their time', as well as those who are so completely 'ahead' of it that they cannot be understood (who are labelled 'mad'). What distinguishes the former from the latter is their communicative competence in existing public forms. What distinguishes them from the rest of us is the extent to which they can live in given structures without being so bound by them. They can therefore see possibilities beyond the constraints of prevailing social codes which they are then able to encode within them and so communicate and realise this vision publicly. It is in these visionaries and experimenters who seize the possibilities for evolution or revolution that the creative interplay between persons and objective forms of social life initially takes place. Given that persons and social structures are co-determinative, social change must be as dependent on individuals and developments in the structures of their communicative competence as is the reverse.[46]

For every new social order there must be new patterns of social integration and communication and vice versa. Viewed from the personal level, social systems are created through the solidification (by repetition) of communicative practices. From the other side, persons are individual exemplars of an 'objective' social structure. Nothing more than this irresolvable dualism is allowable if a proper mid-course is to be steered between individualism and collectivism, or the pure forms of subjectivism and objectivism.

Part III

Interpersonal relations

4

The redemptive transformation
of relations: dialogue

So far I have been trying to show that personal identity is a structure of response sedimented from a significant history of communication. A person is centrally organised and, on that basis, may exercise a degree of autonomy as a subject of communication. Since this subjectivity and autonomy refer to communication, personal centredness does not only indicate the power to integrate one's internal life as a unity, but also denotes the power to enter communication and relation as such an internally unified being. Indeed, as a structure of communication, personhood is to be understood primarily in public terms. The centred way in which we organise ourselves as persons does not arise out of internal processes or out of any qualities or attributes which we hold individually; rather, it takes shape through our communication and relation with others. We cannot be personal centres in ourselves, left – as it were – to our own devices, since centredness is a learned and embedded practice of organising oneself in the public world of interacting with others. This way of centrally organising ourselves is sedimented from a significant history of relations in which the ways in which we are recognised and intended by others whirl around us and gradually become borne in on us. Following on from the position I took in the last chapter, it is my contention that this history will be a specific mediation of the pattern of personal co-intending, of social value and meaning, which is valid in our particular societies.

For persons are structures of response(-ibility) who, being centred and autonomous, may be held and may hold themselves accountable for their actions. Societies, on the other hand, are extended structures of call and response in which the taking of personal responsibility is a social necessity. It is therefore proper to consider both to be moral structures which, as moral, are therefore free and open to distortion. Personal centredness, relations and/or the wider social structures and codes may take distorted forms, taking or locating responsibility in a manner antithetical to the construction of genuine personal identities.

Social processes establish the minimum criteria (centredness) of personal being that require that people co-intend one another as centred, responsible subjects of communication (persons), and that social responsibility is recognised, in some form and to a certain extent. The recognition and location of responsibility for and in communication is an essential aspect of social life. All societies must therefore call their citizens to forms of responsibility, and forms of personhood capable of identifying and accepting their responsibilities, which are socially appropriate. As structures for the location and acceptance of personal responsibility, forms of personal and social organisation may be termed *formally* moral. That a structure is moral in form means that its specific content and what happens in it may be evaluated in moral terms. It does not imply any particular evaluation of its morality or otherwise. That which is socially appropriate in the moral structures of a given society or social situation is not necessarily that which is moral or good. This means that morality is not to be equated with social appropriateness. If it were, then every society would constitute its own moral absolute and social conformity would be a moral imperative. Part of my argument is that there are ideal undistorted structures of person and relation which constitute a moral norm for every society. To conceive of normative codes outside the boundaries of a particular society (and, indeed, beyond all possible societies) entails viewing that society as a limited and less than absolute context of communication. That means seeing it as open to development, change and transformation, as set within a transcendent and expanding horizon of possibilities. As a horizon, it will remain transcendent. Yet movement may be made towards it as the impact of its possibilities are felt in the present situation.

In what follows I shall argue that person and relation become concrete ethical norms for communication, and therefore for all social processes and structures, when viewed in the wider context of relation to God and God's creative and redemptive communication. Further, under the impact of redemption, our social relationships undergo modification through the transformation wrought in relation to God. As our relationship with God is reconstituted through Christ, so are our relations with one another. Redemption provides a new framework of meaning, a new pattern of co-intending in communication. It does not replace the meaning-frame and patterns of the social 'world', for it takes place within them. But it does transform and relativise them by providing a more significant context of communication. The way in which one is addressed by God and the pattern of co-intending in the redeemed community (Church) become decisive in the sedimentation of a transformed personal identity, and therefore for interaction in all other spheres as well. Redemption is a *recontextualisation* which brings a person into a new community with a redeemed pattern of intersubjectivity. Simultaneously, however, he or she is 'returned' to the old community in a new way, as a transformed subject of communication with a new orientation who intends self and others in a new way. In other words, redemption is a transformed way of being in the world with others.

If it is possible for personal identities to be transformed by their incorporation into new relationships and patterns of co-intention, then past relations cannot be determinative of identity in a complete, absolute and mechanistic sense. There is a distinction to be made between a person's history of relations and the ossification of this history into a sedimented structure of personal identity: between the person and the relations which have been formative of his or her identity. That is only to be expected since the history is unfinished. Personal identity is therefore only a temporary 'synthesis' of the past which is open for future formation (information) through that history's subsequent development or transformation. This may lead to a reinterpretation of the past as it is present in a sedimented identity and therefore, whether consciously or otherwise, in communication and relation too. Most of our relations are partly future orientated, especially as they are constituted by commitment and fidelity to ourselves and to one another. Futurity has a special significance, however, in our relations to God. The redemptive presence of God is the presence of something so radically new that it cannot be fully present. God and redemption can only be present in promissory or anticipatory form. The mode of redemption's presence is future. Because of the newness and futurity which it brings, God's presence transforms present structures and forms. In addition to the more mundane sedimentation processes through which past relations push persons into an evolutionary future, God's Word pulls persons into the divine future which so radically differs from the present that it seriously challenges our present identities, relations and social structures in the process.

A person is sedimented from past relations as a unique organisational source of communication with a unique identity which guides future communication and relation. The form which a person's communication takes identifies what I have termed the spirit of the individual.

Individual spirit is the organisational energy through which both oneself and the boundary between oneself and others are structured. Individual spirit organises the form and content of communication by regulating openness and closure, or public representation (output) and the openness of receptivity to others (input). It is individual spirit which is initially transformed in redemption by being placed in the context of relation with God. Such transformation effects a newly organised identity which shows itself in a new patterning of relations around the person – in the way she or he now responds to and addresses others and God. It is through the incorporation of persons into the context of God's interaction with us that persons and relations become properly constituted, although this reconstitution remains incomplete. It is only therefore by viewing persons and relations against the horizon of redemption (i.e. in the divine communication context), and therefore as transformations of what they presently are, that we can come to a proper understanding of them.

In the opening chapters I identified the form of properly constituted relations as dialogue. In dialogue the conditions for personal centredness and autonomy (distance and relation) are met in conformity to the call of Christ and in analogical correspondence to the communicated intention of God. The structure of call and response in dialogue involves a formal reciprocation of personhood: one intends oneself as one intends others and as one is intended by them (see further below). Dialogue is the undistorted form of relation through which undistorted personal identities may be formed, as one becomes a person only by intending others as persons and by being so intended by others. It is therefore a structure of reciprocated intentions, a mutual co-intending.

Call

We are called into being as persons by the expectations others have of us. These are framed and mediated to us through their form of address – the way in which they intended us in their communication. A sedimented personal identity is a restriction in the range of communicative possibilities, the establishment of a tendency to enter relations and communication in a particular way. The partners to a particular relation meet each other as the bearers of these communication tendencies, as persons with particular public identities and as products of their communication histories.

In any particular relation either of the two following possibilities might happen. First, the partners may reduplicate their previously established identities, in no sense being changed by the relation into 'different' persons. Fortunately for shopkeepers and for their customers, they are usually able to conduct their business relations in an entirely routine manner. For few encounters in the shop will be of such decisive moment that either shopkeeper or customer will have to understand their identities in a new way. Alternatively, if the relation proves of great personal significance, the partners' identities may be transformed by it – although such transformation will usually be within certain of the developmental constraints of the sedimented past. New sedimentation is always deposited on a previously sedimented base which is a prime determinant of the meaning and significance the relation has for the person (although that base may be restructured in the process). Illustrations of this are provided by my discussion of the calls to discipleship in Chapter 2. The effect of a particular call may not be immediate but, as it is always open to future interpretation (perhaps based on future recurrence and clarification of the relation), it might play a part in restructuring identity. The identity of a person is formed or deformed through the calls of others and God.

The past establishes a tendency for future communication to take particular forms, but this need not be overdeterminative either for the partners or for their relation. The form of response an individual may make and the identity one may have in any particular relation will never be entirely predictable. But any appearance which defies expectation will usually be explicable after the event as a new, evolutionary development of the old identity. There are personal 'developments', however, which represent a decisive break from one's past, at least in its presently sedimented form. The newness of these is of such a quality that they are best thought of as new beginnings. A particular address, whose power lies perhaps in its obvious discontinuity, may be capable of breaking open a closed person whose identity is overdetermined by his or her past. The reverse is, sadly, also the case. A change in the way a significant other intends one can lead to a breakdown of identity. In either case, although the new identity is a transformation of the old, it so decisively differs from it that it must be considered to be non-developmental. The transformation offered in this way by the call of Christ is emancipatory.[1]

Jesus' personal identity (the way he entered communication and relation) was marked by its liberatory aspect. His address and response to people took the form of an open invitation to establish relations with them on a different basis from those in which they were currently contextualised. In his communication he intended people in a radically different form from others' intention of them and their own self-intention; different, that is, from the prevailing patterns of co-intention from which their personal identities had been sedimented. He could therefore decisively reject the expectations others had of them and which had been ossified into self-identities appropriate to such a network of expectations. Jesus found broken, closed and communicatively distorted people in distorted and closed relational networks. The Gospel set people free by placing them firmly in an alternative communication context from which a new identity could be sedimented, even though their social situation might remain materially unchanged. In relating to people as though they were forgiven, as though they were free of the burden of their sins, Jesus intended them as forgiven and justified sinners before others and God in a new way. He pulled the possibilities of future emancipation into the present and thereby established new possibilities of identity with and for them.

When we say or do anything, we take up a particular stance in relation to our audience. In every address, we make implicit and explicit claims and assumptions concerning our own identities, the identities of those whom we expect to respond, and the relation which ought to pertain between us. An address intends (assumes or seeks to establish) its recipient, his or her response and the relation to take a particular form. It is simultaneously an attempt to communicate something and to effect a desired response which evidences the achievement of a mutual understanding between the partners concerning the form as well as the content of the address. Agreement can therefore be reached on two levels. (1) That what I say or do is true. If I say, 'I'm hungry', we may come to an agreement about whether I really am hungry, or whether I am lying, joking or misinterpreting sensations in my stomach. (2) That how I say or do it, representing the form of relation between us which I assume or intend, is valid. The way in which I say, 'I'm hungry' will be a signal to you of the response I expect and therefore of the relation I intend and of the way I intend both of us in our relationship. I may intend you to debate with me whether and why I am hungry, or I may just expect you to feed me. We may agree about truth at level (1), but you may not reciprocate my intention of you as someone who must drop everything in order to provide me with food whenever the fancy takes me. An address is always in part the intention of a relation in which the desired mutuality of understanding becomes possible and in which the desired form of response to one's address takes place.[2] The form and content of communication are inseparable. A mutuality of understanding occurs when the actual form and content of the relation matches that which is intended in the communication, when agreement is reached on both levels.

This mutual understanding need not be explicit and could be based on a mistaken or hidden premiss. It need not, in other words, involve the autonomy of both partners, but could represent the coercion of one by the other. Although you may feed me whenever I say, 'I'm hungry', this need not indicate a real agreement about the valid primacy of my needs over yours. The understanding which we really share may concern the consequences of your refusal to comply with my wishes. We would then presumably share an understanding about the inequality of our relationship, but not necessarily about the validity of that inequality. Feeding me may be a way of avoiding my petulance or violence which you expect to be the result of non-compliance.

In the first two chapters I tried to show that an enduring feature of God's communication is its creative appeal to personal autonomy. Interpersonal relations conformed to and transformed by the redemptive presence of Christ are dialogical in form. In dialogue an address intends the other as a person, as an autonomous subject of communication. This means that, although a certain response is expected and desired, the addressee is none the less intended and expected as one who is not *wholly* determined by the initiating communication. The form of the address intends the other as independent from this relation and this particular intention, and so acknowledges the other's freedom over against one. It is therefore recognised that the other may resist one's expectations and intentions in the relationship. For she or he is intended as an autonomous, self-centred subject of communication who may manufacture her or his own self-definitions and control appearance in public communication. To recognise and intend the freedom of the other in response is to recognise that the form and content of that response cannot be overdetermined by the address.

This undistorted form of address intends the other as a responsible subject capable of an undistorted and independent response orientated towards a genuine mutuality of understanding in dialogue (one which is free and unforced). The desire is therefore that the respondent should co-intend him or herself and the caller as free and seek an unforced mutuality in undistorted relation. The intention is for the other to be a truly responsible dialogue-partner. The power of the address to secure such a reciprocation of intentions will depend largely on the ability to show in communication that one is being responsible in this way oneself: to communicate this intention of oneself, the other and the relation to the other. Dialogue, then, involves the communicated claim of formal reciprocity, that one is being genuine in self-representation and is seeking the other as an independent partner who is also genuinely present in the relation. Where genuine and responsible call meets genuine and responsible answer, there is conformity to Christ (see Chapter 2).

When a person is, consciously or otherwise, adopting a hidden agenda, and is therefore not genuinely present in communication, that person's address is distorted because it is not aimed at a true mutuality of understanding. The call will be presented as a genuine self-presence in the relation, but there will be a significant distance between real personal identity and self-intention and those communicated to the other in the call. It will seek a response which is genuine in that it intends the partner to be totally and genuinely present in an understanding and identity which accords with the hidden agenda. In other words, distorted communication is orientated towards a form of misunderstanding in which the called falls in with the caller's real intentions and interests without their public communication. Here there is an attempt to manipulate the other towards goals which are probably not in his or her interest as well, or else they could be openly communicated. The interests, and therefore the independence, of one partner are subsumed by those of the other, and the claim to formal reciprocity and genuine self-presence in the relation is false. The distorted call is an attempt to establish both a distorted relation and a distorted self-presence which one wants the other to believe to be a genuine identity.

An undistorted address, on the other hand, recognises the recipient as an independent subject of communication who is not overdetermined by the call. This recognition creates space within the relation for the other's independent communication. It is only through the undistorted call of others that the call of Christ and the conditions of existence in the divine image are socially refracted and mediated in interpersonal relations.

Response

It is my understanding that a person is conformed to Christ in making genuine response to the address of God and others (the latter often mediating the former). In conformity to Christ one becomes a person for others, a centred and autonomous subject orientated towards others who therefore stands within any particular relation as an independent (though not totally closed) locus of communication. Conformity to Christ is never complete and, in any case, can never be held in isolation from others. It is not a static substance, but a radical openness to God and others in which our present way of being and understanding ourselves may be transformed by new information as we recognise God and others as significantly different from oneself and as significant in their difference.

Making responsible answers to others cannot be a simple, mechanical response to a given stimulus which returns the intention in a way overdetermined by the other. That could hardly be called free or responsible. Yet neither may our responses be completely predetermined by our personal identities or intentions of these others which existed prior to their calls. That could hardly be called a response. Response must involve attending and returning to the other as she or he is present in communication. This is a readiness to allow the calls of others to transform us in response. Such transformation is a renewed orientation on oneself (centredness) and others in which the form of punctuation operated between oneself and others undergoes modification. Personal responsibility requires an openness to others and to self-transformation, combined with the closure proper to an individually centred identity which is resistant to external overdetermination. This represents a structure of personhood in which both openness and closure are present, but never total. For personal identity is a form of punctuation between self and others. It is appropriate to talk in terms of partially open or semi-closed structures according to the aspect we are wishing to emphasise. In personal response there is an interplay between the identity intended by the caller and the present self-intention and identity of the called.

The formation of individuals through relations is not a synchronic but a diachronic process. A person is not merely a response to a particular call but has an existence independent of appearance in this relation. He or she has a life prior and subsequent to this relation and a private, internal life within it. He or she may therefore communicate independently of the intentions constitutive of this relation. There is therefore a capacity to initiate relations and communication elsewhere and to do so independently in this relationship, which might mean resisting the other's intentions in response. Call and response, understood as autonomous communication in this sense, are the same reality viewed from the different vantage points of the partners. In the spiralling process of dialogue the response which follows the initial communication has the character of call for the initiator, who must now respond. Even the initiation of communication is in its way a response. Communication is never directed into the void but aimed at the presence of a particular other, intending the other in a particular form. It may thus be considered a response to this presence which may, in its turn, be considered as having implicit communication content itself.

Call and response are bipolarities in the process of communication and exchange which, in dialogue, the partners assume in sequence. In distinguishing between them it is possible to examine relational formation in dialogue as one is alternately the object and subject of the process. Call denotes the way in which one's identity is informed by the spirit in which significant others enter into relation with and intend one in communication. Response refers to the way in which one is defined by one's own spirit of relation, the form in which one intends oneself and others in communication.

There are three possible forms for an individual to take in relation to another: to be manipulated, to manipulate, or truly to seek the other. Strictly speaking, the first of these involves an abandonment of independence and therefore of individual personal identity. It is a non-option for personal being as it identifies the I completely with the intentions of the Thou. It represents the loss rather than a distortion of the person, for the openness to the other is total and therefore unstructured through personal centring. Individuality cannot be constituted by total openness but only by total or partial closure. These are the two options whereby individuality may be sustained in a distorted (monological) or undistorted (dialogical) manner. The question is whether, in the closure which is proper and necessary to personal identity, there is an openness to the other. The spirit of an individual organises the manner of this closure, the form of entrance into communication and relation. The I is constituted by the form of its response in which others are intended either as co-subjects of dialogue (other Is or Thous) or as manipulable objects (Its).

> To man the world is twofold, in accordance with his twofold attitude.
>
> The attitude of man is twofold, in accordance with the twofold nature of the primary words which he speaks.
>
> The primary words are not isolated words, but combined words.
>
> The one primary word is the combination *I–Thou*.
>
> The other primary word is the combination *I–It*; wherein, without a change in the primary word, one of the words *He* and *She* can replace *It*.
>
> Hence the *I* of man is also twofold.
>
> For the *I* of the primary word *I–Thou* is a different *I* from that of the primary word *I–It*.[3]

Individual identity (I) is constituted by the way in which one intends others in entering communication and relation.

Intending someone or something as an object is to intend the relation as a monologue. For an object is intended and perceived as having no independent meaning or existence apart from this relation. It cannot offer a point of moral resistance because it is not perceived as ethically transcendent. The relation can only be exploitative and manipulative. The other as object is intended and experienced as a reflection (appropriate and accommodating response) of the I who returns the image of the I. The I of an I–It relation has an unbounded sense of its proper claims, seeking from the other only that which is a confirmatory repetition of itself. In seeking oneself from the other, one is engaged in one-way communication open only to oneself. The I's feedback mechanism is structured in such a way that any independent communication orientated towards a different understanding cannot be recognised as such, for the other is related to as an object, rather than as a subject, of communication.

A monological I is receptive only to its own echoes; the otherness of the other is therefore effectively silenced as she or he is conformed to the I's image. This I's identity, expansion and growth can only be had at the expense of others. The pluralism which is essential to all communication and relation is effectively replaced by a monism in which the world is identified with the single communicative subject. Everything exists only as it exists for this person, only as it is in this relation, so that communication and relation are based upon identity instead of difference. As difference is a necessary prerequisite for relation this form of individuality is, qualitatively speaking, unrelated. Everything external and non-identical is internalised on the basis of its supposed identity.[4] God and others cannot be transformingly present, for they are not recognised as other, as bringing new information which would make them significant for one. The monological I cannot hear the call to judgment or responsibility because it regards itself as self-constituting and cannot therefore know God as Father or acknowledge any externally constitutive power.

A person with such an identity really ceases to be a subject of inter*personal* interaction, since that would entail the recognition of others as subjects. He or she exists, not so much in a social (i.e. moral) 'world', as in a causal one. That is to say that, as a monological subject of communication, this I becomes an object causally interacting with others in order to bring them under control. The communication of a monological subject is orientated towards success rather than understanding.

In monological communication a person is in relation only in and for her or himself. The other is intended as an object whose existence in the relation coincides with one's own purposes, desires, needs and intentions which have been self-constituted and validated. The communication is orientated towards the success of self-constituted and validated goals, and not towards a genuine mutuality of understanding in which the validity of these goals and of the intention and understanding one has of and for the other and the relation are open to question and negotiation.[5] The monological subject is only partially present in his or her communication and relation. This is so not only where there is a hidden agenda operating, making it impossible for the person to stand behind the communication as a genuine attempt at understanding, but wherever the communication is aimed at the success of one's own understanding, intentions, needs and desires over against others. Here present self-understanding and the understanding of the other are taken as read, as unproblematic; they are not therefore open to resistance, questioning or transformation, for this self-understanding persists in splendid isolation. Real and whole self-identity is taken to be something one has apart from relationship. It is not therefore perceived to be at stake in relations which are not understood as requiring a whole personal presence. Despite this understanding of oneself as self-constituted in seclusion from relation, one cannot escape the fact that we are defined and constituted by the form our relations take, by our spirit of communication; in this case, as a monological subject of communication.

Dual orientation

I have already suggested that the transformations accruing through God's dialogical address do not constitute an abandonment to external, heteronomous determination, but a personal, autonomous response. God's dialogical address creates the possibility of genuine response and, in doing so, of genuine self-constitution too. A person is orientated and centred on him or herself as an autonomous subject of communication. This self-orientation and centring is properly constituted only when it accompanies and serves an external orientation and responds to the communicated presence of God and others. In recognising the form of God's presence and intention of and for us in the divine call we come to a better understanding of ourselves and of our true nature. For the form of God's Word communicates a particular intention and understanding of what it is to be a person in relation to God, and calls us to make this understanding our own in a responsible existence before God and others. In our acceptance of God's call and claim by responding to it aright, God's understanding and intention of and for us inform a new self-understanding. In affirmative responses to God's call to be full and genuine persons, we transform ourselves in a transcending movement beyond what we presently are or take ourselves to be. Although the power of this movement rests with the creativity of God's Word, it is none the less our autonomous, responsible act.

In the genuine relation of I and Thou in dialogue, this self-transformative movement is socially refracted. In dialogue one not only gives oneself to the other, but receives oneself back from the other too. My self-understanding is embedded in my communication, and your understanding and response to it will be embedded in yours. So I receive a reflection of myself in your response. Dialogue may be considered as a process of self-transcendence (movement towards the other) and return (receiving onself back from the other). Through giving and receiving ourselves in this way we can come to a new understanding of ourselves.

If persons are the concrete manifestations of their relations then they cannot be known apart from them. They cannot, then, know themselves except as they are known in their relations. Communication orientated to understanding is not just an orientation on the other but upon oneself, so that one's identity and presence in the relation may become more genuine. In this process both partners may change by comprehending the understanding which others have of them and of their communication. I argued in the previous chapter that one's 'self' cannot be a direct phenomenon of experience. What we experience is the communicated experience God and others have of our 'selves'. Thus self-identity or self-understanding is a sedimented interpretation of our perception of others' experiences and understandings borne to us in their communication. So the way we see ourselves is related to the way we experience and interpret others as seeing, understanding and experiencing us. I am therefore defined in my relations because I am for myself only as I am for God and others. (Though my understanding of others' understanding of me may be mistaken.)

Dialogue provides a formative principle for personal ethics as it demands a particular form of openness in, to, and for others in which one 'puts oneself in their place'. By this I mean that one attempts to understand others' understanding and experience their experience by imaginatively understanding and experiencing the world (including oneself) from their personal locations (points of view and action) as if one were them (i.e. had their autobiographies of relation).

This imaginative occupation of the other's location can only take place through the mediation of systems of public communication and is, in fact, what makes communication and relation possible and so is an inevitable part of every social interaction (though it might only take place in a distorted form). A public semiotic and semantic system grounds the very possibility of understanding in that it facilitates the transmission and reception of information (message, not noise). Competent communication, even when it is strategic or instrumental, involves an understanding of how the message will be received, and this involves understanding the standpoint of another. In distorted communication (monologue) one is not trying to communicate one's self-understanding but to achieve a goal. The commitment in the relation and to the other is of a very different quality from that in dialogue. Because one is not giving one's real 'self' to the other, there is no need to attend to the independent reflection of oneself from the other. Neither, of course, will there be a seeking of the other's independent self-understanding, but only of her or his compliance. In dialogue, however, one's self-understanding is genuinely present in communication. One gives oneself to and seeks the other as a real and independent other who may therefore provide new information about oneself, her or himself, or the world in the making of an autonomous response. Dialogue can only be sought where the meaning one has for oneself is the meaning one seeks to have for others.

Ethical transcendence

A relation which conforms to Christ and images God is a dialogical structure of call and response. In dialogue persons co-intend themselves and their partners as communicatively autonomous, as co-subjects of communication. My argument up to this point has indicated that this requires the persons to be both genuinely present in but also partially discrete from the relation. We are to be truly there for one another, but we are to be there as persons; that is, as subjects of communication, who must therefore retain a certain independence from one another and from the present relation. This discreteness and independence, however, must not be understood as a reservation from genuine and as complete self-presence as is possible and appropriate; it is not a reservation of their being but the designation of the difference and individuality of the partners. Christ is present *in* individuals who are ex-centrically orientated. This means that they are centred only through an external orientation towards personal centres beyond themselves, and are so externally orientated only through personal centredness. The indwelling of Christ in the partners individuates and therefore constitutes them as transcendent personal identities who may thereby be external points of orientation for one another. Christ's presence *between* them is a mediation of their transcendent individual identities to one another, and therefore of the specific claims, calls and responses they make to one another as different persons. (See Chapter 2.)

In a relation conformed to Christ the partners co-intend each other as subjects. This is a creative expectation that each will autonomously respond to the other. The expectation is that there will be a reversal of roles as the recipient of communication becomes its subject, as Thou becomes I, and vice versa. The partners in a dialogue are Thou–Is, persons responsible to each other in dialogue. The identity they share as Thou–Is is formal and does not refer to their content. They are not, therefore, materially exchangeable. More importantly, the ethical content of their existence before the other as alternately I and Thou is also non-identical. Although the existence of another as an independent subject of communication is presupposed and expected in dialogue, the experience an I has of another is of a Thou–I (of an I only in the form of a Thou) and not of an I as such. The I-form of another can be intended, expected, or assumed by its effects but not directly experienced and known. The identity of the other is, strictly speaking and in the last analysis, impenetrable and transcends both experience and expectation in any complete and absolute sense.

Moreover, the Thou and I of the *same* person are non-interchangeable contents of experience. We can never directly experience ourselves as others experience us (as Thous). We can only experience our Thou-ness indirectly through the mediation of others' communication as they respond to us. Similarly, we can be directly experienced by others only as Thou and never as I. They can experience our I-ness only indirectly as it appears in our communication. We remain separate persons even in our closest relations and can only imaginatively dwell within one another's identities and stand in their place. This means that behind every Thou there is an I independent of the relationship in which he or she now stands. A person transcends others' intentions, expectations and experience and also the relations in which these function. I am here echoing Bonhoeffer's position, that the Thou is not merely epistemologically but ethically transcendent.[6] The otherness of other persons therefore presents a real barrier to the claim we may legitimately make on them and places them before us as the bearers of potentially conflicting interests. They may therefore make claims contrary to our interests and thereby create a moral decision for us.

The transcendence of their personal identities constitutes individuals as points of orientation for and resistance to one another which are imbued with moral content. We are called to responsibility before (and by Christ in) others whose interests, understanding and intention of them and ourselves may differ from and be opposed to our own. On the basis of the distinctiveness (ethical transcendence) of their personal identities, persons call others to responsibility before them. They do this by constituting an ethical barrier to others' unjustified claims and by their communicated commitment to others' just claims, which indicates their readiness to be justly called upon and claimed by others. The transcendence of others provides us with points of resistance. Their transcendent reality places our present identities, understanding and intentions in question.

The ethical transcendence of a person becomes obvious when one resists another's communication. But the person's distinct identity cannot be equated with this resistance. The fact of resistance indicates the presence of a non-identical subject without actually identifying him or her. For if a person were identical with a point of resistance, then subsumption by the other would be resisted only by a subsumption of personal identity into the relation. The identity of the Thou would be tied to that of the I (through negation) and would therefore be dependent on it. Negative identification is a form of dependence in which the Thou is bound to image negatively the I. The identity and appearance of this person in the relation would not be self-determined but tied in contradiction to the appearance of the I. She or he would not therefore be an I for her or himself. Furthermore, if the Thou's identity were totally bounded and defined by its resistance to the I, then there could never be mutuality or dialogue between them, only opposition.

The Thou presents an ethical boundary to the I precisely because it is an independent centre of existence which is not immediately related to it (even in contradiction). The I is therefore morally bound not simply to acknowledge the Thou's resistance, but to seek a mutuality of understanding rooted in the distance between them. Dialogue is therefore communication in the expectation of resistance which is also open to the frustration of this expectation by the resistance of the Thou taking unexpected forms at unexpected places. In other words, the expectation of resistance cannot turn into a subtle determination of the Thou by the I. The impenetrableness of the Thou which is the source of ethical transcendence and autonomy must mean that he or she may act unexpectedly.

The presence of Christ in a relation structures both the relation and the participating individual identities such that limits are set to communication which are not generated by either partner. These limits do not refer to the bounds of one's own possibilities and potentialities but to the presence of the independently centred existence of the other as mediated to one by Christ's presence. The ethical limits to communication in a particular relation can only be found, known and understood through the orientation towards a mutuality of understanding which happens in dialogue as relations are in conformity to Christ. The limits may be recognised only where others are recognised and intended as communicative subjects. A person who knows and acknowledges as limits only those of her or his own competence, needs or possibilities cannot acknowledge any external existence, be it God or others, as either claim or limit, as Thou. Such a person cannot therefore answer the call of another as a point of orientation from beyond her or himself. The potentiality and truth of what is other cannot be recognised where others do not exist for one as limit and claim. Where existence and truth are self-imposed and self-bounded, there can be no 'imposition' of them from outside.[7] For then truth is regarded as personally immanent, never personally transcendent.

Expectation

In the recognition and intention of the other as ethically transcendent, ethical space–time within the relation is offered to the other for independent communication. The proffering of this ethical space–time is a recognition of the other's communicative subjectivity, or identity as a Thou–I. This represents an openness to the other which is a precondition for dialogue in which a true mutuality of understanding may take place. What is offered is ethical space–time within a particularly intended relation. It is not abstract, but dimensioned and bounded. The offer therefore mediates an incomplete openness towards the other in the expectation that any resistance will be made within certain limits (i.e. is likely to have a certain form, content and location). This incompleteness is not itself a bad thing. It provides an opening gambit, an initial orientation towards the other which, provided it is open to disappointment, is capable of subsequent revision. It is this openness to the frustration of preconceptions, not the absence of preconceptions altogether, which orientates a person towards others and towards a genuine mutuality of understanding.

A structure of expectations (code or law) is indispensable because communication is a concrete encounter within a determinate social context. It is necessary to assume in dialogue that others will undertake communication within a range of possibilities constrained by their history and by the character of the general and local contexts of communication. Whilst being receptive to contradiction, one must assume that one's perception of this restricted range is accurate. Some of these expectations will be particular, referring to a particular other, perhaps in a particular context, and based upon previous communication, but others will be a mediation of the social assumptions concerning the character of personal being in general and in the abstract.[8] Both are absolutely necessary preconditions for dialogue because, by reducing the range in expectation of possible communication from infinity to a manageable number, they serve to reduce complexity and thereby to ground dialogue in the reciprocally shared expectations of a concrete relation.

Relations are processes of communication and exchange transacted through a public language. A language establishes ground rules for expression and interpretation through its communication codes and exchange values. It thereby operates as a normative structure for the expectation of communication (behaviour, expression and interpretation) and thereby regulates communication and relation. As a meaning-frame, it makes it possible to select a single communication, expectation or interpretation from a restricted range of possibilities whilst keeping others open.[9] If the way one expects another to interpret one's communication matches one's experience of the other's interpretation as this appears in his or her response, then there is an implicit consensus in their relationship concerning the normative expectation structure of the locally valid social code. So long as expectations are not frustrated, communication takes place within a stabilised structure through which validity claims (i.e. that it is valid for the person to make this communication in this way, here and now) and exchange values will be taken as unproblematic.

Meaningful communication and relations depend upon the semi-predictability of lawlike behaviour in which both the ground rules of the relation and the other are often taken for granted. This does not indicate the total determination of the other, but it does imply the assumption that the dimensions of social space–time required by the other in response may be presupposed (though not necessarily accurately). This need not be as impersonal as it might at first seem, for this assumption may, indeed, be directly related to previous experience of a particular person. Expecting a certain constancy from another person is actually an act of loyalty to his or her existence as an integrated individual. It is not a denial of personal freedom but a recognition and intention of her or him as an autonomous, centred and integrated person. The profferment of predetermined social space–time in the recognition of another's communicative subjectivity and personal integrity is an important part of the process in which others learn what is expected of them as persons.

The expectation of another's constancy requires some systematisation into 'law' in order to cope with what would otherwise be an unrestricted range of expectation, i.e. an expectation of personal inconstancy and indeterminacy. The reverse is also true, that being dependable in a relation and to another oneself involves the presentation of a pattern of communication which provides some firmness of expectation. Where communication appears as a pattern, it may be interpreted as structured and intended personal activity with implications for the future. Stable relations depend upon this 'double contingency' whereby each partner may expect the expectation and the expectation of the expectation of the other. In this two-fold expectation communication may take place within a semi-stable environment. The relation does not have to begin again from the beginning at every instant, because certain ground rules are already operating through an implicit consensus. Here I think it is appropriate to talk of the relation as a sedimentation of previous encounters through which its own peculiar law or code evolves and exercises a certain independent power as a common bond.

Personal integrity and centredness are not intrinsic to one in isolation from others, but arise only in the self-obligation to be dependable to and for others. One's dependability for others is a strong source of one's personal sense of identity. In each particular relation one enters a network of mutual obligation for the continuity of personal identity. The identities of the partners within a particular relation are mutually dependent. Any change in the real or perceived identity of one partner in the relation threatens that of the other if it shifts the ground of the terms of their relation sufficiently.[10] Self-consistency within any given social context is therefore tied up with the real or perceived self-consistency of others. Of particularly pronounced effect will be any change in the expectation of veracity, the genuineness and wholeness of self-presence in communication.

The expectation of the other indicates the identity of self and other and the form of relation which are intended and supposed, a mutuality of expectation which may or may not actually exist. Communication is generally undertaken on the assumption that there is a background understanding (i.e. a common code) and is orientated towards further understanding in the elicitation of the response sought and expected. Understanding therefore takes place on two levels: the background understanding concerning the codification of the relation (deep structure) and the explicit understanding to be reached about what is or ought to be in the world (surface structure).[11]

The possibilities of response fall into four categories: (1) compliance, representing the actualisation of a consensus concerning the codification of the relation and therefore the appropriate identities of the partners in the relation; (2) non-understanding, representing the perception of uncoded variety or noise; (3) misunderstanding representing either (a) an ambiguity in the codification, or (b) an implicit but not conscious rejection of the code by the substitution of another; (4) resistance, in which the code is understood but the proposed codification of the relation is rejected. These alternatives may be illustrated in the example of a manager who, whilst speaking on the telephone, indicates the need for a pen to a secretary by finger-snapping. The secretary might respond by: (1) passing a pen; (2) not interpreting it as a communication at all; (3a) realising that the finger-snapping was intended to attract attention to a need but interpreting this as an instruction to keep quiet; (3b) humming along to the tune the manager is thought to be snapping along to; (4) showing irritation at the manager's rudeness.

Monological communication screens out the fourth possibility. The possibility that the proposed codification of a relation may rightly be perceived as unjust or otherwise unacceptable by another can only be entertained in a dialogical recognition in which the other is intended as an ethically transcendent subject who may generate as well as respond to codification proposals. Dialogue therefore contains a feedback loop through which a response may be interpreted as an implicit or explicit counter-proposal. This is not an expectation as such – more an openness to the fact that the communication of the other may escape expectations. As a generalised and therefore formless openness it is to be differentiated from the expectation of resistance derived from previous experience.

In an address analogously corresponding to that of God in Christ, social space–time is offered to the other in the expectation that it will be adequately dimensioned to contain any expansion appropriate to the other within the relation (but which is not so large and free of expectations that the other becomes lost in it). This is carried out in a spirit of letting the other be. It is a non-coercive expectation that the other will conform to one's intention of autonomy within expected limits. An undistorted call is a social refraction and mediation to others of God's call. Its expectations are formally creative whilst materially non-determinative.

In dialogue the structure of expectation relating to the other is orientated towards a genuine mutuality of understanding. But as the Thou remains an impenetrable mystery for the I, there is a gap between the understanding, expectation and intention one has of the other and those the other had of him or herself; so disappointment is always possible. As an independently centred point of orientation, the Thou can be approached through successively refined expectation and understanding, but will never be reached in the sense of being completely understood. There is always something left out of an expectation and, therefore, always something for the Thou to say. An orientation towards a genuine mutuality of understanding demands that the systematised expectations appropriate to a supposedly understood dialogue-partner be coupled with a sensitivity towards the rejection of this understanding. Communication orientated towards genuine mutuality of understanding, or conformity to Christ, is a diachronic spiral of understanding in dialogue, rather than a loop or circle indicating the exchange between static identities. A proposed codification (call) for a relation can elicit a counter-proposal in response which demands, in its turn, acceptance or a further counter-proposal.

When the presence of Christ is a formal principle of the relation, informing expectation, intention and understanding of self and other, then it is understood that the call might be, or might be perceived to be, inappropriate. There is a genuine openness to the other which offers not only a predefined social space but a recognition of the other's right to reshape it. There is a seeking of the other which is truly open to the other on two levels. Social space–time is offered to a communicative subject in the expectation of a response which, even in compliance, may lay a claim upon oneself. The other is formally intended as a communicative subject free, for the purpose of this proposed codification, within certain limits (expectations). Second-level openness refers to the readiness to be openly receptive to the other's communication which may escape this codification.

First-level openness is based upon an understanding of the other which, at the second level, is recognised as incomplete. Second-level openness represents but a formal recognition of the otherness and mystery of others. In dialogical relations both levels combine in a positive celebration of the other as the mysterious and independent basis of one's understanding of them.[12] Both levels are absolutely necessary and imply each other.

Reflection
In dialogue the social space–time offered to another is a recognition, acceptance and celebration of the other as partially understood and as, in the final analysis, a positive mystery. As such, the structure of expectations and present understanding is prevented from becoming rigid and stereotypical, and thereby from slipping into monological forms of domination. The other is invited to fill this predimensioned space–time but also to sweep it away. The social space–time offered to the other is not

constituted by one's evacuation from that point in the relation, but is ethically dimensioned by the form of one's presence as passive, rather than absent, at certain points. The communicated offer therefore has an ethical meaning and content predetermined by one's presence and intending of oneself and the other in it and in the relation.

The proffering of space–time in the relation for the other's autonomous response does not represent a withdrawal of oneself from that point in the relation, but one's presence there and then having a specific quality and form. It is what might be termed a 'passive' moment in which the active communication of the I is curtailed so the Thou may be 'attended' to. This attention to the other's response by restricting the activity and expansion of the I is in itself an acknowledgement of the former's ethical transcendence in the expectation that the I's overexpansion would and should be resisted. This is a letting-be of the other in recognition that the other's independent communicative subjectivity requires an area for independent response and codification. This communicative pause in which the other is let be is an essential constituent of dialogue, representing the intention of the other as an autonomous subject of communication. It is only by attending to the independence of the other that more refinement in mutual understanding may develop through the process of call and response:

> Precisely by 'giving space' to the other, an interaction comes into being which is not simply dominated by the subject; there is an expansion of the interaction to allow for the other to 'be'. While this constitutes that being as truth for the subject also, it does not neces- sarily have to be seen simply in the effect on its subject ... But the truth of the being of the other as it arises in the interaction with the other can equally well be spoken of objectively, as the truth which emerges through the 'self-utterance' or self-presentation of the other, so far as it is given primacy by the subject and so far as the relation between them is corrected by its self-presentation. (In other words, the objectivity of the other is not a 'brute objectivity' but one which occurs in its interaction with the subject.)[13]

The understanding and expectation of the other in dialogue are referred to and ultimately derived from the independent communication which reflects the independent and unique being of the other. Where this structure of expectations is not related to the independence and otherness of the other, there is an attempt to collapse the relation into a monologue. The independence of the other from the I and of the I's proposed codification of the relation is abrogated as she or he is desired only as an object whose existence is totally bounded by this particular intention in relation. The independent reality of the other as a communicative subject can only be sought through moments of 'silence' before the other.

The 'silence' involved in letting-be is a passive moment of communication pregnant with proffered possibilities, a moment of receptivity appropriate to the perceived form and content of the other open to disappointment. The fact that there is a *readiness* to pause, to be silent before the mystery of the other, is more important then the precise *content* which this pause has in one's structure of expectation. In this pause one seeks ever fuller understanding and ever fuller presence of the other in the relation by offering space–time for the other to be fully her or himself. What is invited, therefore, is an expansion in both the understanding and the presence of the other. It is only in such an offer that the other may be present as a Thou–I for the I, and that dialogue may take place.

In this passive moment there is reflection on oneself and the other. It may therefore by subdivided into two bipolar moments of self- and other-reflection. Self-reflection is a self-checking in which one's communication and its interpretation (as evidenced in the other's response) are considered as to their accuracy, efficacy and validity. It thereby functions as a means of bringing oneself more genuinely into communication and relation as, on the basis of this new information provided by the other, one may alter one's public appearance (self-communication) or transform one's personal identity (the 'self' behind communication). Through reflection on oneself as one is, and is perceived by the other to be, in the relation, one may come to a more genuine understanding of oneself, the other and the relation. On this basis, one may undertake more genuine or more adequate communication.[14]

There is, then, a dual aspect to self-reflection. On the one hand, one checks one's self-understanding and knowledge, which must be adequate for communication to be honest and genuine. This represents attending to oneself.[15] On the other, there is a receptivity to being misunderstood, representing attending to the other's communicated interpretation of one and one's own communication. Self-reflection therefore involves attending to the other and cannot therefore be viewed as a withdrawal from the relation. For the new information which one is primarily attending to is the reflection of oneself and one's communication in the other's response. It is primarily through the other's response that one may be made aware of latent or alternative meanings in one's communication and of alternative understandings of oneself. Self-reflection is orientated towards more genuine self-communication and therefore towards refinement in one's own identity in communication for others, but also one's identity as it is in and for oneself. Other-reflection is similarly orientated towards the identity of the other both in and 'behind' communication.

In other-reflection, the I seeks to reflect, within him or herself, the self-understanding of the Thou and the accompanying understandings of the I and of the world as they are embedded in Thou's communication. This is an essential aspect of dialogue in which the partners are trying to interrelate their understanding *about* themselves, the other and the world with that of the other in order to reach an understanding *with* the other. To understand the understanding of the other, one must pause in the active communication and manufacture of one's own understanding and be prepared to accept the other beyond expectations without prejudgment. The pause which acknowledges the ethical transcendence of the other is a suspension of judgment in every sense, seeking to comprehend (so far as is possible) an understanding connected with another's unique identity and social location (as a specific point of view and action). Instead of immediately opposing or denying the validity of an alternative understanding, an attempt is made to explore and comprehend it. This understanding of understanding may appear either explicitly[16] or implicitly in subsequent communication which is undertaken as the self- and other-understandings resulting from the reflective moment are brought together.

Interpenetration and distance

The partners' reflection of each other represents their 'dwelling in' the other. By this 'indwelling' I mean an empathetic occupation of the other's social location and identity in the attempt to understand the understanding and to experience the experience of the other. These moments of interpermeation are those in which the relational identities of the partners in dialogue are only as they are 'in' each other. But how can this interpermeation be possible if the impenetrableness and ethical transcendence of the partners is to be maintained?

The interpenetration of the partners, mediated by the presence of Christ both within and between them, may be neither literal nor complete; but is, rather, metaphorical and limited. Furthermore, the understanding so reached will be neither complete nor direct, but inferential and intimated. The ethical distance between the partners therefore remains, and their presence 'in' each other does not imply a unification, but a community between them. (Compare my discussion of trinitarian interpermeation in Chapter 1.) The other's experience is not directly accessible to one, but the other can be experienced as experiencing (i.e. as a centred subject) and therefore as having a distinct social location and identity. Thus it is necessary to say that the attempt to participate in the other is an intention and recognition, and therefore maintenance, of the other's individuality, the other's existence as a distinct and ethically transcendent Thou–I. In the partners' mutual co-intention as Thou–Is alongside each other and in Christ, their orientation towards a mutual 'indwelling' is compulsory.

The structure of dialogue depends upon the partners alternately taking on the inexchangeable dialogue roles of I and Thou, alternating as the subjects and recipients of communication. 'I' and 'Thou' index a person together with her or his communication relative to others and their communication. In an extended dialogue both persons will become I, but never at the same point in social space–time. I and Thou do not refer to single, constant substances, but index the present subject and recipient of communication, their present attitudes in the relation and in relation to one another. The exchange which occurs as I becomes Thou and vice versa is of dialogue roles and not of individual identities. The exchangeability of dialogue roles does not therefore indicate the exchangeability or identity of individual identities. It does, however, indicate a mutual engagement and unity which may be indexed in the matrix of persons by the plural pronouns 'us', 'we', 'them', 'they', 'you'.

The mutuality of understanding which dialogue represents is based upon the non-identity of the partners. The independent subjectivity of each may be apprehended only through their self-communication in the locally valid communication code. Particularly as one registers disagreement or reservation concerning the other's understanding, one's existence as an individual identity who transcends both the other and the relation is indirectly communicated and may thus become an aspect of the indirect experience of the other.[17] In the awareness and intention of another ethically transcendent I behind the Thou–I of the relation, there is already an indirect formal participation in that reality.

Our status as Is, as ethically transcendent individual identities who are autonomous subjects of communication, is derived from our participation in public communication. There is no relationally bare individual essence, no subjectivity in complete opposition to or isolation from the intersubjectivity of mutual understanding. There is neither a complete identity nor a total alienation between the transcendent I (deep 'self') and its public appearance in communication. Communication is not an inappropriate objectification of a properly incommunicable subjectivity; on the contrary, it is only through the lawlike structure of mutual expectations contained in dialogue that subjectivity becomes possible through the process of intersubjectivity. Communication orientated towards mutual understanding depends upon a public meaning-structure stable enough to support the expectation of expectation and understanding of understanding. Thus communication may proceed on the assumption that the meaning of a symbol will be reciprocally recognised. One may therefore anticipate the interpretation of one's communication by the other. This entails the empathetic occupation of the other's identity and social location within the limits I have described.[18] One understands the meaning of one's communication from both dialogue roles simultaneously in the passive moment of self- and other-reflection.

This moment is a passive intention of oneself and the other as Thou–Is. It is therefore an intention of reciprocity in the relation, of both as simultaneously Thou and I from their different perspectives. Hence there is a differentiation in the partners' content through their identity in form. Putting oneself in the other's place represents a formal intention and recognition of the other as an I like oneself who therefore has a specific and unique content which is only partially known and understood.[19] If the other were either not formally identical or not materially distinct, then there would be no point in putting oneself in his or her place. For if the other were not an I, then there would be no independent communication, experience and understanding to comprehend, and if they were materially identical, then all this would already be comprehended and would not be informative.

Because Christ's presence is the structuring element of the other's unique identity which constitutes it as ethically transcendent, one's dwelling in and genuine orientation towards the other must be an orientation towards Christ. In this orientation the identity (content) of the other will be recognised and intended as unique and ethically transcendent. Further, in trying to understand this unique identity, the understandings or expectations specific to it must be considered as potentially one's own, as if one had the same history, location and identity. There is a recognition of a formal identity between self and others.[20]

Mutual expectations

In the partners' co-intention of each other as formally identical with themselves, they co-constitute themselves as interdependent partners in the dialogical, and therefore reciprocal, process of active and passive communication ('speaking' and 'hearing'). In intending the other as an autonomous subject of communication, one cannot expect her or his response in an overdetermined way. This response will be a selection from a range of possibilities made on the basis of his or her own structures of expectation and previous understanding. This is why the expectation of the other's response and understanding is an expectation of the other's expectation of one's own expectation (and so on, ad infinitum). In other words, all communication is related to a network of anticipatory expectations. One's own communication may affect another through his or her own structure of expectations on three levels: (i) the communication may conform to or disappoint it; (ii) this may affect the stability of the structure and thereby (iii) effect some change in individual identity and, consequently, in the codification of the relation. An example given by Luhmann to illustrate this point may aid clarification here:

> It is only with a three-tier reflexivity that one can, for example, not only preserve the other's momentary security of self-presentation by tact, but beyond that the security of expectation as well. If, for example, the wife always only serves a cold evening meal, expecting that her husband expects that, he will on his part have to expect his expectation of expectation: He would otherwise not understand that he does not just cause inconvenience by his unexpected wish for hot soup, but further also undermines the security of expectation related to him on the part of his wife, and can thus get into a new equilibrium in which he has to expect his wife to be someone who expects him to be moody and unpredictable.[21]

The structure of expectations which one operates in a particular relation corresponds to one's identity with and for a particular other. It will be related directly to one's own history apart from and within this relation. The perceived identity and dependability of the other will be a determinative feature of the latter. But if the identity within the relation (dependability in communication) of one partner may be disturbed by a real or perceived change in the identity of the other then, from another side, it must again be said that the two identities are mutually dependent. This is a property peculiar to dialogical relations in which Christ is present. For monologically identified individuals would operate an overstable and static expectation structure, resistant to disturbance precisely because it is not open to the other. That does not imply that all stable structures of expectation are inherently monological, but that all monological structures are resistant to change by virtue of being resistant to anything truly other.

Where there is a conformity between one's expectation of another and that other's self-expectation which is reciprocated (i.e. where A's expectation of B conforms to B's self-expectation and vice versa), then a stable mutuality of understanding has been achieved. Both the code and the codification of the relation are agreed upon and, in this consensus, both the relation and the individual identities involved become stable (but not necessarily static) structures. The stability of the relation through consensus and reciprocated expectations is not, however, sufficient to guarantee its conformity to Christ, its undistorted and dialogical character. That is, in fact, the case even where A's structure of expectations of B is open to, but does not receive, disappointment by B.

The situation is rather more subtle than this view could allow. For the partners' mutuality of understanding might be based upon a distorted understanding of what each of them is, and what their relationship should be. Given the rupture of relations in a fallen world in which persons are socialised after a distorted pattern, intending themselves and others in distorted ways, the consensual achievement of mutual understanding should be regarded with some reservation as an indication of an undistorted relation.

As a result of the sedimentation of previous relations and of the social expectations communicated to me relating to my social location (for instance my caste or status), I might come to expect myself to be dominated or dominating in certain relations. I may therefore anticipate the corresponding expectations of others. In other words, I may accept my identity as subordinate or superordinate within a certain context and may expect and anticipate others' expectations that I will have this identity in relation to them. Others may therefore be expected to enter into relation with me on the basis of this sub- or superordinate identity. In this case, there may be a mutuality of understanding in my relation to another, but this will be distorted because one of us is present in an overbearing way which coerces the other's identity and communication in the relation, even though this coercion may not be realised. There may be nothing wrong in the feedback mechanisms which mediate our understanding of the other's understanding to us in self- and other-reflection. The relation and our identities may well be based on an accurate perception of the other's understanding of him or herself and of myself. The problem arises with the distorted form in which we both seek the other and in which we both seek to establish ourselves: sin.

Relations in which anything goes so long as it is by mutual consent are not conformed to Christ, no matter how good the structure is for establishing mutually informed consent by attending to the other's self-understanding. For the other's self-understanding may be distorted. An undistorted relation is the result of attending not only to the other but to God. This represents a recontextualisation of the relation into the divine communication context in which it becomes possible to attend to the other as she or he really should be. The response to the self-understanding and call of the person is to be a response to the call of Christ. The call of the person is genuinely heard when it is heard as the call of Christ present in that person as structuring a genuine individual identity. And the response is genuine when it is orientated towards a mutuality of understanding which is conformed to Christ.

It must also be the case that even a genuine intention of the other responding to the call of Christ in him or her may be disappointed and frustrated by the other. A genuine seeking of the other might encounter the other as present in an under-reaching or overbearing way. It might then become necessary to resist the self-definition and intention of another in order to maintain a genuine orientation towards and intention of him or her. It is only by resisting the distorted presence of another (and therefore also the understanding, expectations and intention the other has of him or herself, oneself and the relation) that the other may become genuinely present in a relation in which Christ also would be present.

The genuine and open attending to another is a means, not an end. It is entirely necessary to the process of coming to an undistorted mutuality of understanding, but it is insufficient to secure such a relation in and of itself. Refining one's own communication and understanding of the other so it more accurately reflects the other's presence, self-understanding, expectations and intention will only repeat and reduplicate the distortion. It is no less sinful to accept the distorted self-intending of the other than it is to intend the other in a distorted way oneself. That personal identity transcends any particular relation within which, and particular other before whom, it is present means that a person is a locus of individual responsibility for the other. One's response is not overdetermined by the other's self-understanding and intention, but is a free, responsible act which may therefore resist the other when distorted. It is not what we receive from others in communication, but what we give which determines our identity as distorted or undistorted.[22]

Whilst the other is always to be attended to and his or her self-understanding taken with the utmost seriousness, it can never be taken as the last word or as necessarily determinative for the relationship. In the final analysis an undistorted relation takes neither partner's understanding, intentions, expectations or identity as the final word. For the final Word in this respect can only be God's. The relation is structured and ordered by the redemptive presence of the Word, not by the words of the partners, and the openness of one to another is empowered by the Holy Spirit, not by some force of the partners' own. An undistorted relation is not constituted solely in the matching of intention, expectations and understanding, of call with response (though it must include these). It is constituted only as all of these are in conformity to Christ. An individual whose fidelity, commitment and response to the other is mediated through Christ may have deliberately to frustrate the other's expectations and self-understanding in order to transform the other's self-identity through Christ's presence in the relation between them.

Referring one's understanding, intention and experience of the other to the other is an essential element in checking that one is truly attending to the other and not just reflecting oneself. The question which now arises is how the genuine interests of the other can be maintained free of distortion once they are no longer identified with the other's self-understanding. This is a practical difficulty of some magnitude but it is not, I believe, insurmountable in principle. It is clear that the dangers of paternalism or worse arise where one of the partners becomes the formative principle of the relation and of the other's identity. On a theoretical level it may be sufficient to be clear about the fact that, in the rejection of another's self-understanding, it is Christ rather than the other or oneself who is the formative principle. But this still leaves immense practical problems in determining what is a call to conformity to Christ and what is a call to conform to another or to oneself in denial of Christ. Whilst the problem will always be present, the dialogical structure of relations conformed to Christ provides some means for clarification.

Formal reciprocity in dialogue

In a non-dialogical relation, the partners may reach a mutuality of understanding in which the understanding one has of oneself and of the other matches the other's understanding. There is then an accurate reflection of the one in the other such that there may, for example, be an identity between my expectation, intention and understanding of myself and your expectation, intention and understanding of me and vice versa. In a dialogical relation conformed to Christ, the mutuality of understanding takes the form of a formal reciprocity between the understood, expected and intended identities of us both. In undistorted communication, the understanding, expectation and intention I have of myself is of the same form (but not content) as my understanding, expectation, and intention of you. I therefore intend both myself and you in a formally identical way. When you reciprocate this intention, we have achieved an undistorted mutuality of understanding. My self-understanding, my understanding of you, your understanding of me and of yourself will all be formally identical. There is, in other words, a formally reciprocal co-intending.

A genuine call to another will therefore intend and expect a formal reciprocation of intention in response; it will seek the other as formally identical with oneself – that is, as a co-subject of communication in the relation. It is impossible to seek another and oneself in the same distorted form. Distorted identities seek mirror-images which are formally nonidentical. If I intend myself as dominant over you, I cannot simultaneously intend you in the same form (as a dominant and overbearing presence in the relation), but must seek you in a form which is compatible but nonidentical (subservient and compliant). Only an undistorted identity may seek another who is formally identical but materially non-identical. It is only, of course, in this genuine seeking that an identity may avoid distortion itself.

This means that both the identity and the relation it seeks to call into being are distorted where the intended pattern (proposed codification) of giving and receiving, passive and active communication, call and response between the two partners is not reciprocal in form. If one seeks where (as opposed to what) one is unwilling to give, or vice versa, then one's intentions, expectation and understanding are distorted, and one's presence (identity) in the relation only partial. The proposed codification is self-generated and not a conformation to Christ. A genuine relation may be described as a form of mutuality in which the partners are fully and genuinely present to each other, with each other, for each other, and 'in' each other. It is a formal reciprocity in which 'I am as Thou art.'[23] The full presence to and with each other represents the active and passive moments of a relation of full and genuine presence which still pertains even in the absence of active communication. The being for each other represents the orientation of each upon the other in a seeking for the other's true and full being in Christ, whilst their presence 'in' each other represents the moments of self- and other-reflection in the 'indwelling' receptivity of the partners to each other.

The reciprocal nature of this full and genuine presence, and it can only really be full and genuine in reciprocity, means that there is a formal equality in the relation. Formal equality requires that, at the very least, there must be an equal distribution of dialogue roles. There must be sufficient space–time allocated within the relation for the active and passive communication appropriate to both partners in this relation. Otherwise, the social space–time proper to one will be overrun by the overexpansion of the other. Dialogue is not founded upon a fixed and stereotyped mutuality of expectation in which the distribution of communication roles would be fixed. Rather, it is characterised by a certain fluidity and openness in which each can be and is an initiator and receiver of communication, a Thou–I, in ways appropriate to their specific identities in this particular relation as it unfolds between them. This can be expected but not predetermined in advance.

In dialogue, equality refers to a formal identity between the partners, to the quality of their intersubjective engagement. It does not refer to their material identities, or to an equality in the quantity of the social space–time they occupy, or yet to their taking on the dialogue roles of I and Thou an equal number of times. A purely quantitative notion of equality issues in a tit-for-tat understanding of personal relationships where every communication has to receive a response equal in quantity, where every gift has to be returned. As people are materially non-identical they have different needs and capacities for self-communication. A dialogical understanding of equality will be based upon and reflect these differences. In what sense, then, does it still deserve to be termed equality? Equality in this sense is concerned with the meeting of needs and the celebration of differences in ability, aptitude, and so forth which are connected with differences in identity – it is not concerned with ensuring people occupy equal quantities of social space–time.

Formal equality in the distribution of dialogue roles governs the access of each partner to communication, and secures the right of each to take up different dialogue roles at different moments within the relation. What it does not do is establish equal and inalienable rights of both to have access to the same social space and time, which would represent a strict, quantitative notion of equality. The space and time appropriate to each will be asymmetrical for two reasons. First, a dialogue between two people who try to assume the same dialogue roles simultaneously amounts to two simultaneous monologues in which no information can be exchanged because both either 'speak' or 'listen' at the same time. Both would only really be present to and communicating with themselves. Second, there is a material non-identity between the partners in which each has different needs and potentialities. Consequently, there is a material inequality between them and therefore in their rights to occupy different dialogue roles as appropriate to them in the here and now of their particular relation.

Formal equality and reciprocity within a relation occur in the recognition and intention by both of themselves and the other as communicative subjects who, as such, may initiate or interrupt communication. The fact remains, however, that an asymmetrical relation will usually be a requirement of their material non-identity. This means that the space–time of the relation is imbued with ethical content and is relative in value. It is proper for me to intend and recognise you as an autonomous subject of communication (an I), but that does not make it proper for you to do or say whatever you like whenever you like. Although we must both intend and regard you as an I for yourself, it may not be equally proper for you to assume the dialogue role of I at any particular point in our relation. The appropriate expansion and occupation of social space–time in the relation is determined by our unique needs and identities. The redeemed pattern of intersubjectivity means being in need of others and being at the disposal of others in their need. There will be times when the orientation upon the other demands that the codification of a relation be determined solely by the call (i.e. the needs) of the other, in which case one's own needs are (temporarily) set aside.

In a medical consultation, it could be positively unhelpful for the relation between doctor and patient to be symmetrical. The social space–time appropriate to each is quite properly bounded by the professional relationship orientated towards the health needs of the patient. Within certain limits and safeguards, the dialogue roles of the consultation are distributed according to the different identities, understanding and experience (attributable to their different social locations and histories) of each. The doctor has a certain medical and therapeutic expertise and the patient has an experience of the illness. Both the doctor's diagnosis (interpretation of the patient) and the self-understanding (presentation) of the patient may sometimes have to be resisted by the other but, in general, the response of the doctor will be moulded by the content of the patient's communication. The communication (diagnosis and therapy) of the doctor is to be directed towards the genuine health needs of the patient (whether implicitly or explicitly communicated). It is only, I think, a light overstatement of the case to say that the patient's communicative subjectivity in the relation is confined to self-presentation and that of the doctor to other-reflection, which both understand to be only a partial self-identity specific to this relation and social role. On the basis of the material disparity in their being and the orientation of the relation upon the patient, there is an asymmetry in the rights of occupation of dialogue roles and in the location of ethical resistance. The doctor does not make a self-presentation of her or his own state of health, and the patient does not write a prescription for either of them.

Similarly, it is sometimes appropriate for one's being at the disposal of another to be exclusively passive ('listening' rather than 'speaking') as well as mono-directional. Sometimes all the other needs is a 'listening ear', a passive presence, when all that is appropriate is an open presence with another rather than communication on his or her behalf. There will, of course, be communication, but it will tend to be passive and implicit in the simple being there, in grunts of affirmation, or in the simplest affirmative body language or touch. There is no independent communication, but a passive reflection of the other.

These examples do not, however, represent an abandonment of individuality. One is present in one's particularity even where only passively present. Presence, however passive, is still the communication of a particular personal identity. It therefore bears the form and content of a unique communicational spirit. An implicit self-presentation is unavoidable, and this has some determining effect upon the relation and the communication of the other, and the way in which one is and is perceived to be present.

In the second example, the one's identity in the relation is defined in terms of his or her passive presence (indexed, if at all, as Thou) with the other, as such a one who is able to be passively present with the other in this particular way. The content as well as the form of this identity is implicitly reflected in the communication of the other which takes appropriate form. The other's communication is structured in the expectation of the form of one's presence as a sympathetic listener who will not occupy the social space–time necessary for the former to talk through his or her problems. Communication can only continue on this basis so long as the form and content of the one's presence implies consent, a reciprocal co-intention. As soon as the form changes (by, say, beginning to take on an active communicative role by providing explicit interpretations of what is said or by passing judgment), or else as soon as the content of the passivity changes (say, from a posture of interestedness to yawns), then the other's communicative form and content will change too. The content of the other's communication must, on this basis, be expected to vary as different people are present with him or her, perhaps in identical (passive) form but non-identical in content. However much it may seem that all another needs is an 'ear', that ear is always attached to a whole person, the individual character of whose presence can make a decisive difference. Indeed, the one who comes to another as just an ear and who imagines that all other forms of self-presence in the relation are unimportant generally fails to be even an ear. For the relation demands a complete presence which is always implicitly communicated in one's total disposal towards the other.

Asymmetry in a relation need not be an indication of distortion, provided it is intended as a momentary rather than a permanent structure: that is, provided the asymmetry is informed by a formal reciprocity in the partners' co-intending of one another. All relations are necessarily asymmetrical, given the non-identity of the partners. It is not asymmetry and material inequality in a relation which cause distortion, but the sedimentation of particular forms of asymmetry and inequality into hard structures of relation or personal identity which resist the free exchange of dialogue roles even in intention: vicious cycles of dependency or even of gratitude.

In undistorted communication there is an intention of the other as a co-subject of communication. In the first case, the history and future of the relation will contain different symmetrical codifications in which the imbalance in its orientation is reversed and reciprocated. In the second, it is recognised that in the other's personal life apart from this relation, she or he will have occasion to occupy the opposite dialogue role. So the identity in this relation here and now is understood to be particular, limited and partial. This recognition of the person's transcendence of this relation will make a concrete difference to the intention of her or him in this one.

In a medical consultation, for example, the distribution of dialogue roles is structured according to the peculiar limitations of this encounter. There are, indeed, limitations to every encounter, but in a professional relationship these are static and repeatable. Such static, repeatable structures are undistorted only if they are bound to an implicit recognition of the other as an ethically transcendent and autonomous subject of communication – although such autonomy and subjectivity may be restricted in its appearance in this relation. Although a completely free (indeterminate) exchange of dialogue roles is disallowed (which, incidentally, would destroy the character and usefulness of the consultation), the relationship may none the less be structured by a co-intention of the patient as a free and full subject which operates as a guiding ideal. This implicit orientation will, in fact, make a difference to the codification and communicative content of the consultation, though it may rarely have to be made the subject of explicit communication. It should, for instance, prevent the total reduction of the patient to an objective syndrome. This example also indicates how an undistorted personal relationship may be maintained with those who, for whatever reason (e.g. mental illness or handicap), cannot assume the autonomy proper for an I in a relation themselves. The counterfactual intention of such people as full subjects of communication remains necessary. (I discuss this further in Chapter 6.)

Where a relation is asymmetrically codified, there is a material inequality in the identities of the partners, and the distribution of dialogue roles between them. If, however, this material inequality takes place within a formally reciprocated and genuine co-intention by each of the other, then the relation is undistorted. The inequality will probably be understood to be either a temporary phenomenon of the relationship or the result of personal identities particular to this one relation.

An asymmetrical relation may, however, be distorted even if the asymmetry is only temporary. The temporary nature of asymmetry is not, then, a guarantor of non-distortion. For not every call to be at the disposal of another can be justified on the basis of its momentariness. Some proposed codifications have, therefore, to be resisted irrespective of their duration. Identifying just when such resistance is necessary is extremely difficult because it is bound up with claims about what is proper to oneself or another as we are and should be ourselves and in our relation together. It can be difficult to distinguish an unbounded self-intention and orientation from their more genuine forms. These difficulties can be relieved only by a proper understanding of the nature of individual integrity and the means for the mediation (and only sometimes the resolution) of conflicting codification proposals in the orientation upon an undistorted dialogical relation and conformity to Christ.

In this discussion of dialogue in interpersonal relations I have tried to draw together some of the insights concerning personhood and identity which were thrown up by my argument in earlier chapters. Most important among these are: that dialogue, whilst a relation which might contain considerable proximity, rests upon the maintenance of difference between the partners – despite the fact that they might be changed by it; that individual identities are defined by the form which their relations take and that individuality is therefore the way one is for others; that personal being denotes the capacity to organise oneself in a centred way and act autonomously as a subject in relation with others; that this is acquired through the processes of social relation which are conducted through communication codes and other institutionalised forms of interaction valid in the wider society; that one is properly centred only by being externally directed towards the reality of others; that relating to others as subjects entails acknowledging and giving space for their freedom.

The emphasis of the last chapter was on the relational determination of personal identity at the societal level. By contrast, this chapter is concerned with matters at the interpersonal level, early parts of it attending to the determination of identity in and through interpersonal relationships. Following on from that discussion, my concern in the rest of the chapter has been to explore further and elaborate the implications of dialogue in interpersonal relations and to advance towards an intimation of the ideal conditions of personal being and interrelation. Essentially, what I have been trying to work out is what it means in practice to regard oneself and others as (partly) independent, transcendent and autonomous subjects of communication; or, to put it another way, what it means to be a centred person orientated on and respectful of other personal centres. What, in fact, is implied by the dual orientation implied by an ex-centrically structured being, and how might the integrity and freedom proper to each individual be maintained and recognised by both in their orientation on themselves and one another? How may one be oneself in being for a range of particular others? In the following chapter I shall develop my position further by considering its implications in terms of integrity, fidelity and commitment.

The following chapter therefore develops a key issue of the discussion up to this point – centredness and external orientation – through the language of fidelity and integrity. The same questions and concerns have been aired in this chapter in terms of the encoding and structuring of relationships and of identities. That led to specific suggestions regarding what a genuine attending to another in his or her otherness and autonomy might mean if there is to be genuine mutuality and open encounter. Openness is a crucial feature of dialogue, although it is never total or complete, since it has to be patterned and structured according to the anticipated needs of the partners. Various difficulties in ensuring genuine openness have been discussed in the foregoing. In particular I have been concerned to show that, whilst dialogue is orientated towards a genuine mutuality founded on the freely given reciprocity of the partners, indicating the achievement of a consensus, this is an insufficient condition to guarantee dialogue. It is therefore necessary to check whether one is really orientated on and attending to the other, even where agreement has been secured. Conversely, it is necessary to check whether resistance to consensus on the basis one has suggested is valid or not. My discussion so far has left unanswered the question of what one may do on encountering resistance. How may one check whether it is justified, and what may one do if the answer appears to be no? This question is of quite central importance in practice and will be taken up properly in Chapter 6.

5

Personal integrity: centredness and orientation on others

The locus of fidelity

My argument so far has constructed a relational understanding of personal identity as the form of punctuation operating between oneself and others. Our personal identity is the way we relate to others. We are the way we are for others. For who and what we are as persons is immediately evidenced in the formation of a 'boundary' between our 'selves' and the world. This 'boundary' is organised and deployed by our own individual spirit of communication which has, in its turn, been laid down and moulded through past relationships of some significance. Crucial to the formation of personhood is the centring of one's experience, consciousness and activity on oneself so that one may interact and communicate in an autonomous way. It has been a major part of the burden of my argument that we learn to become personally integrated and centred subjects only through our interaction with others who regard us as and expect us to be such. Furthermore, I have offered a normative conception of the structure of personhood as well as relation according to the pattern of dialogue. Basic to this is the understanding that we are properly centred as persons only by being directed towards the true reality of other personal centres: we become truly ourselves when we are truly for others. Self-interested and self-seeking individuals who, in relation, are only there in, for and with themselves are destructive of the possibilities of genuine relation and identity. For true persons are centres directed beyond themselves in a process of self-transcendence and return.

This being so, fidelity and commitment are crucial factors in personal identity. Extreme self-centredness, fidelity and commitment exclusively to oneself lead to distortions in personal identity. The giving of

one's 'self' to and orientation upon others which is the mark of the ex-
centricity proper to personhood is impossible if one is bound to and hemmed
in upon oneself in an exclusive self-orientation. For such a self-centred
identity as this there arises a total opposition between 'self' and other, so
that any real self-transcendence, any giving of 'self' to another, is seen as
threatening the disintegration of the 'self'. If everything beyond the borders
of 'self' is held in simple opposition as not-self, then it follows that one can
only be oneself by keeping within one's own borders and existing on one's
own terms. Since, in this case, what is other can be neither informative nor
of value for the 'self', others may not be trusted or met on their own
distinctive terms. One's entrance into society can then only be disruptive,
since others may be placed at one's disposal, but any commensurate self-
giving must be avoided because it is supposed to represent a disloyalty to
oneself, an apparent renunciation of one's right to an individual and
inalienable identity. The need to stand upon one's right to maintain an
identity which is inalienable (self-enclosed and non-transcendent) is based
on the understanding that all manipulation and use by others must be
resisted in order to remain an integrated and secure centre.

Christ's call and His presence both reconstitute and transform
individuals as they respond to Him as persons who claim no rights as
inalienably their own. Such rights as they do have exist only in concrete
relation with others for whom those rights are maintained. I do not mean to
imply by this that one is nothing whilst others are everything, but that to
assist and serve God and others one must be something. There is therefore a
right and proper place for personal centredness and, indeed, for resistance to
others, but only as a means for being there as really needed by others. In
other words, centredness and resistance are to be in conformity to Christ
and directed in a genuine orientation on God and others. So any rights one
has are not inalienable in any strict sense, but belong to one only in and for
relation to others. The duality and distinction between rights and duties is
hereby eroded and blurred. The limits and demands of putting oneself at
others' disposal are therefore identical: the needs of others. In a genuine
orientation upon others the same person may rightly allow her or himself to
be manipulated at a particular moment in a relation, but may also rightly
resist exactly the same sort of manipulation on another occasion or in a
relation with someone else. Personal integrity is not a matter of being
predictable no matter what the context. It means maintaining the same
spirit of being for others in a variety of contexts, a formally identical pattern
of intending others. The identity one should maintain before others changes

with context and according to the needs of oneself and specific others in these particular situations as they occur at particular points in the partners' biographies.

A person is an integrated, centred and autonomous subject of communication. Consequently, what a person does or says is not random, but centrally organised. There is, therefore, a continuity between public appearance and communication at different times and in different places as a person leads an integrated and centred existence turning individual history into an autobiography. The personal integrity of others makes them dependable for us. We can expect future communication as integrated with their past because personal identity is a continuity through time and space. Our sense of others' dependability is a recognition of the continuing integrity of the identities they have as particular personal centres. However, persons are also subjects of communication who are not therefore overdetermined by their past. Because they are dependable for us as *persons*, to turn this dependability into an expectation of total predictability would be a serious distortion of what it means to relate to another subject who, whilst integrated, continuous and therefore dependable, remains free. Personal identity is diachronic, open to others and to change. Since persons are autonomous subjects, their communication is neither random nor predictable. Its non-random character means that we can expect and depend on the personal integrity of others. But its non-predictability indicates that what we are depending on and expecting is not a repetition of previous identity, communication and relation; it is, rather, that future communication, relation and identity will continue to be organised by and in the same spirit. On this basis we may expect and depend upon others as integrated persons, not to say or do the same things, or even to be precisely the same person for ever and a day, but to organise themselves and their communication in the same ex-centric orientation on 'self' and others. Because persons are integrated beings, they are dependable for others. Because they are depended on by others, they may learn to integrate their own lives.

As the integration of a personal life indicates neither a material nor formal identity of communication in different times and places, so a person is free to incarnate her or his spirit of communication as may be appropriate to particular situations. The way it is appropriate to be with a particular other here and now, what it is appropriate to do or say, is not determined by the form or content of one's previous communication in this or any other relation. So long as one's identity and communication here and now represent a continuity in the intending of oneself and others, then they are organised by and incarnate the same spirit which has structured personal centredness and external orientation in the past and elsewhere. It is constancy in one's spirit which determines personal constancy and integrity and which means that one's dependability for others may take a variety of forms.

By the same token, the way one is for others at a particular moment of a particular relation cannot threaten personal identity and integrity, provided it is an incarnation of one's own spirit and that one's identity transcends this relation. This is so even in moments of the most radical manipulation by others. It might be appropriate, for instance, to become a verbal or even physical punch-bag for others for whom this is the only expression of personal power available. An apparently total self-surrender to others' manipulation may be the most constructive way of being for them here and now.[1]

There is no 'self' in itself, but only as it is with and for others. A person who is only loyal to him or herself will appear as disloyal for others. Personal integrity must be understood in terms of public appearance in communication through which the form of one's commitment (spirit of communication) to oneself and others materialises, is experienced and may henceforth be expected by others. Personal integrity can also be seen as a sedimented acceptance of others and of others' acceptance of one. For persons are defined by their integrity in communication and called into being by that of others whilst, simultaneously, through their own integrity they call out that of others.

Continuity, integrity and public integration

Personal integrity is a matter of maintaining continuity in personal organisation so that the same spirit of communication may become incarnate in different relations. Since spirit structures and organises internal as well as external life, this means that there will be a continuity between the I transcending any particular relation and the Thou–I of a concrete and particular relation. There is, in other words, a continuity between deep 'self' and local 'self'. This is a matter of continuity between public and private and between the particular appearance in a relation and the enduring identity which transcends particular relations.

In genuine communication, in which one responds to Christ's presence in others, there is a match between internal forms of unity and external appearance, an integration of private and public life, in the seeking of a genuine mutuality of understanding. It is only through and for this public incarnation that the internal integration (centring) takes place. A person becomes a centred, ordered and self-consistent whole only in the process of public communication and external, self-transcending orientation, a subject (of communication) only through the processes of intersubjectivity. This is one reason why distorted individual identities and distorted relations presuppose each other. Distorted individuals cannot, on their own resources, enter an undistorted relation, whilst a distorted relation indicates the presence of at least one distorted identity. Individuality, in its distorted form, is orientated upon and loyal only to itself and cannot therefore be genuine in communication claiming to be orientated on and loyal to the other, or towards a genuine mutuality of understanding (conformity to Christ).

A distorted relation indicates the collapse of mutuality into individual self-seeking, of co-humanity into solitude; that is to say, it represents (for at least one partner) a corrupt form of individuation and identity discrete from relation. Communication based on the fiction of an essence withdrawn from relation represents a fracture in the internal constitution of a person as well as in one's identity in the relation. In distorted communication one is orientated towards oneself and intends the misunderstanding of the other. Soul ('self')[2] and body disintegrate since the individual spirit which patterns their interrelation as well as outward communication requires their separation. Thus, soul becomes an internal, relationally pure sphere, whilst body becomes an inauthentic mode of public appearance. The great paradox is that the more unensouled the body becomes, the more it is at the disposal of the power of outside forces. By being rejected as a vehicle for the soul it becomes subjected to the causality of apersonal and other-personal forces. And because the only sustainable life for a soul is embodiment, the soul is lost too.[3] The absence of wholeness in 'private' life and from public communication coincide. The lack of integration between soul and body, their polarisation into two quite distinct spheres, directly corresponds to the polarisation between public and private.

Individual spirit is the energy which organises a personal life, which structures centredness and external orientation. The Holy Spirit may also be understood in terms of energy, as the divine energiser which dwells and acts in the world as the life-giving organisational energy of open systems.[4] The Holy Spirit may indwell and empower an individual's spirit, and so inform the person's orientation towards 'self' (centredness) and openness to others, the world and God. Where the presence of the Holy

Spirit co-inheres with that of Christ, divine energy is divinely ordered. When this co-inherence occurs within a personal life, centredness and self-transcendence are genuinely structured as one is for oneself and others in a genuine way. In contradistinction, the disintegration of personal identity, in which public identity (appearance in communication) is alienated from and non-identical with private identity, exhibits an anarchic, individual spirit whose energies are tending towards entropy, a removal of identity from communication. This may be understood as a misdirected and overbearing autonomy which displaces the Holy Spirit and the form of Christ in favour of an isolated form of life which is the death of the person.

The disintegration of soul from body arises as one seeks a personal essence or identity either in opposition to that deployed in communication with others, or by otherwise withdrawing it from relation altogether. This represents the death of whole personal life because there is essence and personal identity only in communication.[5] The body has a dual aspect as the hinge between public and private existence and must be understood as the medium through which the soul is present both privately, to itself, and publicly, to others.[6] It is only through physical and social embodiment that the soul is established in and expresses its particularity. As soul a person is a distinct, centred being who, only as such, may provide an ethically transcendent point of orientation for another as an independent communicative subject; as body, this centre may be fully incarnate in the concreteness of physical and social life.[7] In this embodiment a person is addressed and called into being as ensouled body and embodied soul. The mode of integration or organisation (spirit) of soul and body is a sedimented response to the call of others. The possibility of maintaining a genuine order between the bipolarities of personal being (centredness and transcendence, or ex-centricity) is created in the genuine call of a genuine other mediating the presence and call of Christ and empowered by the Holy Spirit.[8] Thus genuine address grounds the possibility of genuine responsibility by calling forth another whose existence is concretely integrated.

Individual integrity cannot therefore be secured through strategies of seclusion or withdrawal from relation. It arises only in the orientation of others towards one and of one towards others – only, that is, through the co-inhering indwelling of Christ and the Holy Spirit in individuals and the conformity of their relations to Christ. The anxious seeking of self without others leads to a loss of self as well as a loss of community, for truly to find oneself one must go beyond or 'lose' oneself. The integrity of body and soul cannot be bound together without binding oneself to others. Personal integrity arises as one is bound to others in public appearance in various communication contexts. For a person

> does not find identity in this life, in remaining isolated and in keeping his soul for himself, but only in going out of himself and becoming personally, socially and politically incarnate.[9]

Self-seeking is inextricably bound to self-giving. One's own personal integrity is simultaneously a response and call to that of others.

There is a personal sense of security which undergirds such ex-centricity, which enables the self-transcendent 'indwelling' and acceptance of others which I have described. But this self-security is not something removed from relations; it is derived from them through the process of sedimentation. One is able to love and accept others on the basis of being loved and accepted by others and/or by God.[10] A secure personal identity is one capable of being shared with others, capable of sustaining others in their brokenness and suffering by becoming broken or suffering oneself; that is, by following Christ. The otherness of other people, including their brokenness, does not pose a threat of disintegration for those who live in the knowledge that they are upheld as integral beings in the presence of Christ, the indwelling of the Holy Spirit and in the love and acceptance of God and/or others: who are, in other words, empowered by the Spirit, conformed to Christ and called into responsibility before God and others.

In the ordered integration of soul and body a person is genuinely present to her or himself and, on this basis, may be a genuine presence before others. An ordered unity of soul and body represents the maintenance of undistorted internal communication which is a necessary, though in itself insufficient, condition for undistorted communication with others. False modes of self-understanding, on the other hand, such as that in neurosis, lead to an inability to order external communication. In this case there is a breakdown in the processes of self-communication through which aspects of an historically sedimented identity would otherwise be ordered together into a whole and consciously made present in communication. A disordered identity and presence in communication is the incarnation of a disordered spirit. Because aspects of the personality, which may actually be guiding interests in themselves and may therefore be guiding communication too, remain repressed or unconscious, they cannot be made explicitly present in communication. There can be no personal integration in neurotic communication, which will therefore have the character of untrustworthiness or untruthfulness for others as for the self. In disintegrated communication the distorted person cannot be present in the reflective moments of him or herself or those of others. None the less, the fact that there is some discrepancy between 'self' as I and as Thou–I in communication can be picked up by others and interpreted as an indication of the person's inconsistency and non-dependability. This might be apparent in the lack of control evidenced by, for example, discrepancies between bodily and verbal, or past and present communication. Alternatively, such discrepancies might be perceived, for instance in special modes of interpretation such as psychoanalysis, as symptoms of an inner distorted state for which a specific interpretation may be provided.

In integrated personal communication, however, one is present to oneself in an undistorted way. One's communication is neither self-alienating nor self-deceptive, and on the basis of this accurate self-understanding, one can control one's appearance in communication, one's identity for others as an integrated centre and subject of communication. Yet this lack of *self*-deception, which makes the internal control of communication possible, also creates the possibility of deliberately distorting communication in order to deceive *others*. This is why undistorted internal communication, as reflected in accurate self-understanding, is not a sufficient condition to secure the non-distortion of external communication. For, on the basis of an accurate self-understanding, one may intentionally distort one's communication and the presentation of oneself to and for others. In this case, the claim is false that there is a close match between one's identity for oneself and that communicated to others, and that one is orientated towards a truthful, genuine and whole presence before the other (a genuine mutuality of understanding).

Locus of commitment

Personal identity can be understood, on this basis, as the locus of commitment to which one's integral being, one's personal *Gestalt*, is directed.[11] It is a matter of where one places one's trust – in God, others, oneself – and therefore of the manner of punctuation operating between oneself and others. Personal identity is bound to concrete communication directed towards others; that is, to the way one is concretely for others. Self-consistency is directly related to one's constancy before and fidelity to others, one's dependability for others. A person whose communication is founded only upon a self-trust and self-seeking cannot be dependable for another as, from the other's point of view, the former's disposition in the form of love or hope for the latter will seem occasional and arbitrary. It escapes the character of arbitrariness only when viewed in terms of the self-seeking person, and thereby being redefined as self-love and a hope buried in the self.

A person's dependability (representing constancy in identity for others) is the fulfilment of promises given to others about the nature of one's fidelity and commitment to them. It is through the giving of promises and the fulfilling of one's own and others' hopes that one is personally identifiable by the form of one's presence in communication.[12] The structure of promise and fulfilment is implicit in all communication which represents a claim to a certain personal continuity through time.[13] This, in turn, is both based upon and grounds the diachronic natures of the individual identity and of the relation. It is an invitation to enter into a joint future together on the basis of trustworthiness and dependability. Thus personal identity lies between the sedimented past and the future in which one hopes and places one's trust and which one proleptically anticipates by the manner in which promises are given and hope shared with others, the way in which one intends oneself and others.[14] Structures of co-intention always have a future aspect.[15] Duplicity and intentionally distorted communication represent a hope and trust only in oneself and an intended future in isolation and dreamed of self-sufficiency.

In a relation conformed to Christ there is a mutuality of trust in which a hope is shared, not in the identity of interest, but precisely in the non-identity of the partners; not, then, in the identity of needs but in the fact that one can be there as the other has need, that both can be truly and, therefore, reliably present in communication orientated towards the other. The promised and expected identities of the partners are formally reciprocated in the mutuality of trust and fidelity which, whilst it can be distorted or disappointed, can also be forgiven. The relation has something of an independent power which continues to bind the partners together through infidelities and misunderstandings because it represents a real and whole commitment of the partners to each other in the reciprocated co-intention of both as full autonomous subjects of communication. This commitment is therefore to the freedom of their mutuality, rather than to a 'contract'. In this relation there is neither the promise of absolute predictability nor the absence of the pain of disappointment, but an area of free play in which all the pain, misunderstanding and bitterness of personal life are secured in the promises of genuine interest in the other as other and therefore as transcendent and unpredictable.

The very possibility of personal integrity involves a double acceptance structure, in that it represents an acceptance of oneself which is based on others' acceptance of oneself as this has been sedimented into a personal identity. The self-acceptance which characterises personal integrity is the acceptance of (significant particular) others' acceptance of oneself. One's formal identity as a communicative subject is, as I have already argued, derived from the expectations others have of one as a personally integrated centre of communication. It is in this expectation of communicative subjectivity that one's communication will be interpreted and understood as rationally based, centred and therefore intended. This applies whether or not it is, or is perceived to be, distorted (for instance a strategic communication aimed at manipulation). Rationally based and centred communication is simply that which is non-arbitrary: i.e. attributable to the centred and controlled activity of a person and therefore understandable as intended, purposeful or designed.[16] The assumption of rational centring facilitates the distinction between distorted and undistorted communication since rational communication can be subjected to questioning and common rational criteria. (This will be developed further in the following chapters.)

In genuine communication one's personal integrity is not just held within oneself but orientated towards others. It does not exist behind communication merely as the source of intentional activity, but is present in communication as a pledge of trustworthiness for others. In other words, in genuine communication there is no disparity between the reasons which may be given for or implied within communication and those which are actually operating for the 'self'. Real and declared interests and intentions are identical (so far as one can tell) because the communication seeks a genuine mutuality of understanding, a conformation to Christ in which both partners are wholly present in an orientation on the other.

Genuine communication, then, involves trusting oneself and trusting others. Trust of oneself indicates the ability to put out of play all unconscious motives and therefore to be fully incarnate in communication on the basis of one's personal integrity. This means being fully present to and for others as one is present to and for oneself. The command 'to love your neighbour as yourself'[17] is a recognition of the fact of the bipolarities of a genuinely orientated, ex-centric existence. Personal integrity arises only in the orientation on another, but this orientation on the other can only be maintained as that between independently centred persons in whom Christ dwells (and possibly also co-inheres with the Spirit). Trust of others is also necessary in the expectation that their communication may also be orientated towards a genuine mutuality of understanding (conformity to Christ) empowered by the Spirit. A genuine communication is simultaneously a declaration of one's own trustworthiness and an invitation for another to be correspondingly trusting and trusted.

The formal reciprocity of a genuine relation conformed to Christ is represented in this double-integrity, double-trust, structure, in that both expect the integrity of the other as they present and incarnate their own. However, the genuineness of one partner's response to Christ's call in another, which invites and intends the free response of the other, is insufficient to guarantee the genuineness of the relation. A genuine relation cannot, by definition, be assured from one side alone. A genuine relation is nothing more or less than formal reciprocity in expectation and integrity. As such it must be understood in terms of an *orientation* towards a full and genuine mutuality of understanding rather than its present achievement. It is the state of both partners communicating in an open rationality in which (rationally based) misunderstanding is still possible, and therefore in which further accommodation of one to another, further transformation in the presence of Christ is still necessary.

The conception of personhood as an ex-centric structure which I arrived at in previous chapters, in which one is centred only by being externally directed, can also be expressed in terms of personal integrity – as I hope I have now shown. The integrity of an ex-centrically constituted person is not something which happens in an entirely private sphere. Instead, personal integrity has to be conceived as intimately linked with one's integration with the public domain of communication and relation with others. Genuine personhood is primarily derived from one's fidelity and commitment to others. Fidelity and commitment to oneself do have a rightful and important place – but they are secondary and valid only in so far as they are required by commitment to others. My brief discussion of this above has once again returned to the practical difficulties of being genuine in communication and, in particular, of how it is possible to seek a genuine mutuality of understanding where this is being resisted. It is to this problem which I now turn in the following chapter, where I will examine the ways in which distortions in relation and communication, arising out of either intentional misrepresentation or rational disagreement and misunderstanding, should be approached and resisted if the relation is still to be genuinely orientated towards the partners' full presence and a conformation to Christ.

6

Ethical resistance: testing the validity of disagreements

The concluding remarks of the previous chapter return the discussion to an issue I raised earlier but have not yet answered; how conflicts in understanding and in expectation are to be dealt with. Every communication involves the claim to be genuine (rational and truthful) and to be orientated towards an appropriate mutuality of understanding (reasonable codification of the relation), but not every such claim will be capable of vindication, for communication and relation may be subject to intentional or unintentional distortion. This immediately raises the questions: how can we tell when a claim is false, and what do we do when we think it is? In discerning the validity and truth of a claim and the proper course of action, the main issue will be the proper location of ethical resistance. This may be re-expressed in the question: when and how is it right to resist another's codification proposal and the intention, expectation and understanding of the partners with which this is intertwined?

A genuine openness to the other in answer to Christ's call is not unstructured in such a way that it could allow the other to become the formative principle of the relation. That would entail an abandonment of one's own individuality, which is structured by Christ's presence as a transcendent point of orientation to and for others and therefore as a point of resistance to them. In this case, the relation would be orientated towards an uncritical conformation to the other as the other understands him or herself, rather than towards a conformation to Christ. Being there for the other cannot, of course, mean an abandonment of the other by withdrawing oneself from the relation. But neither can it mean an abandonment of oneself as an independent, centred and autonomous subject through which one would cease to be an independent point of orientation, and therefore cease to be really there for the other at all. Resistance may therefore be justified on behalf of one's own individual integrity as that is a minimum requirement for personal presence before the other. Yet, given the formal reciprocity of genuine relations, such resistance must simultaneously be justified on the basis of the other's integrity. The proposed codification of a relation contains and conveys the intention for an understanding and expectation of both partners and may be resisted where the intention, expectation or understanding of either threatens or denies the integrity proper to a person as a subject of communication.

When our own codification proposal is resisted and the allied intentions and expectations disappointed, two related questions arise: (i) is our communication a genuine self-representation founded on a rational self-understanding, or is it guided by hidden interests? (ii) are our expectations and intention of the other reasonable and therefore justified? This is a real problem, as it is not always easy to discern the demands of formal reciprocity in terms of positive content within a particular relation. There is always the possibility of making formal and/or material errors, either through an inadequate self-understanding and subsequent presentation in communication or a genuine misunderstanding of the needs of the other. Because of the transcendence and mystery of the other as an independent point of action and experience with a unique history, the supposed rightness of a communication can only be tested through dialogue – it can only be tested, that is, in a relation which involves the explicit autonomous communication of the other's independent understanding. A genuine seeking of the other must entail, then, a process for handling disappointment and returning to the other in loyalty in a dialogical spiral of understanding.

This process is orientated towards a mutuality of understanding which genuinely reflects the being and interests of the partners. Our understanding of independent others cannot just be internally manufactured by ourselves, but must be referred to them. The securing of social space–time for the other's independent communication is therefore a strict necessity. The structure of intention, expectation and understanding which another has become evident to one as the other initiates communication or resists one's address in her or his response (codification and recodification respectively). This structure raises three questions for one corresponding to those above: (iv) is the other's understanding rational (not self-deceptive)? (v) is his or her communication genuine? Does the other really understand him or herself, oneself and the world in the way presented, or is there an attempt at deception? (vi) are the structure of expectations and the proposed codification reasonable? The other's claim that the answer to each of these is in the affirmative may only be redeemed through further dialogue in which there is explication of the understanding and claims of both.

The questions concerning a person's rationality and reasonableness in communication have already been answered by the person for her or himself. But this answer, however honestly believed, may be mistaken, for a person is never fully transparent to him or herself. This has only partly to do with the complexity of human being; it has equally well to do with the fact that personal identity is not something which can be known by itself, but only in its orientation towards others – only, that is, in communication. A person's self-reflection must be open to others' reflection of him or herself in their communication too. Openly attending to others affords an understanding of the others' understanding. The truth about a person is as much present in others' reply (return or feedback) as it is in self-communication. If another is seeking a genuine mutuality of understanding, then he or she will reflect on one's resistance to, reflection and questioning of him or her.

In genuine communication there is a correspondence between the public representation we make of ourselves and the understanding we have of ourselves. We actually believe the claims we make in communication to truth, veracity and reasonableness. Genuine communication is therefore an attempt to share our understanding of ourselves, the other and the world with another. In so doing, we seek the genuine (rational and unforced) agreement of the other. Our communication is therefore orientated towards a mutuality of understanding, or conformity to Christ, in which it is necessary to be open to the resistance and presence of Christ in the other.

Resisting the distorted other

Rational understanding is based upon the cogency of reasons given for the pursuit of interests and for the intentions claimed to be guiding communication. The claim to rationality is a claim that others may be rationally motivated to accept our intentions, interests and understanding as based on a valid and generalisable norm. Rationality is one thing; truthfulness, however, another. So the question of truthfulness has to be raised alongside that of rationality in order to discern the genuineness of communication. For, whilst one might agree that what is said or done is rational, given the intentions and understanding the other claims to be her or his own, we must also discern whether they are actually guiding the other's communication, or whether in this claim the other is deceiving us or him or herself. The question to be established discursively, or else naively accepted, is whether the other is genuinely present in the relation or is being deliberately or unconsciously deceptive: whether, that is, she or he is genuinely intending, seeking and respecting both us and him or herself as independent and autonomous subjects of communication. The recognition of and orientation upon the other as a participative partner in the achievement of understanding is the essence of the ethics of dialogue.

In conformity to Christ this recognition and orientation is mutual (i.e. there is a reciprocated orientation on Christ's presence in the other). It is also, in principle, unrestricted so that all others are intended as subjects and therefore as equal participants in the task of naming and transforming the world given to all human beings in the Genesis creation accounts. The intended distribution of this sharing comes under scrutiny in the discursive explication of the norms and interests displayed in communication. Claims we make for ourselves must be shown to be part of a genuine orientation towards mutual understanding and sharing with others, and must therefore be shown to be generalisable, at least in form if not in content.

A genuine mutuality of understanding is sought wherein the partners' agreement is rationally based and involves their mutual and reciprocal recognition. Whether communication and understanding are rational can be established only through a discussion in which the norms and understanding in question are subjected to an open process of explication in order to test whether they are redeemable (non-theological sense) in dialogue with others and therefore valid. In order to decide this, the communication will have to be free of constraints, coercion and all other forms of distortion. For if the understanding which resulted from this process of explication were the result of coercion, constraint or some other type of distortion, it would clearly not be the product of the free exercise of reason. The process through which such claims are explicated and tested, since it is free of distortion, provides a pure model and ideal form of dialogue.

In this process of explication, the crucial question is whether one is truly attending to the other and her or his understanding, or whether one is subsuming the otherness of the other into oneself by assuming that one can understand the understanding of the other without the other. That, however, would be a denial of the other's identity as an independent and autonomous subject, and therefore a denial of Christ's presence in him or her as an independently structuring element. We can only really understand others by attending to their communication of themselves and their understanding of themselves, us and the world which is drawn from their individually unique identity and location. We can, of course, help facilitate their self-communication by showing in ours that we recognise and intend them as autonomous and regard their being and communication as indispensable to ourselves and our understanding. For true understanding cannot be had alone but only together; but understanding can only be had together if both are allowed to communicate and to do so in a way which is restricted in no other way than by the structure necessary to ensure the respect due to both partners (i.e. communication must be non-coercive).[1] Conformity to Christ in dialogue indicates a process of mutual, open discovery through radical respect, not the imposition of one's life, desires, needs and understanding on others.

The respect due to another as an autonomous subject of communication, who is an equal and necessary participant in the task of sharing and transforming the world, is an active commitment to the other as a transcendent point of orientation (constituted by Christ's presence). This means a commitment to seek mutual understanding in which it will be necessary to act in love and solidarity with the other to remove all fetters distorting communication, whether self-generated or the product of external domination (including, of course, one's own as this is revealed in the course of interaction). Adjusting one's communication and the understanding on which it is grounded involves trusting the other (but not necessarily naively) and/or one's own ability to discern genuine from deceptive communication in the course of explication. By coming to a better understanding of the other, one may orientate oneself upon the real, as opposed to the deceptive, understanding of the other; that is, on Christ as He is present in the other.

The openness to the other and, in particular, the readiness to abandon previously held understanding in order to move towards a genuine mutuality represent a love, trust and hope of such dimensions that it cannot be attributable to the other alone. The conditions of fallen human interaction are such that expectation, love, hope and trust are continually disappointed. The hope of reaching a genuine mutuality of understanding can be sustained by faith neither in oneself nor in the other, much less in mutual trustworthiness, but only in the empowering co-inherence of Father, Son and Spirit – that is, in God as the one hoped for. It is only in the power of this hope that one can genuinely hope with and for others, and continue to trust oneself and others despite the bitterest disappointments.

As communication genuinely seeking the other is sustained in a trust and hope more basic than that of this particular relation, it is capable

of handling disappointments in a distinctive way: by maintaining commitment and reference to the other. This is actually what constitutes
communication as genuine. For it is in taking the other's communication
seriously, as demanding a further response which also genuinely seeks the
other, that one is genuinely orientated upon another. In dialogue one seeks
an understanding of the other by intending and recognising his or her
ethical transcendence and by allotting appropriate space and time for
independent communication. Dialogue is therefore open to resistance and
disappointment of expectations because of their inappropriateness, to
misunderstanding, and to one's self-deception or unconscious deception of
oneself or the other. But it is also open to disappointment of trust in the
recognition that the other might be deceitful. Being open to disappointment
is being open to the true reality of the other in Christ.

If we are genuine in communication, then, when we encounter
disappointment, we must entertain the possibility that the other's resistance is rational, reasonable and justified, and that the other is also
orientated towards a genuine mutuality. It is openness to this possibility
which leads to explication in order to find a codification mutually
acceptable on rational grounds. Disappointment represents a disturbance
in the deep structure of normative assumptions guiding communication
which, until then, had been assumed to be unproblematic. Others resist us
and frustrate our expectations when they select a communication as
appropriate, rational and reasonable which had been screened out by our
structure of expectations and our understanding of the norms operating in
(i.e. codifying) the relation.[2]

Resistance to us is initially, in part, 'noise' in feedback or shock in
circuit, since it refuses to be integrated or understood in the structure of
understanding and expectation being operated by us. The resistance cannot
be understood without a new consensus as to code and/or appropriate
codification. Taking others seriously as independent, rational subjects of
communication means acknowledging that our understandings are not
absolute and that others' resistance may therefore be justified. On
encountering disappointment, then, we must subject the prevailing social
code and our structures of expectation and understanding to discursive
testing, as we recognise that it is these rather than the person before us
which are immediately questionable.[3] There is then immediate recourse to
explication in which another is sought as an expanding presence before us.
This represents the reverse of monological options as represented by, say,
recourse to restrictive strategies of blame which are designed either to

mould the other into the contours of the norm (one's own understanding), or to restrict the application of the norm to 'normal' people (implying that resistance denotes abnormality. So neither the resistance nor the other, who is now an expected exception, will be taken seriously).[4]

When genuine communication meets resistance there is an obligation to subject ourselves to the questioning of others (as implicit in the initial resistance and as subsequently explicated), and to question them. The disappointed partner, having first reflected on the validity of his or her expectations and the codification of the relation as may be appropriate, is obliged, if they still seem to be valid, to clarify them publicly, offering them to the other so that he or she may simultaneously clarify the reasons for resistance to them. The immediate future direction of the relation will depend upon whether the initial expectations are dropped, insisted upon or suspended.[5]

Genuine communication deals with disappointment by recognising and respecting the other, but seeks to alleviate the tension between contradictory intentions, understanding and expectations by coming to an unforced mutuality of understanding. The understanding is to be genuine as well as mutual. This is crucial, because it means that distortions in understanding cannot be acceded to for the sake of 'peace', nor can the other's obstinacy be submitted to for the sake of maintaining a consensual relation. If disappointment cannot be alleviated by explication, the orientation upon the other translates into an obligation to resist the other's understanding where this is distorted. Resistance of resistance can only come, however, after clarification and explication involving the other has failed; that is, it must come after – and, further, must include – the open recognition of the other.

The fact of the other's resistance is to be respected, and the autonomy appropriate to a communicative subject recognised and intended, throughout one's own resistance. One's own resistance cannot be justified if it slips into obstinacy or distorted, restrictive structures of expectation. This can only be prevented by maintaining openness to the other and ceaselessly referring one's understanding to that conveyed explicitly or implicitly in the other's communication (by empathetic 'indwelling'). The letting-be of the other is neither (necessarily or usually) a letting alone nor a letting-be-as-self-defined, but a seeking of the other as she or he truly is before God and as constituted by the presence of Christ. Another's self-definition and orientation may be distanced from what they genuinely should be. One's orientation upon the other is an obligation to resist false self-understanding and orientation whilst being acutely aware of all the inherent dangers of such resistance being unconsciously distorted or misplaced. There is therefore a need for continually testing that one's own resistance is orientated towards a future mutuality between oneself and the other as mediated by Christ.

The expansion appropriate to the other's presence in the relation is not unlimited; and so the other is to be sought in a particular economy – as a particular other. The precise contours and content of this economy cannot be understood, predetermined, prescribed and expected by oneself in any totalistic way. It is, however, possible to detect an inappropriately expansive presence as it tends to infinity, in the other's self-intention as an absolute and monological subject. Similarly, the restrictions appropriate to a genuine presence cannot be infinite either, as that would reduce the other to a manipulable object. Genuine communication arises from the bipolar orientation on 'self' and other. In seeking genuine understanding one is orientated towards more perfect forms of the other's presence in which there is an overflowing of the other's particularity within the proper bounds of relation. In other words, the particularity of the other overflows one's expectations (and possibly those of the other too) as the other responds to one's call in his or her own ex-centric orientation.[6] Genuine communication therefore has an inbuilt warrant and duty to resist overbearing or under-reaching forms of understanding. Resistance may be justified, then, by distortions in another's intention, expectation or understanding of him or herself, of others and of the world. Such resistance must be non-coercive, in that it must represent an orientation towards, and therefore an invitation for the other to join in, a genuine, unconstrained, mutuality of understanding, the form and content of which might exceed either's expectations.

Resistance as recodification

Whether we are facing either the overexpansion or the under-expansion of the other, we have no right of withdrawal from the relation. Resistance to improper codification is to be a maintenance of the relation, even where this can only be one-sided. Such resistance is a recodification (or sometimes relocation[7]) offer which maintains loyalty to the other even after the other's withdrawal. Some recodifications which maintain the relationship on a different level might, however, easily be mistaken for withdrawal. An alcoholic or drug addict, for instance, might be ejected from the home out of genuine love, in the wish that he or she experience sufficient discomfort to accept the fact that there is a problem for which help is needed.

Even this extreme case ought not to be considered a withdrawal from the relation, but a (temporary) relocation of it on to a level of non-proximity. The addict may be present in a very real and painful way to the family during the enforced absence, which is a communication of their love, concern and desperation (which is certain of misunderstanding at least in the short term).

In this instance, the relocation and recodification of the relation, which the family hope and perhaps even expect to be temporary, is done for the addict's good. His or her needs are uppermost in the family's minds when they decide upon this course of action. But the ejection might still be justified if the family have their own needs most in mind, provided that continuing as they were represented a real risk that they would be destroyed as a family or severely incapacitated in their joint or individual ability to maintain their identities and so be for others. Whether this amounts to a withdrawal from the relation depends on the family's future intention of it – on whether it represents the imposition of firm conditions for the return to home, or a straightforward 'Enough is enough! We will take no more under any conditions.' Even in the second case, what is tantamount to a withdrawal is not justified on the basis of any individual or familial *right* to choose not to be related to this person which may be exercised at any time or in any circumstance; it is based, rather, on the *obligation and duty* to be for others which requires the maintenance of one's own being for oneself, and so also requires the resistance of its dissipation.

There can be no right of withdrawal from a relation as such because it is Christ, rather than either of the partners, who is its formative principle. Instead of withdrawal there is the open entrance into the suffering caused by a person whose presence in the relation, and possibly her or his identity as well, is distorted. Whether this means allowing the other to inflict suffering on oneself, or standing with the other as suffering is inflicted upon her or him, it inevitably means undergoing suffering oneself. We cannot close ourselves off from others, even if they are trying to close themselves off from us, and remain true persons. For complete closure means death, the absence of communication and exchange, total silence. People whose boundary with the world is too hard, tending towards complete closure, are orientated on death and, in some metaphorical sense, are dead already. Closure cuts one off from otherness, and so from the possibilities of self-transcending movement through which one can live and grow as a person. That is why trying to maintain genuinely open relation with someone who is closed in upon her or himself is sure to involve suffering. Trying to be with, for and 'in' a person who is orientated on the personal death signalled by closure from otherness and the future (because it inhibits change) means entering into their orientation on death.

Entering into the death-orientation of another, being open to a closed person, means following the path of death oneself for the sake of life. Paradigmatically, it means following God in Christ, restoring and maintaining communication, celebrating and proclaiming the power of life in its apparent contradiction. This is not a self-righteous imposition of one's own life on another, but an enabling of the other to live her or his own life. One can only be for another in this radical way if one's own life is also open to the other and therefore to life together on terms which are only generated through the spiralling dialogue between one and another. It can only mean, in other words, being open to transcendence and change, and therefore to suffering.

> We can . . . call salvation in history the divine opening of 'closed systems'. The closed or isolated person is freed for liberty and for his own future . . . But because closed or isolated systems can only be opened again by means of renewed communication with others (if they are not to be destroyed), the opening to God takes place through God's suffering over their isolation. Because God himself suffers over man's closedness towards him, he keeps his communication with man alive in spite of opposition, creating the domain where isolated man can open up and transform himself. Thus man's openness to God is brought about by grace, and grace springs from the suffering of God in his faithfulness to isolated man. The opening of man's closed society for openness towards man's neighbour and towards the world can be conceived analogously. Closed systems bar themselves against suffering and self-transformation. They grow rigid and condemn themselves to death. The opening of closed systems and the breaking down of their isolation and immunization will have to come about through the acceptance of suffering. But the only living beings that are capable of doing this are the ones which display a high degree of vulnerability and capacity for change. They are not merely alive; they can make other things live as well.[8]

Christ's path cannot be followed in one's own strength or on one's own resources (that would imply another form of self-closure), but only in the life-giving power of the Spirit, the energy of organisational openness. In extreme cases, the call to follow Christ may mean following that path to the end. Whilst no one may justifiably demand the surrender of one's life, such a surrender may be the only way for one to fulfil the concrete Command of God.

Even when one is faced with the overexpansion of another in which one is sought only as a manipulable object, the proper response is never total resistance to the other, but only to the distortion of the other. Maintaining oneself in an orientation upon the other's genuine interests and identity, one cannot stand upon or solely in one's own. In particular, the distorted form of communication is not to be returned. If it were to be returned, then the mutuality of understanding in the relation would be conformed to the distortion of the other and not to Christ. It is not reception, but communication which may defile, not the coming in but the going out (Matt. 15:11). Christ's call is to 'turn the other cheek', to 'pray for those who persecute you' (Matt. 5:39, 44), to accept rather than redirect suffering. The return of the violence which is being done to your personhood, identity, rights and interests constructs a vicious spiral of escalating conflict and suffering. The only way out of that spiral is to refuse to accept its logic whilst accepting its consequences. For accepting its logic would be to accept as truth the other's distorted structures of expectation and understanding; refusing its consequences would only be possible by withdrawal from the relation. Thus the spiral of violence is to be entered, but its values and reciprocity are to be rejected.[9] In this rejection resistance becomes loyalty to and acceptance of the other.

Because the recodification which it proposed will often be quite subtle, resistance which maintains the relation can easily be mistaken for compliance or collaboration. In suggesting that we should happily go an extra mile when asked to go one (Matt. 5: 41), Jesus was referring to the obligation to carry the kit of any member of the Roman occupying force one mile when ordered to do so. In this instance, the resistance defies the structure of expectation by communicating a readiness to be joyfully at the other's disposal, even when the demand is an unjust imposition expecting only churlish compliance on pain of physical punishment. Perhaps more usually, resistance incarnates the duty to be there, in proper humility, as a limit for the other and, as such, as a transcendent point of orientation. Another's overexpansion may justifiably be met on one's own part either by what may seem to be underexpansion, but is actually expansion in a different direction (subtle recodification), or by a gentle but firm resistance to invalid incursions which may be mistaken for, but must never become, an overexpansion of oneself. One does not have inalienable rights or interests, but only a joyous duty to be there for the other as she or he really needs. Sometimes this must mean resistance, but such resistance must never be the servant of one's own interests and must constantly be tested for this sort of distortion.

Another's underexpansion is also to be met by one's own redirected expansiveness which, in terms of the other's intention, expectation and understanding, may be experienced as an underexpansion, a refusal to occupy the overlarge position offered in the other's call. Underexpansiveness here represents the other's distorted understanding of him or herself as more an object than a subject of communication, whose proper form of response either generally or in particular moments is thought to be deference, silence or compliance. This may simply be the mirror-image of the distorted and overexpansive understanding the other has of oneself and/or it may be part of a much wider network of relations which have been sedimented as a form of relational incapacity. Whether it has been appropriated externally as the ossification of the overarching codification of relations (e.g. through oppression), or whether it is the result of internally generated distortion in understanding (e.g. psychological repression), the only way of restoring such distortion is through another's unprecedented acts of loyalty.

Great care is needed so that, in meeting another's needs, the distorted form of the relation is not reinforced. Another's underexpansion reflects a conviction of his or her own incapacity as a subject of communication. The other therefore understands him or herself more as an object of communication requiring overassistance in the relation which verges on a need for manipulation. In very extreme instances, underexpansion can even reflect a self-understanding of total helplessness: the other's state is so low that he or she would not respond to anyone's intervention. It is not the situation of being in need which represents the underexpansion (and, indeed, the other's assessment of the situation may be realistic), but the tendency towards isolation, utter despair and self-closure in it. In other words, it is the other's interpretation of him or herself (as opposed to the situation) as guilty, unpardonable, unclean, unacceptable and fit for nothing which has to be broken into and broken open by responding to the call and presence of Christ in the other, which show the person's acceptability as a fully human partner. This may well require practical acts of assistance, but these should always be orientated upon a genuine presence of the other and referred constantly to reflective and discursive examination in order to avoid giving assistance where it is inappropriate, which would tend to reinforce the other's incapacity to act as a subject for her or himself. A person's genuine needs cannot be legislated in advance in an abstract formula which holds good for all people at all times. But what can be said is that the forms of assistance should always be related to the economic expansion appropriate to the person and should never become permanent or stereotypical forms of interaction, no matter how well intentioned.

The danger of all forms of active assistance (speaking or acting for another) is that they quickly become a permanent means of substituting one's own activity for that of the other, with no eye on the other's hoped for expansion. Such a permanent activism does not have the futurity and openness to transformation, change and the other which is the hallmark of the activity of the Holy Spirit. Being for another must never become an overbearing form of presence in which the other may only live at second hand. Sorting out someone's problems *for* him or her, doing everything on his or her behalf, is not always enabling because it can remove the person from any possibilities of subjective engagement. What is enabling is the presence of one with another in tackling difficulties together. This may mean doing things on the other's behalf, but only in the presence of the other and with continual reference to the demands of his or her autonomy both now and in the future. Assistance in being must never remove the assisted person from the communicative contexts of his or her own life. Personal autonomy and responsibility can be shared, but they must never be removed. The other is to remain ethically transcendent so that she or he may remain the organisational centre of her or his life. That centre must never be transferred to another.

The assistance appropriate to another is determined by the intention of the other as a dialogue-partner, an ethically transcendent co-subject of the relation. Yet it is just this intention which the other resists in underexpansion. This resistance must, in turn, be resisted through a form of acceptance determined to raise the restricted person to an appropriate expansion: praise. This is an open acceptance of the other despite what may seem to be an overdetermining past. This entails a proleptic intending, understanding and expectation of the other as in a future communication situation in which she or he is a full and equal subject of communication. In Christian terms, it means intending the other as she or he will be before God as a co-member of God's future kingdom (a fully redeemed communication situation) towards which both partners are being drawn by the transformative power of the Spirit. In this way the person is raised up and attached to expectations, is trusted and accepted, in a way which is unrealistic on the basis of present and past predicates. Only in this way can a relation offer something decisively new and personally liberative. The liberating person brings a basic trust to a situation where it could not otherwise exist. It is not a case of awaiting some sign that trust will not be betrayed, but of trusting anyway and, in this openness which is a mediation of Christ's call, opening the possibility for others to become trustworthy and acceptable partners conformed to that call.

People become incapacitated for genuine relations by their communication history. They become closed from the inside, though often only as a response to strategies excluding them from social participation in significant contexts which become sedimented into structures of self-identity. This closure can only be broken open from the outside by communication which, responding to Christ's call, exhibits unprecedented loyalty and devotion, thereby reversing the disabling history. This process is not abstract; it does not decontextualise the person from the present network of relations within which the person has his or her being. On the contrary, it takes these with profound seriousness as the cause or expression of a distorted identity. But it does qualify the importance of these relations by setting them in the horizon of the person's existence in God's image as a fully human partner, one to be addressed as a Thou–I. The person and the present self-understanding are recontextualised in the perspective of relation to God and to God's creative–redemptive interaction with us. In communication one may mediate, in anticipatory and provisional form, the reality of the other as a person before God as one tries to reflect, not just the other's understanding of him or herself, but God's – in so far as this is falteringly grasped in the acceptance and celebration of the other 'warts and all'.

Disputing validity claims

As I have already suggested, whenever we undertake communication we make a claim to be appropriate in a number of different ways. The most basic of these is the claim to be comprehensible in the supposition of a shared code. It is only on the basis of this shared supposition that attempts, which may be more or less successful, may be made to encode and decode information, to understand one another with reference to a common 'language'. It is only in and through a shared code that claims may be made, examined, redeemed or rejected. The assumed existence of a shared code and mutual competence in it is the necessary background assumption, or deep structure, of all communication. Against such a background, together with the assumption of competence in the code, an understanding may be reached *about* a given topic. I have already adverted (on p. 131 above) to the fact that achievement of understanding *about* may be the basis on which an understanding *with* another is reached. Understanding on this second level indicates acceptance of the offer of fidelity and truthfulness in the communication. These may be accepted or rejected on the basis of their validity or acceptability to others.[10] For the proposed codification of the relation to be acceptable, three further types of validity claim must be redeemable.

These are raised, usually only implicitly, in all communication. They represent the claim that the communication is properly coordinated with the objective, subjective and intersubjective worlds, so that the communicating person can be relied upon.[11] It is therefore claimed that: the content of the communication is true (i.e. that it is or depends upon an accurate representation of the world); the communicator is veracious or truthful regarding his or her intentions (i.e. that it is a genuine self-representation); the proposed codification of the relation is appropriate or reasonable (i.e. satisfies a legitimate norm or normative context).[12] Genuine communication is undertaken in the belief that one is fulfilling these conditions and that a mutual understanding can therefore be reached on the basis of a consensus regarding the conditions and the manner of their fulfilment. Because it is orientated towards the achievements of a consensus, it is simultaneously orientated towards the autonomous communication of the other, represented by the possibility of resistance.

The validity claims are actually claims that one is being rational – that one is a communicative subject integrated rationally into different communication contexts. Integration with the 'objective' world is claimed in communication as it either is, promises or describes an interaction with it, or refers to a state of affairs in it. The claim to truthfulness is a claim to have rationally integrated conscious, inner identity, understanding and intention with their public expression. The claim to rightness is of integration in a social, moral world. Each of these claims is, then, a claim to be integrated into a public world as a rational follower of the rules for interaction applicable in it. The belief that one is being rational is the belief that the intentions and understanding guiding communication may be shared with, understood and accepted by others without coercion or deception. The claim that communication is rationally grounded and genuinely orientated towards the other as a rational and autonomous subject of communication makes it an offer which is open to questioning. The fact that it seeks the consent of another whose understanding may be different, yet just as honestly believed to be rational, means that the offer simultaneously intends the other as rational and autonomous. The other is only expected to accept the offer if convinced of one's seriousness and sincerity on rational grounds. The claim to rationality in which the other's understanding is sought is simultaneously an offer to provide grounds.

Communication may be shown to be rationally grounded if it is publicly redeemable. By this I mean, first, that the understanding of the world and of the codification legitimate in the relation can be shared with (explained to) others and accepted by them as a rationally understandable (grounded) understanding. Second, I mean that others may be convinced as to the sincerity of the self-representation, in that what is said or done can be understood as a rational incarnation of the person's publicly declared intentions.

Both are principles of universalisability. The first tests whether the communication represents an understanding anyone might come to; the second, whether anyone, given that intention, might make the same communication. The claims to rationality are, then, claims to universality on the basis of the communication's undistorted character: that it neither emanates from, say, prejudice or neurotic disturbance nor represents malevolent intentions; that it is not based on a 'mad' understanding of the world and that it is morally justifiable. The orientation towards a mutuality of understanding necessarily involves a readiness to explain oneself to others as soon as the validity claims made cease to be unproblematic. When this happens communication will continue at a different level whilst a norm moves from the background to the surface, becoming the subject of discussion as it is reflected on and explicated. All communication, of course, requires some background agreement concerning valid norms, and the explication process is no different. So, at the very least, there must be a continuing background consensus as to the general structures of rationality and comprehensibility, or else participants could neither be nor make themselves understood. Interruptions in surface structure consensus regarding the reasonableness, truth and sincerity of the partners require explication and clarification, but this can only happen against a background consensus.[13]

In an undistorted relation, there is a formal reciprocity in the partners' co-intending in which they recognise themselves and one another as rational subjects of communication. This means that they regard their own communication as rationally understandable by, and therefore demonstrable to, the other. The other is intended and understood as a formally identical, ethically transcendent, personally centred structure of rationality. The other's understanding, especially as it differs from one's own, is therefore to be taken with the utmost seriousness. The other's misunderstanding of or disagreement with oneself indicates the really problematic nature of one's communication for the other. The apparently conflicting expectations or understanding of the other cannot be dismissed out of hand if the other is to be taken seriously, for they represent a questioning of oneself and the questionability of one's own communicated identity, intention, expectations and understanding. What is required is an open explication process whereby the rational grounding of one's communication may be examined by the other. It also means, in the passive moment of self-reflection, that one questions oneself as one's questionability for the other is communicated to one in her or his response. The formal reciprocity of the relation requires that the other be expected to explain and give reasons for her or his communication too. The other's resistance and questioning must also be understood to be rationally grounded before one's acceptance can be secured.

All communication seeking to establish some sort of relation with another does, in fact, claim to be rational, though the claim and the communication may, of course, be deceptive, manipulative or mistaken. Relations which function smoothly in a double consensus structure (i.e. both background and surface) actually rest upon the supposition that the rationality of the content of communication, the codification of the relation, and the sincerity of the partners could, if necessary, be demonstrated to be rational. This double consensus therefore represents a mutuality of understanding (which may still be distorted) in which there is 'reciprocal understanding, shared knowledge, mutual trust, and accord with one another'.[14] When consensus and the validity claims which it supports become problematic, the relation may be orientated towards a genuine mutuality of understanding if the partners attend to one another and to themselves in a particularly refined way in a dialogical process of explication. A relation conforming to Christ, involving a genuine mutuality of understanding between the partners, is only achievable by explicitly or implicitly undergoing, or having already undergone, this process. Through a description of the process of dialogical explication, a better understanding of the structure of dialogue should emerge.

The explication process

In dialogical explication at least one of the validity claims is made the theme of explicit communication (though, as they are interdependent, there will be some implicit reference to the others). This can happen in a variety of ways and need not, in principle, involve speech. All that is necessary is that we take reponsibility for our communication and personal identity before, and in the orientation towards, particular others.

The naturally unequal distribution of capacities to express or even come to an understanding indicates only the need for particularly refined modes of interpretation and feedback (i.e. of continually referring interpretation of the other to the other), and does not justify the exclusion of less capable persons from the process. The indwelling of Christ and the possibilities of participating in a relation conformed to and mediated by Him are not constrained by mental capacities. Where the level of communicative competence is too low for another to explicate his or her understanding, or to make the grounds for his or her resistance plain, one has to 'stand in for the other'. This means attempting to reconstruct an understanding from an imaginary, empathetic 'indwelling' of the other's identity and social location. This is guided by one's enduring intention of formal reciprocity in the relation which indicates that one's own communication is unjust if it would be resisted by oneself were positions reversed. Formal reciprocity yields an understanding, admittedly only approximate and vague, of universal and reciprocal interests or rights of the person. The imaginary and empathetic 'indwelling' of another gives this abstract and formal understanding a content specific to a particular person, although this too can only be approximate because of the ethical transcendence of persons.

The supplementation of others' communicative incapacities, in which the rational grounds of their behaviour are examined and explained on their behalf, is not such a special case as it may at first seem. It will, in fact, be a fairly regular aspect in most of our histories of communication and relation, especially for those of us who have frequent contact with children, the mentally handicapped, the mentally ill and the very elderly. Most of these people will be able to communicate their resistance and their alternative understanding, at least as a brute fact, in some way, although they may be incapable of speech, sophisticated explanation, or the fairly complex mental procedures which make reflection possible. If, through the process of empathetic 'indwelling', one is able to detect rational grounds for such resistance, there are at least two options open. If it is thought that the resistance rests upon a misunderstanding of intentions, effects, or rights of performance, then there is a duty to provide appropriate reassurance before continuing, whilst being open to further resistance and to the possibility that one may have misunderstood.

An elderly female patient, severely demented and physically disabled by the effects of the dementia, might resist the attentions of a male nurse attempting to bathe her by thinking that: the nurse intended to assault her; the water was too hot; this man should not touch her. The nurse could reassure the patient by: a show of gentleness and concern (for example cuddling – provided the feared assault was not sexual); immersing his elbow in the water; drawing attention to the nurse's uniform (assuming the woman was confused about her situation). But it must also be borne in mind, especially if reassurance is resisted, that the woman's understanding might represent a genuine alternative interpretation. This must lead to self-questioning on the nurse's part as to whether: unnecessary terseness or force had been employed in moving the woman; the water may be too hot for the woman (considering her physical state and personal preference); the woman may simply object to being seen naked by a man. (The particular problems posed by failure to reach understanding together will be raised later.)

Inequalities between the nurse and the woman in the ability to communicate do not justify her exclusion from the dialogical explication process. In Chapter 1, I argued that dialogue is a universal, ontological structure of human being, distorted but not destroyed through sin and transformed through redemption. The mutual intentions of autonomy, responsibility and relatedness which coincide in the structure of reciprocal questioning and answering are unrestricted. There is no one who does not have the right to put one in question, to elicit an appropriate response from one. Mere personal presence is enough to make some sort of claim for recognition as a point of orientation towards whom one ought to be directed – not as a process of thought, but as a whole process of being: being there for another. Regardless of age, sex, race or mental capacity, there is no one who does not call others to responsibility before her or him, and towards whose autonomous existence communication and structures of intention, expectation and understanding cannot be referred.

The ethical transcendence of persons constituted by the presence of Christ is the grounding for explicative communication. Because a person, though identifiable only *through* communication, is not identical *with* that communication, the claimed relational identity may be, or may be considered to be, untrue. A person is distinguishable from the content and context of his or her communication. It is therefore possible to ask questions concerning the rationality of the structures of intention, expectation and understanding by which the person expresses attachment to the world which is referred to in communication (content) and in which that communication takes place (context). It is possible, therefore, to examine the punctuation operating implicitly or explicitly within communication between 'self' and world (private self-identity and public, 'objective' reality), 'self' and the content of communication, or what is said or done ('essence' and public appearance), and between 'self' and normative social context (what is and ought to be). In explication, the question of these differences becomes the explicit theme of communication in which there is an obligation to show (immediately) or justify (mediately) through argument the claim that: a reference to or proposition about the world is true; the norms governing communication and the codification of the relation are right; the intention claimed to be guiding communication actually is doing so, thereby proving trustworthy by virtue of the consistency of subsequent behaviour.[15]

Where surface consensus cannot be regained immediately, then, consensual communication must either be abandoned (by resorting to non-consensual and manipulative forms of interaction or by giving up altogether), or else postponed whilst mediate processes of explication are followed. This usually means becoming gradually more abstract in argument and moving beyond the immediate communication situation. The failure to restore surface consensus usually indicates that the background norm against which the attempt to demonstrate the validity of the communication has been made is also problematic. Mediate explication usually does rely on speech (less competent speakers may be 'stood in for' and have interpretations provided on their behalf) as the medium through which conflicting or problematic understandings are examined. The claim to sincerity, however, is only mediately redeemable as subsequent communication shows a person's commitment and fidelity in practice. Theoretical propositions and reconstructions 'proving' fidelity are secondary to the commitment shown in practice. A point is very quickly reached where the questioning of truthfulness makes further consensual communication impossible. If truthfulness remains in question – if, in other words, one understands the other's engagement to be deceptive, strategic or manipulative – then further explication is rendered impossible, as this too would be distrusted as another means of manipulating one towards the desired goal. Doubt about a person's sincerity which remains unrelieved within the immediate communication situation undercuts the possibility of moving the discussion on to a different level. Mediate explication also depends on the sincerity of the partners' intention to reach a genuine mutuality of understanding founded on the reciprocation of respect, and it is just this sincerity that is doubted.

If, on the other hand, the original communication can be accepted as sincere, though possibly mistaken, then an avenue is opened for further communication regarding the other validity claims on the basis of mutual respect and trust. In any subsequent moment of explication regarding these other claims, the question of sincerity may again be raised. Explication may only continue once the claim of sincerity has been redeemed on the same basis of assurance or subsequent continuity. In particular, a readiness to accept the consequences of rational argument (e.g. abandoning beliefs or behaviour shown in explication to be irrational) will have to be shown.

Explication therefore represents something of an ideal-type of communication conformed to Christ, since it can only be founded upon the reciprocated consent of the partners to be genuine in communication and so act towards one another out of mutual respect. It is structured by formally reciprocated co-intending in which the partners are orientated towards a genuine mutuality of understanding. Explication is orientated towards the achievement of a rational (and therefore generally acceptable) consensus regarding the truth of an understanding of the world, or the valid distribution of social space–time (the rightness of a particular relation or communication). It may only be entered in the mutual recognition and intention of sincerity and may only be continued in the securing of a continuing consensus regarding the rights of each to social space–time and therefore to make particular claims and statements. The background 'norm' of explication is the reciprocated co-intention of the partners as rational subjects of communication who may question themselves and place each other in question.

The principle of generalisability

As I have indicated in the foregoing discussion, communication is only justifiable if it would receive the rational consent of all (potentially) participating persons: if it would be acceptable to others on a rational basis. The guiding principle of ethical communication is therefore the rational basis of its universal acceptability. This returns the discussion to the notion of universalisability raised earlier. Testing universality depends upon being able to 'exchange places' in imagination with others, to assess the acceptability of the communication from others' social locations and identities. In addition, it means securing (often only in imagination) the consent of neutral third parties to ensure that the tested or expected consent of the partners to a relation does not depend wholly upon the idiosyncrasy of their identities and of the relation, but could be enjoined by any significant third party in his or her position with his or her particular commitments, interests and intentions.

This principle of universal rationality is not as Kantian as it might at first seem. Maxims for dialogical communication are not the idiosyncratic generation of an isolated subject, but arise in an individual 'self' which is itself the sediment of social life-processes. In particular, the self-consciousness on which Kantian ethical procedures depend is not considered here to be private and discrete, but to be sedimented from processes of intersubjectivity. There is a corresponding procedural difference too. For Kant it was only necessary to carry out tests of universal acceptability of a maxim in the mind of the isolated subject. I have already argued in contradistinction, however, that information about the universal acceptability of a maxim can be received only through the independent communication and reality of others, as it is offered to them in the form of a codification proposal. If their consent is withheld, then further communication on that same basis is only justifiable if there are reasons for supposing that resistance was guided by non-rational reasons or self-interest. This must of course be done with extreme caution (see below), and once again offered to themselves and/or to third parties for subsequent communication of their understanding and testing through explication.

What is supposed to be universal must be submitted to a real test of universal consensus which is open to the resistance of others. This is necessary if the conceptions of universality and of individuality are to escape the abstraction of individualism which Kant, for one, operates. The universality of a rational ethical maxim for Kant is a function of the identity and interchangeability of individuals as the bearers of a universal and abstract individual essence (characterised by reason). It is on the basis of this universality that individual life-histories and social settings are not considered to affect or determine the structure of rationality universally shared by all. The individual is here abstracted from forms of social determination by becoming abstracted from his or her individual identity; only saved from social determinism by being thrust into a determination by the idea of individuality in which what is known of one is known of all. In the fiction of the ontological priority and independence of the individual from relations, each may be considered as merely the bearer of the rational characteristics and universal dispositions which constitute universal individuality: an abstract form of individuality with no significant individual content.[16] It is therefore unnecessary, on this view, to refer one's ethical maxims to others because their existence as rational subjects cannot be truly other, there being a single rational will which can be known by each alone. The consent of all rational subjects to a rational ethical maxim may be presupposed without testing, as the possibility of ethical resistance has been severed. A maxim is considered on this view to be rational if one may attribute it to all others as having equally binding force.

> The moral laws are abstractly universal in the sense that, as they hold as universal for me, they must *eo ipso* be thought of as holding for all rational beings. As a result, interaction under such laws dissolves into the actions of solitary and self-sufficient subjects, each of whom must act as though he were the sole existing consciousness; and yet each subject can at the same time be certain that all his actions under moral laws are necessarily and from the outset in harmony with the moral actions of all possible other subjects.[17]

There is a corresponding difference between Kantian ethical individualism and the position I am taking here in the manner in which consensus is secured. In both there is an attempt to occupy the other's vantage point, but in individualism this need never involve the participation of the other. For the reality of the other can supposedly be known independently of the other, without requiring any independent communication on her or his part, by virtue of a universally shared, abstract, identity. Because individualism may not acknowledge essential differences in individual identities as essential, they can have no ethical significance. Consequently, the form of trancscendence existing between individuals is spatial and accidental rather than ethical and personally formative. The form of 'indwelling' required cannot, therefore, be empathetic or respectful of difference or of material personal particularity. The person into whose position we are instructed by Kant to think ourselves is not a particular, but an abstract individual. A maxim is to be subjected to a universal rational standpoint which does not, in fact, exist. It is my contention, however, that the consent of (sometimes imaginary) third parties is to be sought in the concrete, and that every stage of the reflection is to be referred to the other as a real and ethically transcendent person.[18]

One cannot find what is rational and reasonable on one's own, but only in reponse to the call of Christ – only, that is, in the give and take of dialogue. In conformity to Christ the understandings and identities of both partners are open to change. This indicates that through – and only through – dialogue, rational motivation and understanding are not simply discovered, but are actually formed. Rational interests do not precede their relational testing, but are generated through it as Christ becomes increasingly present in the relation. In subjecting one's interests, understanding, intentions and communication to redemption in dialogue with others, one enters a process of mutual will-formation. Genuine communication therefore seeks the genuine interests of the other through a rationally valid normative framework which can only be found through the self-transcending, dialogical process of responding to Christ in the other, and by being mediated to the other through Christ. Through the process of explication in dialogue it is possible to determine which interests guiding communication are merely particular and which generalisable.

In ethical individualism interests are particularised on the basis of their abstract identity; that is, all individuals have the formally identical (self-) interest in expansion. In pursuing self-expansion, however, each person's self-interest, whilst formally identical with others', is actually in diametrical opposition to them. Because the space around each self is not a social vacuum but inhabited and claimed by everyone else, everyone has an interest in limiting the expansion (i.e. the pursuit of self-interest) of everyone else. In individualism social space–time can only be exclusively occupied and, because its possession is tied up with individual identity and security, it must be jealously guarded. Interest is thereby universally particularised. The recognition of the identical interests of the other from a different social location is a recognition and intention of the other as competitor with whom one may only join together when these interests are temporarily compatible.

In ethical individualism anything really particular is considered pathological. A reason which has been generated by the particularity of an individual identity cannot be universal because it defies predication of all other rational subjects. Therefore, every interest, desire or need one has as a direct consequence of one's history or social location is invalidated. By bending over backwards to secure the conditions for autonomy and loyalty to oneself in extreme forms as *universal* and therefore valid, ethical individualism actually annihilates both. It does so by validating them in terms of obedience to a universal law (which legislates the resolution of conflicting interests), by equating autonomy with the non-contingently motivated exercise of duty under a universal norm. Social relations can then only be contractual, and loyalty both to oneself and to others is replaced by that to the contract. This represents a severance of the 'internal' motivation proper to autonomy, a subjugation of the will to a preordinate, heteronomous norm of interaction which, as such, is open neither to change nor to questioning. It represents, then, a disintegration of the will and of individual spirit and the norms for their public communication.[19]

Explication is a concrete practice for discerning the acceptability of particular interests and intentions directing communication on the basis of their generalisability. Explication does not seek agreement concerning the universal nature of an interest, need or desire (the reduction of particular interests to a maxim that all should follow). What it seeks is a consensus regarding a universal norm by which the rationality (generalisability) of interests which never cease to be particular can be judged. Such a norm can only be identified and established through concrete dialogue. Interests do not, therefore, need to be identical or shared by all in order to be rational. They must, instead, be acceptable to all who are affected by them, and with whom they must be tested in dialogue.

In order for consensus or disagreement to be rational, the discussion must be guided by the common interest of all parties to come to a genuine understanding together. All other interests are to be discarded or discounted when detected because they can only distort understanding. The dialogue is therefore to be unforced. This will involve a common sensitivity to the inequalities in proficiency and therefore to the asymmetrical need for access to social space–time for the partners to receive equal attention and understanding.

A rational consensus may only result from communication and relations which are unforced and non-manipulative and where, to prevent a dissolution into ethical formalism, the parameters of the dialogue are unconstrained. This is an extended dialogue in which the partners are not merely choosing between pre-established alternatives, but engaged in a process in which they are transformed by the call of Christ present in the other and the enlivening energies of the Spirit through which their intentions and wills are formed anew in dialogue. No pre-existent norm is above question (though not all norms can be questioned at once if the dialogue is to remain comprehensible), and there can, in principle, be no limit to the newness of norms found in dialogue. The seeking of agreement of all those partially affected by a particular communication makes ethics concrete. Further, because no norm can be unquestionable, it is impossible for a norm derived in one relation to become an abstract universal, legislating further relations or even disallowing future discussion within the same partnership. For the real ethical norm is not an abstract principle but a person to whose call ethics is a conforming response.

Clearly an ethic founded in the social consciousness of an

individual human partner cannot be confined to a private morality, but must become political at this point. For it is not only the norms and interests governing a particular relation which are open to question, but those of the wider social and political context in which the relation is embedded. This will be the subject of the final chapters of the book.

Ideal interpersonal communication

Unlimited, constraint-free explication, in which the autonomy and responsibility of each partner in and for communication is respected and intended as means are found to ensure formal reciprocity in the relation (i.e. non-privileged distribution of dialogue roles, or symmetrical binding by norms), exhibits a formal ideal for communication. It is this ideal to which all communication is or pretends to be orientated (it is therefore anticipated even in its distortion), and which presents the codification proper to the ideal form of life in God's image. In that it entails mutually seeking 'objective', rational truth, the mutual truthfulness of the partners in their autonomy and their formal reciprocity, it establishes the normative ideals of truth, freedom and justice.

> (1) In the case of unrestrained discussion (in which no prejudiced opinion cannot be taken up or criticized) it is possible to develop strategies for reaching unconstrained consensus; (2) on the basis of mutuality of unimpaired self-representation (which includes the self-representation of the Other as well) it is possible to achieve a significant rapport despite the inviolable distance of the partners, and that means communication under conditions of individuation; (3) in the case of full complementarity of expectations (which excludes unilaterally constraining norms) the claim of universal understanding exists, as well as the necessity of universalized norms. These three symmetries represent, incidentally, a linguistic conceptualization of what are traditionally known as the ideas of truth, freedom, and justice.[20]

This indicates the form of interpersonal life as intended by God at creation, distorted through the fall and subsequently modified through redemption. For it incarnates the relational form in which the independence and relatedness of persons may be undistorted: the horizontal image of God in which there is formally reciprocal co-intending organised by the Spirit and structured by the Word.

The consensus sought concerns the norms of interaction, and it is only through such a consensus, at some level and in the background, that communication may be maintained. This is the case even with explication, for if there were no consensus as to any norms of interaction, it would be impossible to subject any other norms to discursive redemption. In other words, explication also operates against a background consensus. The understanding sought concerns the rational cogency of communicated interests, understanding, identities and intentions, which are redeemable through norms of interaction (ultimately of truth, freedom, justice) which are not presently, but may in the future, be subjected to scrutiny.

Consensus regarding background norms enables the movement towards mutual understanding at a higher level. This mutuality is founded on the differences in the individual identities of the partners, and cannot be equated with their reduction. The reciprocated co-intention of communicative subjectivity in it entails the recognition of the particularity of individual interests (as generalisable), and therefore of the transcendent, irreducible and inexchangeable individuality of the partners. Understanding is only possible between non-identical communicative subjects who are related through a shared code through which mutually acceptable codifications of call and response are possible. The situation of understanding represents the differentiation and relation of the partners within the limits of absolute difference and absolute identity. What I mean by coming to a mutuality of understanding concerns the conditions for the emergence of formally reciprocal identities, and therefore includes the very conditions of undistorted differentiation and relation: Christ's presence and Christ's mediation of one to another as the codification of the relation is brought into conformity with Him.

Christ's presence structures individual identities as distinct and ethically transcendent. Conformity to Christ in relation cannot therefore indicate a complete and total understanding, for the identity between the partners indicated by their mutuality of understanding is formal and not material. A total understanding would swallow up ethical transcendence, which is the condition of both relation and individuality.[21] The further point must be made that a mutuality of understanding, even if consensually achievable, would not in itself guarantee the rightness of the norms or interests agreed upon, as all relations are subject to constraints set by the real world (such as limited space and time with competing demands on them, and limitations in knowledge and understanding). If achievable it would, however, guarantee that the codification of relations and the understanding of truth would be guided by genuinely shared interests in truth, freedom and justice. The inadequacies of the understanding, which might be the best achievable under present circumstances, would then be open to further unrestricted questioning as soon as this inadequacy is apparent and becomes important.

Within the limits set by the concrete situation Christ's call sets one in a self-transcendent movement towards Christ in others and, thereby, towards transformed forms of self-identity. In the opening energies of the Spirit, the process of explication and understanding through which one becomes autonomously (in that the understanding is engaged) responsible before God and others, and the understanding, intentions and expectations one has of and for oneself, God and others which emerge through it, may never have the character of finality, but are continually open to question.

Relating to others as subjects of communication with particular identities therefore commits one to engage in a permanent dialogue which, in principle, has no limits. It is only by integrating oneself into such undistorted structures of relation that one may become an integrated and centred subject, genuinely for oneself and for others: a truly responsible person. In this and the previous two chapters I have been concerned with working out what my understanding of personhood means in interpersonal – that is, small-scale, person-to-person – relations. But even maintaining the discussion at this level it has been necessary, time and again, to refer to structures of communication which are larger than the individual and interpersonal interaction. Even at this level, person-to-person relations very quickly achieve an institutionalised form and framework of interaction between the partners. This is partly produced through the dynamic specific to this particular interaction; partly by the previous experiences, identities and expectations of the partners; but partly also by prevailing social institutions regulating all communication and exchange in the wider context within which this relation takes place. As I have tried to make particularly clear in this chapter, it is not possible to communicate without reference to the general conditions for communication and relation which pertain to a particular society – not least the prevailing social code or 'language'. In particular, it is often not possible to raise questions as to the rightness of a particular communication or proposed codification or institutionalisation of the relation, without also bringing wider social codes and institutions into question. Furthermore, in order to justify the validity and rightness of an identity, codification proposal or communication as rational and valid it is necessary to refer them to the wider community of potential participants.

Questions concerning the right practice of interpersonal relations which I have been dealing with in this part of the book lead on to questions about the overarching socio-political context, and the nature, form, structure and content of relations at this level. Turning towards relations at this level was also required by the content of Chapter 3. There the discussion of the social and societal dimensions of the formation of personal identity presses for some clarification of the ideal conditions of communication at that level which will facilitate the formation of proper personal identities. I shall address these concerns in the final chapters of the book.

Part IV

Political relations

7

Theology, Church and politics

A crucial strand in my argument is the understanding that a person is a structure of communication sedimented from a history of relations which take place within an overarching communication context. The specific nature of this wider network of relations, a determinate social world, will therefore be significant for the determination of relations and of the individuals who live within its frame. This social determinacy involves the very broadest connotations of the word 'social', including such things as social mores, tradition, language, culture and kinship groupings as well as political institutions. The wider social context provides rules for the social regulation of communication. My purpose throughout Part IV is to try to discern the socio-political practice and organisation which is required by the theory of the person developed thus far.

Before addressing this central theme, however, I will very briefly outline the way in which individuals are socio-politically determinate. I think this might be helpful because there is a deep-rooted suspicion in Western thought (a heritage of individualism, personalism and liberalism) that private rights, interests and freedoms are in principle opposed to their limitation in socio-political order. Socio-political structures, in that view, may be a necessary evil, but they cannot contribute anything essential to the individual. Individuals are not therefore considered to be determined in any sense by the socio-political structures within which they live. On the contrary, these structures are thought to be determined by the activity of asocial individuals. The state is then the minimum structure required for the coordination of private interests. Given the widespread currency of this kind of view, I cannot take it as self-evident, but must first establish, that the polity and the complex of socio-political relations have any internal relation to personal identity and liberty.

Socio-political structures set the situation within which persons may be related and differentiated (individualised). The polity is what broadly constitutes a society. The regulation of the distribution of social status and material goods and services may be understood as a semi-stable structure of communication and exchange – the codification of relations – which is the institutionalised pattern of recognition in a society. What it regulates is the way in which people, either as individuals or as members of a group (which itself has a particular identity in communication) are habitually addressed and responded to: how they appear in public communication. The pattern of this recognition incorporates a shared perception of social, economic or political value or power which both reflects and establishes the distribution of communication rights. That is, the distribution of social, economic and political value is intertwined with the distribution of communication rights: the ways in which persons and groups are recognised as valuable contributors to the communication processes which constitute the socio-political world (through rights of access to social space–time). The polity is the matrix of persons, together with the rules and structures which regulate their appearance as valid subjects of communication in a range of local communication contexts (a communication code): the form of socio-political organisation.

In previous chapters I have argued that even the innermost aspects of the person, such as consciousness, are determined (weak sense) through the communicated intention of them by others which itself takes socially relative form. A person, as a subject of communication, is born through incorporation into processes of intersubjectivity which are regulated by socially valid rules of communication. The structures of subjectivity and intersubjectivity encode, represent and reflect the form of social reproduction across its entire range, from family life to economic organisation. (This is where Marx goes beyond Hegel.) The social communication processes which I have described in Chapter 3 must therefore be understood as having a profoundly material aspect, distributing the means for material life as well as meaning.

Furthermore, I will later argue (Chapter 9) that the stability necessary for a determinate and dependable personal identity can only be provided through institutionalisation or otherwise organised and structured social relations. Socio-political institutions do not, then, necessarily distort personal integrity or genuine communication. In Chapter 3 I argued that subjective and 'objective' processes are reciprocally formed. It must follow from this that socio-political processes which stabilise distorted communication will coincide with distorted structures of personal identity. On the other hand, undistorted communication can only really be possible in a free society. Personal identity must therefore be both a personal and a political project.

The reproduction of society takes place through communication processes. It therefore requires the reproduction of people competent to participate appropriately in these processes. An oppressive society will therefore reproduce particular (here meaning non-generalisable) interests by institutionalising distorted patterns of communication which distribute communication roles unequally so that non-conformist interests and non-privileged groups are prevented from guiding communication. People will therefore be socialised through distorted patterns of communication, carried in the communication code itself, which frustrates the formation of an undistorted communicative subjectivity or autonomy. A free society, on the other hand, will reproduce itself through communication which is free from constraint and based upon mutual understanding and free recognition. The communicative autonomy of its subjects is the reciprocal requirement of a free society.

Redemption and social transformation

Engagement in social communication, and therefore in socio-political structures, is a necessary aspect of life in God's image, but it is a refraction of the relation with God which therefore remains the primary determinant of human being and personhood, even though it requires social mediation. It is God's address which creates human being as a structure of response. By taking dialogical form it creates the space necessary for communicative subjectivity and autonomy in response and must be considered the ontological precondition for the taking of personal and communal responsibility. This address is therefore ontologically prior to anything which happens in society; yet it can only be directed towards the concrete reality of socially determinate persons or an historically determinate community. Undistorted relations and socio-political structures can be social mediations of God's call, as I have already suggested. But, whilst God's address can bypass explicit social mediation in the direct address to individuals, these individuals exist only as members of a determinate historical situation and community, and this determinacy makes a difference to the possibilities of cognition and consciousness. In what might be understood as a divine self-limitation, God's address is encoded in determinate form in order to be understandable (though not unambiguous) and so invite a response: the Word is incarnate in a determinate social world.

In Christian understanding, however, the determinate conditions of human life are fallen, and so social communication can only be more or less distorted. Fully undistorted personhood and relations are exclusively features of God's kingdom which, because of the pervasiveness of sin, may be fully realised only through divine grace. It cannot come in its fullness through human effort in history and, in this sense, cannot be called an historical, but rather an eschatological, and therefore permanently future, reality. It may, however, be anticipated in promissory form where God's communication in history elicits appropriate human responses, but – because of its radical, qualitative newness – it is not achievable as the result of normal, fallen, historical processes. Salvation cannot be achieved through historical projects of liberation. To believe that it can is to succumb to a form of works-righteousness and an idolisation of political structures or movements which directly distort the relation to God by supposing that we can achieve salvation on our own: a supposition which closes us off from God. But without the maintenance of a proper openness in our relation to God, political structures, movements, social relations and personal identities will fall to distortion.

Here we are confronted with the paradox that persons and relations free from distortion are political projects which are politically unrealisable. In one form or another, a perennial problem for Christian political commitment has been how to take the political realm seriously without imbuing it with ultimate significance. The Christian vision of the kingdom of God is of an undistorted political community under God's rule established at the end of history by divine fiat. God's rule is not the result of evolutionary or revolutionary historical processes; yet Jesus' earliest preaching none the less concerned the inbreaking presence of the kingdom within determinate social relations and socialised persons (Matt. 4:17). The problem of political theology arises out of the tension of an incomplete discontinuity: the partial appearance of God's future kingdom within a determinate society with which it is both historically and ontologically discontinuous. The transformations of the present which these inbreakings represent are also historically, though not ontologically, discontinuous with the future promised reality in the sense that they do not deliver it up to human possibility and are to be considered as anticipations or partial fulfilments, with a still unfulfilled promissory element. The kingdom is a future reality and the mode of its presence is therefore futural (e.g. in the form of promise, hope or anticipation).

A determinate socio-political situation is essential to human life, but it is not our ultimate environment, which is God and the kingdom. It is, none the less, essential and of decisive significance as the concrete place wherein personal identity projects of responsibility take place, and where the address of God and others must be heard and responded to. The particular society within which we live is a local horizon for our communication and commitment, and can be understood as a mediation or representation of our relation to God.[1] That this horizon is necessary (although not absolute) means that faith's commitment has a 'Green' tinge to it: act locally; think eschatologically! (Compare the Green slogan, 'Think global; act local.')

The social 'place' in which we find ourselves does therefore achieve a penultimate significance and importance. It does so, however, not only as the situation in which individual transformation may occur – where we are found and empowered in a new spirit by God – but as a world which may itself be reconstituted by God's redemptive activity. If redemption is thought of in relational and social, rather than simply individualistic, terms, then it must be the case that it effects new forms of relation, community and society. Individuals who respond aright to God's redemptive address become ex-centrically structured: that is, directed towards the real nature of God and others. Such openness, however, requires the order of a new determinate community. So the impact of God's redemptive address on people within a determinate social 'world' (which may, of course, be mediated by others in it) will issue in transformations of the forms and structures of common life – although such transformations may be restricted to particular 'places' and times within the society. God's active entrance into determinate social orders transforms, or recodifies, relations into a conformity to Christ, or a correspondence to God's kingdom. Socio-political orders, personal relations and personal identities are all transformed through God's activity, which binds people together into a new community. But the transformation is only partial because the transforming presence takes a form appropriate to and therefore limited by the determinate situation – as well as by the present forms and contents of identity – and so is itself transformed by it. In terms of Christian tradition, this new community is termed Church – at least in its ideal, if not in its empirical form. (To use Christian terminology to reflect upon this reality does not imply that 'redeemed' forms of community may not be found beyond the borders of the Church.)

The universality of the Church

The Church is the historical community which understands its identity to be an encoded communal response (i.e. a structure of intersubjectivity) to the communication of God in history. It also comprehends the fact that God is Word-present in its own communication and structure as a transforming power. Yet the Church, as a human community within a determinate situation, exists only in a partial or distorted form. The tension between the complete redemption of communication in the future and the conditions of the present is not annulled but heightened within the Church. As a universal ideal of a communication community, the Church is historically, socially and politically indeterminate; yet, as an enduring and identifiable human community, it has to acquire historically determinate forms particular and relative to different times and places. The Church, as the place where God's rule is present in a locus of outer-directed communication, is necessarily engaged with its determinate situation towards which it is orientated and from which it appropriates, *whilst relativising them*, the social, historical and cultural institutions through which it endures.[2] The Church is *in*, but not *of*, the world.

The Church as ideal is historically transcendent. Whilst it requires historical determinacy, it can never acquire complete historical realisation. As ideal communication community, the Church requires a specific order within a determinate, overarching socio-political order of which it is, in some sense, a part, and towards which its mission for the universalisation of ideal conditions of communication (God's kingdom) is proximately orientated. The universal ideality of the Church cannot be exhaustively identified with its determination within any situation. For, given that the structure of intersubjectivity in the social world informs the structure and the possible forms and contents of subjective consciousness (Chapter 3), the actual content of the Church and of revelation as such will undergo modification and transformation alongside its objective social form. It is not simply a matter, therefore, of the universal alongside the particular, but of the universal taking particular form and being transformed by it with the addition of new content.[3] This process is not necessarily corrupting for the Church, as it is part of its nature to achieve this modification and addition of content, to be in and towards a determinate world, to be concrete.

In a sense, however, the Church forms a social world *alongside* as much as *within* its concrete context. For its structure of intersubjectivity – the pattern of co-intending within the community – and therefore also the subjective forms and contents peculiar to it, despite their transformation, are not general properties of the situation; they are the transformed contents of faith in a determinate situation and are therefore unique to the Church. They are transformations of the ideal communication community which is the Church, and not annihilations of it. The universal ideality of the Church is a co-determinate with its social context of the Church's determinate form. The ideal of the Church can therefore govern the way in which the double transformation, of ideal community by social world and of social world by the determinate form taken by that ideal, occurs. A particular and determinate church is a transform of the universal, abstract ideal by its particular, determinate social world.

The Church must also be said to be *alongside* as well as *in* a concrete and particular social world, by virtue of its orientation or mission. As a universal ideal of ordered intersubjectivity (communication community) in a concrete and determinate form, the Church is both an anticipation and a projection of its future. The Church has a mission for the universal redemption of communication. In this mission it moves beyond itself both temporally and spatially, extending into different times and new places. To achieve this it must reform the form and content of its communication, and therefore the structure of its identity, and, simultaneously, reform the surrounding social world. The alongsidedness of the Church is consequently to be conceived in terms of open identity. It does not form a world apart, yet neither is it a simple part of 'the' world. It is a distinct community which expresses the realities of distorted communication as they occur within itself and its social context, the brokenness of patterns and structures of communication, whilst proclaiming the realised possibility of their forgiveness and redemption in Christ. It proclaims the divine liberation, the conditions of free communication and personhood, within and to an unfree world. In other words, the Church permeates its communication context.

> If faith's community, cultus, and language express this fundamental
> human problem of bondage and freedom, then faith will not be an
> isolated stratum of the life-world. It will re-form the life-world after its
> own image. Faith's inclination though not accomplishment is utopian.
> Through the centuries faith has constantly labored to overcome
> attempts in its own community to isolate it. Intrinsic to faith is a
> resistance to restriction to *gnosis* without *agape*, to individual love
> without societal concern, to emotions without reason, to redemption
> without creation.[4]

The utopian vision of undistorted communication as God's kingdom is of an unbounded, universal community. The knowledge of the ultimate unity of all disparate social worlds as God's creation and kingdom informs the form and content of the Church's internal order and of its communication directed externally towards its social context. There is therefore an essential imperialism about the Church simply because its primary information is inclusive and total. Yet this 'imperialism' is not the totalitarian imposition of one world or vision of the world on another. The world which is the Church's prime informant and towards which it is orientated is the kingdom. This is not 'another world', but the eschatological, and hence radically new, future of this one. It is a hope for *this* world, even for *this* society, which is of such a different quality from the present that it can be spoken of as a new creation, since it arises only out of the creative possibilities of God, who makes all things new. 'New creation' is a metaphorical, not a literal, ascription. The kingdom is an ultimate horizon for the Church's commitment in and to its particular time and place. The nature of the kingdom as a transformation of *this* world requires such proximate commitment in the local situation to its eschatological future. Our local commitment and communication may be a mediation of our commitment and communication to God, just as our understanding of God and the kingdom is mediated and filtered by our social situation.[5]

Iconoclasm and anticipation

The mission of the Church necessarily takes place in a determinate context for two reasons. First, the community is a part, and its members simultaneously also members, of an overarching society which is a co-determinant of the structure, form and content which subjectivity and intersubjectivity may take. Second, the social world within which a church is contextualised will be unique. It will have problems and potentialities peculiar to it as well as incarnating the universal conditions of sin, or distorted communication, in unique ways. For the Church to fulfil its function as redemptive community, it has to address its situations in a form appropriate to the ways in which communication is concretely distorted and bound in them. For the Church to redeem and transform distorted structures of communication, it has to function within the same world within which that distortion occurs. It is to open the conditions of communication to the future it hopes for and anticipates, in which there will be truth, freedom, justice and equality – the conditions of undistorted communication and community. It must therefore be an iconoclast against the idolatries of its world which bind and distort communication. But it must do all this from within the same structure of intersubjectivity and co-intending from whence such distortions arise.[6] This seems to require a pattern of identity within a world without identification with it, so that the Church may represent the transcendental, ideal structures of undistorted communication and community within and to its determinate social world. This may be termed a determinate recodification exercise.

In so far as a particular church's communication and achievement is committed to the redemption of its situation (of the prevailing conditions of communication), Christ becomes concretely present in and to it. The identity of the Church as the presence of Christ, of God's redemptive communication, can occur only within a determinate situation. This means two things. First, the unique form of intersubjectivity which constitutes the Church is institutionalised in its internal structures of communication (e.g. liturgy, pastoral care of members, church order), for which the social situation is a co-determinant. Second, Christ's presence creates ex-centric structures of communication and identity. The Church can only therefore be centred in Christ as it is directed and committed to the wider social 'world' by undertaking situation-relevant (and therefore also relative) socio-political commitments which further extend, in anticipative and incomplete form, the conditions of undistorted communication.

In Christian tradition, the Church is constituted by the presence of Christ. In the terms of my argument, His presence will structure the Church and order its communication and identity in the same way that His presence structures that of an individual. Personal identity refers to the spirit of communication, the form of punctuation operating between 'self' and other, the way one is committed to and orientated on others. Further, 'self' is not a *substantial*, but an *organisational*, reality; not some*thing* which is individually derived and held, but a *means* of organising oneself which is socially acquired. This means that a person's identity is inseparable from the concrete ways in which one commits oneself to others. The same is true for the Church, that its identity as the location of Christ's presence is coincident with the pattern of its commitment to and orientation towards others. For Christ is not only present *in* the Church, structuring its internal communication, but also stands *between* the Church and its world, structuring its missionary communication. In following Christ the Church is directed into the world. Through its determinate situation the Church is engaged in a mission for the universal redemption of the conditions of communication.

Because the redeemed communication situation towards which the Church is orientated is eschatological (its content therefore cannot be fully known or realised in any historical present) and universal (it includes all times, places and people), it is an historically unreachable ideal. It is therefore an ideal, the content of which will overreach any particular anticipation of it. The permanent transcendence of the kingdom's actual content over the content of any anticipation of it in theory or practice serves as a formal principle for the Church's commitment and identity: they must always be open towards the kingdom's transcendence of the present. The identity of a particular church in a particular here and now can only be provisional, limited and relative. The Church must find a form of identity in the here and now which remains open before the universal time and space of the eschatological kingdom. Yet, because there is a requirement for determinate and concrete identity in the here and now, this openness can be neither boundless nor indeterminate. There is therefore a double openness about the Church's identity: it is to be open both to its particular situation and to its universal and transcendent horizon. Open identity refers to a permanently transformable and transformative structure which denies the claim to absoluteness to any determinate form (including its own). Absoluteness is a premature form of closure in social space–time. The Church's mission, by contrast, is towards the eschatological redemption of communication, to transform – in a proleptic and anticipatory way – the distorting and distorted structures in its situation through the power of the Holy Spirit which opens prematurely closed systems.

The form of the Church's commitment is therefore iconoclastic. Idolatry fetters or prematurely arrests communication by universalising a particular space and time. The Church is therefore to remind its world of its provisionality by placing it within the wider context of God's communication in creation–redemption. This will involve negating aspects of the situation through socio-political critique and commitment. Because redemption is an eschatological and universal future, such communication must be understood to be provisional and anticipatory. The Church, in its socio-political communication, must make an explicit theme of the distance between any particular political commitment and order and the kingdom. It will thereby resist any and all forms of totalitarianism which equate the kingdom with the here and now. It must also thematise the distortions of communication which are institutionalised in its particular situation: the specific and concrete ways in which its situation (and the Church itself) contradicts the kingdom.

It is not a social reality's particularity or its nature as provisional and penultimate but, rather, the *forgettting* of that as its nature which is sinful. What is particular and determinate should not be considered evil on the grounds that it lacks the perfection of the kingdom, for the provisional realisation of the kingdom – which is a necessary step on the path to its full realisation – can only happen through the particular and determinate. Emancipatory transformations occur in the present under the impact of redemption on that which most contradicts the coming liberation of the kingdom in the present, thus negating those elements which most bind and distort communication here and now. None the less this is a transformation of the present, and not its substitution by a completely new social 'world' created by divine fiat. It is therefore simultaneously an affirmation of the present – even, perhaps, a celebration of it – since it takes its specific nature seriously in directing it towards its complete liberation. It is this present which is redeemed and reorientated towards the horizon of a new future, and so it cannot be annulled in the process. Setting a particular society or a socio-political movement within the eschatological horizon of redemption therefore has a positive aspect too. For the particular social world may contain provisional and limited anticipations of the future kingdom as it is the place where God's call may be heard and is to be answered, where human being in God's image is at stake. It is therefore to be taken with appropriate seriousness.

The form of political commitment appropriate to redemption which will be universal and is eschatological and therefore future has a double openness. It is open to the needs of the present and to the requirements of the future. That is to say, it sees the need of the particular present from the perspective of the universal future and engages with the present and particular in order to bring it into close approximation to it. The Church engages in a dialogue between its particular present and its future in which the 'otherness', the 'so much more', of the future has to be maintained. The Church's political commitment should thereby remain open to the future and acknowledge its own provisionality. It must make a principle of the permanent requirement of transformation by probing and questioning all political forms and structures in their supposed finality.

The Church's socio-political commitments and its vision of the kingdom can only be anticipatory and therefore provisional and determinate. The question of their truth and rightness cannot therefore be resolved by testing whether there is a direct correspondence with the kingdom. That would either make what is actually a provisional and determinate cognition, understanding or practice absolute, or make any concrete commitment and understanding impossible because none could be perceived as perfectly corresponding with the kingdom. Instead, the truth and rightness of an understanding of the kingdom and of the commitments and activity informed by it may be tested by relating them not only to the futurity of the kingdom, but also to its concrete inbreaking within the movement of the historical present. The truth and rightness of redemptive commitment and engagement are to be found in their appropriateness for the redemption of present communication: enabling a meaningful anticipation of the kingdom in the concrete here and now. This can only be tested through dialogue.

A political commitment may be verified in a dialogue concerning its historical as well as eschatological appropriateness. The kingdom is a community structured so that the conditions of dialogue are universalised. Both the universal extent and the form of communication (dialogue) in redemption are prime informants for the process through which the truth and rightness of a political commitment can be verified. A political commitment is true if it is part of the contemporary discussion concerning meaning and necessary and right order (i.e. is historically relevant), and if it deepens and extends the quality of this discussion as the way towards better approximations to a genuine and true community – i.e. it further extends the conditions of dialogue, and so is eschatologically anticipative. It is not that political commitments are verified as true through dialogue, so much as that they become true through the realisation and extension of dialogue which they bring about or propose. In other words, the test of the truth and rightness of a political commitment is whether it furthers the conditions of dialogue in the present by improving the quality of communication or increasing the quantity of those freely admitted as subjects to socio-political processes. Truth is a relation between a socio-political context and the kingdom in which the former is opened and moves towards the latter through the transformation of distorted structures of communication in the concrete situation. A crucial part of the truth is the intrinsic relation pertaining between distortions in the vertical and horizontal dimensions of human life.

The code of a true society based upon God's communication in creation–redemption cannot be explicated, then, in terms of universally valid structures, political maxims or commitments. For that would not take the qualitative newness offered by God and required for our redemption seriously. The only theological-political universal is the means for testing the truth of socio-political commitments in dialogue. Redemption will be a universal extension of the conditions of dialogue in terms of both quality and quantity. The appropriateness of a programme or order of communication can only therefore be tested in dialogue.

In the following chapters I shall be describing the organisation of the polity consistent with this view of Christian political commitment and the nature of undistorted personal life outlined in the preceding argument. My immediate concern is with universal conditions, a philosophy of politics, rather than with immediate and concrete political application. But the fact that this is carried out in a determinate situation, where the institutionalised presence or absence of certain issues from socio-political discourse is informative for participation in such discourse, means that it is none the less directed towards its determinate situation.

8

Political community

Understanding and participation

As I argued in the opening chapters, God's interaction with us is dialogical in form. In communication God intends and informs our human being as an autonomous structure of response: we are autonomous subjects of communication responsible before God. Our constitution as persons through our relation with God, which requires social refraction and mediation, generates a specific conception of the person, which was elaborated in Part II. The form which God's communication takes is normative for practice in social relations, and I have already discussed the implications of such a view for the practice of small-scale interpersonal relations in which the free, reciprocated recognition and co-intention of the partners as autonomous subjects of communication becomes a norm for practice. But it was impossible to restrict the discussion to this level of social reality alone, since interaction of this kind is intimately intertwined with social structures and interactions at higher levels of organisation.

What is required now, therefore, is a similar theory which can ground the right practice of relations on a larger scale. In the political sphere, the dialogical norm for communication generates a formal principle for legitimating political practice and order: the extension of free and equal participation in a political structure or movement in which people are recognised, or rather structurally co-intended, as autonomous subjects of political communication. As participating subjects of and in political processes, people are acknowledged in both their freedom and their difference. This clearly makes participation the key to political legitimacy. In political structures and processes people must be acknowledged and intended as political subjects. They must therefore be allowed sufficient social space–time for subjective and autonomous engagement. For they are unique persons whose independent communication is essential because it provides unique information.

Personal identity is unique and irreducible. By virtue of the uniqueness of their autobiographies of relation and of their distinct social locations, people have different contents of understanding and experience: they experience, understand and interact with the world on different bases (sedimented identities) and from different social locations. Because the world is experienced differently by, and holds different possibilities of communication for, each person, and because of the uniqueness of personal identity, everyone has a unique understanding of and interest in the world. The understanding and interest unique to a person as a unique social location may only be comprehended through its self-communication. It therefore makes a difference to the prevailing conception of what is good, true and right whether and how this location is indexed in processes of socio-political communication. The exercise of socio-political power and the structuring of societal relations is to conform to the norm for participation in dialogue: freedom as autonomy in communication. But that freedom is itself to conform in its exercise to the norm for commitment to others, which is also set in dialogue.

Furthermore, political power is to be conformed to the way power is exercised by God in the eschatological kingdom and to the form which God's communication takes in creation–redemption. The form and content of God's communication in salvation history is not that of an absolute, totalitarian ruler (monologue); it is an overspilling of the internal trinitarian process of communication. The form and the content of this communication are inseparable, in that it is the trinitarian life-process which communicates itself through itself. The dialogical form of God's communication cannot be understood apart from the Father's sending of the Son and the empowering of the Holy Spirit. God's rule is an abandonment of absolute, transcendent power in favour of the grace by which creative appeal is made to human freedom and rational understanding: i.e. to the incorporation of human subjectivity in the relation.[1] Human rule and the exercise of power in this image are to be referred to the understanding held by free political subjects.

This recalls the Puritan covenantal theology which, despite its subsequent misuse, created space for individuals' moral autonomy in the political order by institutionalising appeals to their rational understanding, and to their autonomous subjectivity, as a reflection of God's rule.[2] Political rule faithful to God is to engage the rational participation of persons as communicative subjects. The heteronomous aspect of rule must, then, be grounded in a genuine mutuality of understanding arrived at and agreed upon by all relevant political subjects in conditions free from coercion and arbitrary constraint. A structure of accountability on the part of political institutions is to correspond to that of freedom (communicative rather than individualistic) on the part of the subjects. This means that the public questioning of the exercise of power must be institutionalised.[3]

In communication terms, power must be conceived of as the accessibility of effective means of participation in public communication and exchange. The demand that political power be referred to the rationality and autonomy of subjects of communication is immediately translatable into a demand for a more equitable distribution of the rights of access to effective public communication: a sharing of power. As I hope to show, this has implications for participation in political and societal processes. There are implications for all institutions of public life (i.e. all institutionalised forms of intersubjectivity) in which socio-political power is exercised in a way that either includes or excludes the rational participation of those subject to it, by their removal from or inclusion in that sphere of communication.

Political understanding, interests, expectations and priorities are to be justified by public explication. The form which this discussion takes (as more or less dialogical) will determine the genuineness of mutual understanding achieved in it. The form which this 'public sphere' – where interests can be communicated, exchanged, understood and coordinated – takes is crucial. For only as it tends towards the freedom, equality and openness of dialogue will understanding and communication be genuine. The dialogical form of the public sphere in which political objectives and interests are debated therefore functions as a normative referent for the exercise of political power. Political interests and priorities are legitimated by the form public discussion about them takes as much as by the conclusion reached in such a discussion. For it is only if the discussion can be shown to be free of significant distortions that the conclusion arrived at in it as to the justice, or otherwise, of a political interest or objective will be valid. A political order is similarly justified, not so much by conclusions attained in public debate, but by the form which that public debate takes, which is determined by the general structures of public communication: by the extent to which public explication procedures are *dialogically* secured in institutions. The recognition of 'public opinion' as having a valid content for inclusion in the formation of political goals and processes, and therefore in the steering of political society, entails its recognition as a form of rational (more or less) free communication and therefore as more than a realm of special pleading on behalf of private interests.[4]

Consensus

In Chapter 6 I described the link between rational understanding and the generalisability of interests. Explication is the attempt to motivate others rationally to recognise that the interests guiding communication are based on a generalisable norm. The mutuality of understanding which may be reached through explication can only be genuine if communication is undistorted: if, that is, it really does appeal to the understanding of the partners, is free from coercion and constraint and structurally intends the communicative subjectivity of all concerned. The crucial point to comprehend here is that basing political legitimacy on the achievement of understanding does not entail a commitment to anything like a contract view of society for the coordination of self-understood and self-validated particular interests. On the contrary, it establishes the universality of justice as the principle of political legitimation. It does so, however, not in the way of an abstract norm, but as the means for the rational redemption of norms through a public dialogue determining common interest; determining, that is, which norms for the codification of relations are generalisable.

It is not the actual achievement of consensus, however, which establishes the generalisability of a political norm or commitment and thereby legitimates it, but the extent to which such a consensus (mutual understanding), and the explication process used to reach it, anticipate the ideal communication situation (the kingdom). The kingdom represents the eschatological reality of communication under the conditions of full redemption. It therefore functions as a critical ideal against which present structures of communication may be judged and legitimated. Because of its eschatological and universal nature, the reality of the kingdom overflows any particular anticipation of it. It therefore remains a critical ideal even in a situation of actual consensus which, under the conditions of the fall, will be at least partially distorted and not universally extensive (chiefly because, whilst death remains an unconquered reality, communication cannot incorporate past persons as subjects in the full sense). In other words, it is not the actuality of consensus which is normative, but the consensus which *would* result in the present, were there undistorted conditions. An actual consensus may only therefore be legitimated by showing that (a) it was achieved in the absence of significant distortion, and therefore that (b) any communicatively competent third party would be rationally compelled to concur.[5]

An actual consensus cannot be normative in itself, because it could be based on significant distortions in communication. This does not, however, mean that the norm for political interaction remains a lofty ideal, an abstract principle removed from particular conditions. For it refers to the relatively undistorted consensus which *would* result *in the here and now* if significant distortions in and impediments to communication were removed. The norm is concrete for two reasons.

First, the communicatively competent potential third parties whose concurrence is sought are members of a specific (and relevant) communication community. This means that discussion with them concerning the rightness or justice of a political norm may take place against a background consensus concerning other norms of interaction. They are therefore competent in the social codes through which explication may be conducted. This makes the reality and understanding of the participants determinate. They are, in other words, concretely socialised persons. Second, third-party compliance cannot just be assumed; it has to be sought since the only means of understanding the understanding of others is via their self-communication. A consensus need not be reached with these third parties, but the absence of agreement must be explicable as the result of distortions in communication if the norm is to retain validity. This means that when potential become actual third parties, either through invitation or independent communication, they are to be accepted as partners in the process of explication through dialogue because their presence brings new information.

The claim that a political practice or order incarnates a valid norm can only be legitimated through concrete explication with those who are significant others. In the political arena these will be those whose social location and identity is other and whose interests may therefore be non-identical. The legitimacy of norms of political interaction and the determination of right acting under them cannot, in principle, be restricted to the internal communication of any single group. Neither personal nor political ethics can be monological, because the claim to universality (that it would achieve rational consensus) can be tested only by explication in a dialogue which is orientated towards an undistorted consensus with all potential third parties. Within a concrete situation relations are codified according to a relevant norm of interaction. To recommend a norm is to propose a codification of relations in which the distribution of public recognition – and therefore of communication rights, including the chances for need satisfaction – is regulated after a particular pattern. The distribution of communication which it represents must prove capable of undistorted consensus by all potential third parties – i.e. all those potentially affected by it. Through explication in an extended public dialogue the interests or needs which, in interaction under the norm, are met by this particular distribution, will be shown to be either generalisable and common (consensual), or particular (unjustified or else admitting of compromise with competing particular interests).[6]

The requirement of equality in dialogue is necessary in political, just as in personal, ethics. In the socio-political sphere, where explication is generally carried on by persons as representatives of a group (a constellation of social locations), the asymmetrical distribution of dialogue roles is more likely to have, and to be seen to have, a political character. Privileges and disadvantages of individuals and groups in public communication may be perceived to reflect the pattern of distribution operating in the overarching socio-political communication context. That is not to say that political considerations may not be significantly present and explicitly thematised in a matter of personal ethics, but merely that such thematisation *must* occur at the socio-political level *whenever* inequalities occur. If explication of political norms is to take dialogical form, then the partners' communication must be free and unconstrained. The partners are therefore equal in quality. Dialogue in wider society and the polity therefore requires socio-political equality: the equal distribution of rights and chances for effective communication (socio-political power), the institutionalised co-intention of all members of a communication community as free and equal.[7]

Freedom is a function of equality in the communicative sense. The removal from effective communication represented by inequality (the variable degree to which persons are co-intended as communicative subjects) inhibits both internal and external self-communication (autonomy). In a situation of inequality there is a mismatch between the way some experience and understand the world (their subjective content) and the experiences and understandings which are publicly expressible as intersubjectively recognised contents of experience. If oppression and inequality can be conceived in terms of silence or removal from significant areas of public communication and life, then it is impossible for those who are outcast to know or to communicate what they want, think or experience, because such unique subjective content has been removed from the public code. It must also be the case that the inability to bring this perspective on the world to expression makes it impossible for them to understand their experience themselves – or at least impossible without the substitution of a new code or the construction of an alternative community.[8] Equality and freedom for self-communication are the necessary conditions for the achievement of an undistorted consensus, as they mark the absence of constraint or force. It is only under these conditions that interests, needs, understanding and experience may be understood and communicated and thereby participate in the consensual determination of generalisable interests.

If concrete communication is to be undistorted, it must also be unconstrained in its scope, so that there are, in principle, no limits to the political norms and interests which may be questioned. Communication may therefore become wider and more radical in its reference. If, in explicating a particular norm, the inequality of social codification becomes clear and significant, the explicative process must be widened to include other norms and, ultimately, the code itself. For if the social code is obstructing the interpretation and communication of needs, then explication (in which the encoding of needs is proposed and supported by general suppositions concerning the priorities of need-satisfaction under other socially valid norms) and the consensus which may follow it are bound to be distorted. Just as in personal ethics, explication has to be free to metamorphose into a metaethical and political discourse. So socio-political explication must be free to become metapolitical once traditional need interpretations become problematic. There is no norm or code which can be withdrawn in principle from public explication, including, ultimately, the overarching codification of intersubjectivity (the social code) itself.

Democratic will-formation

Through the dialogical process of explication there may be a change in the partners' understanding of themselves and of one another as they approach a mutuality of understanding together. The partners gain a new understanding of themselves, of the world and of their respective needs and interests. They can therefore come to an understanding together about which needs and interests ought to have priority in their relation here and now; an understanding, that is, concerning the structure and codification of their relation. By coming to a more genuine understanding of who they are, and of what their needs, interests and capacities are, they come to an understanding of what they can and ought to be to each other, and therefore of what their relationship is to be. As their relationship comes into conformity to Christ through the power of the Holy Spirit there is a new and real understanding of the other[9] as a partner in the divine image, an external point of orientation whose real needs constitute a concrete mediation of the call of Christ. This happens in the political context too, and indicates that interests, needs and wills are not predetermined and brought into the relation from outside as given and unchangeable, but are actually formed and discovered within the dialogical process of explication. In other words, explication is a cognitive process.

It is only as interests and need interpretations are formed through a genuine dialogue that they may be considered to be rational *qua* generalisable and not the product of monological, self-interested wills. An interest or a norm which is just is one which has been shaped and discovered through dialogue – that is, through reference to the otherness of others – and which can therefore be redeemed in a further dialogue with others.[10] Explication cannot simply be a matter of coordinating pre-established interests, understandings and needs, but of forming them anew through dialogue. The consent of third parties to a proposed norm or interest is not a simple coordination of their current understanding of needs and interests, and therefore of the proper norms of interaction, but a new mutuality of understanding – a new relationship. Where agreement over the needs and interests to be met in a political order changes significantly, the norms of interaction by which the society is structured and relations codified may also undergo change. The consent of others to proposed norms or interests which is sought is that which would follow were they to enter a genuine dialogue.

In the socio-political sphere this process – through which understanding, norms, interests, needs and therefore wills are shaped in dialogue – is a participative process in which wills are democratically formed. Viewed from the other side, it is the formation of democracy through participation. Explication of understanding, norms, needs, interests and wills in a genuine way through dialogue ensures the incorporation of the particular, but generalisable, interests of particular groups into the democratic structures of communal communication. It represents, in other words, the democratic steering of public structures.[11]

The mutuality of understanding, the needs which are understood, the identities of the partners, and the democratic processes through which wills are formed and needs interpreted are all concrete and determinate. People and their interests are determinate in terms of their social location and history of relations. Their real interests may be determined, however, only through undistorted communication in which reason functions as the bearer of generalisability (rather than as the carrier of the abstract, formally universal, yet concretely incompatible interests of individualistic ethics and politics). Interests and needs are also socially determinate in terms of the real or perceived possibilities for need satisfaction in a concrete situation, since the determinate structures of cognition (and therefore of understanding and knowing interests and needs) are directly linked to the forms of production and distribution and to the level of technological expertise. It may therefore be necessary in the course of explication to examine the norms and interests guiding knowledge as such in the situation. For they will be fundamental (though probably hidden) determinants of societal structure, including socially valid interpretations and cognitions of need:

> the cognitive processes to which social life is indissolubly linked function not only as the means to the reproduction of life; for in equal measure they themselves determine the definitions of this life. What may appear as naked survival is always in its roots a historical phenomenon. For it is subject to the criterion of what a society intends for itself as the good life.[12]

What we consider to be 'essential needs' or 'life-interests' – that which no one can or should do without – are in fact socially determinate and relative.

Life-interests which really are essential and generalisable *in the determinate situation* may only be formulated through a dialogue in which interests are legitimated and priorities for need satisfaction agreed. The real and abiding *universal* life interest is primarily, then, in the institutionalisation of dialogue in concrete socio-political situations, without which those interests in a situation which are generalisable could be neither thematised nor democratically formed.[13]

There is consequently a universal interest in democratic forms of socio-political structure, the appropriate form of which will vary according to the requirements and possibilities of the situation. The universality of this democratic interest corresponds to the universality of human creation in God's image, to God's intention of all people as autonomous subjects of communication, as under God's rule and as sharing in the democratic dominion over the earth. The democratic form of life is the socio-political reality of persons co-intending one another as free and equal subjects of communication in an anticipation of the kingdom's ideal for communication and community. Democracy occurs wherever relations in which there is formal reciprocity in personal recognition solidify into socio-political structures.

Democracy is here characterised by an ex-centricity of will and concern and is therefore to be distinguished from its form in liberal individualism. In the liberal version, wills and interests (as are individuals themselves) are self-bounded and constituted. Democracy is then the coordination of such individual wills and interests which regulates their maximum satisfaction. Against this notion, democracy may be understood as the external direction of individual wills and interests towards the constitution of other individuals and groups as free and equal subjects of communication. This entails the recognition of others' genuine interests – as these appear in dialogue – as claims on the community at large.[14] By participating in democratic processes of will-formation, people commit themselves to meet the claims of others which are shown to be just in explication, and to subject their own claims to testing by explication in dialogue with others.[15]

Universal political community
Despite the social determinacy of democratic processes of will-formation and the meeting of need, there is a sense in which what is justifiable has a universal reference. For potential third parties may be drawn from a wider range than membership of the determinate communication community. Rights to participate in explication are still to be limited to those potentially affected by the interest or norm. But this may include those who are not a part of that time and/or place, as well as those not presently included in democratic processes. The boundaries of potentiality need not coincide with those of the determinate situation. The ramifications of a communally pursued interest generally overreach those who participated in its formation and who may, in all integrity, suppose it to be general. It is therefore necessary to examine the contours of internal and external exclusion from participation and question whether they really do demarcate the interest in the norm.

This has, in fact, already been established in the foregoing in the case of internal boundaries. Internal boundaries refer to the general unevenness and asymmetry in the distribution of communication rights which is institutionalised in the social structure. These may unjustly limit the participation of some members of a particular society and may thereby remove some relevant interests from consideration in the processes of communal will-formation. Where these inequalities are relevant, the explicative dialogue must henceforth widen to include those who regard themselves as potentially affected, rather than being confined to those whose interest is either conventionally established or falsely understood to be coincident or irrelevant. Those whose wills, needs and interests are excluded, by a denial of their full subjectivity in communication, from democratic will-formation where they genuinely have an interest are effectively engaged in a political monologue. They receive communication (they are usually at the sharp end of the effects of policy decisions) but are unable to transmit effectively, and so are denied effective subjective integration into socio-political structures.

External boundaries, by definition not *fully* open, are necessary in the pursuit of distinct identity. Within those boundaries will lie a distinct, determinate communication community. Quite clearly, whilst membership of that community need be neither privileged nor jealously exclusive, those outside cannot be admitted to communication on the same terms as those within it. There are different demands of communicative competence, for example, which may actually compose disadvantages for 'outsiders' who inappropriately attempt to take part in the democratic will-formation of another community. Clearly, distance can make it inappropriate for members of one community to 'interfere' with the affairs of another in which they have no potential just interest. That distance, however, cannot and must not function as a permanent barrier to interest-laden communication.

Discerning just which groups and communities should rightly enter this process is extremely difficult, since even the internal decisions of one community can affect another. There are networks of communication and exchange which link the world into a universal community, the use of which can determine the legitimate need satisfaction of other communities. Interaction within the physical/biological environment, for example, may prejudice the life-interests of others distant in space and/or time, for whom the one world will also form an essential context for communication and exchange, as in the case of practices which cause pollution. The pursuit of group self-interest through the structures of world trade may have similarly catastrophic effects for other communities and unborn generations. For justice to be determined in these instances, it is clearly necessary to subject the interest and norm of interaction guiding these exchanges to universal explication. This is so even if the community concerned is operating on the basis of a consensus achieved under fully undistorted internal conditions. For that may be an insufficient criterion of generalisability, and hence justice, if relevant extra-communal interests have not been included in the democratic formation of communal will:

> The members of the communication community (and this implies all thinking beings) are also committed to considering all the potential claims of all the potential members – and this means all human 'needs' inasmuch as they could be affected by norms and consequently make *claims* on their fellow human beings. As potential claims that can be communicated interpersonally, all human 'needs' are ethically *relevant* ... [and] must be made the concern of the communication community.[16]

For the purposes of deciding the justice of some political and ethical interests it may be necessary to index the needs of a universal, and therefore indeterminate, communication community. For political decisions are ultimately to be legitimated in the context of humanity as such. This, however, does not indicate that such universal explication is indeterminate, since – even though it may potentially refer to all present and future societies and people – it can only take place within a particular situation, and so the forms of recognition and understanding of need, right and value will therefore be determinate. Future generations, for instance, may be indexed through empathetic indwelling and other-reflection which, however refined, can only make them present in an abstract way: that is, as bearers of interests which appear from the perspective of *this* determinate situation to be relevant or universal. They cannot appear as real persons, members of their own determinate situation which, in retrospect, might claim that other interests should have been met in our time which we failed to see as connected to our own or to understand as interests.

The more precise way in which explication with a universal referent remains determinate is that interests or needs are (more or less adequately) thematised as claims; that is, as capable of satisfaction within the concretely foreseeable possibilities of distribution and production of this situation. The relevance and recognition of needs cannot be anything but determinate – not least because the understanding and recognition of what counts as a need or life-essential is grounded in the material and social conditions of a particular society, and arises from communication and exchange between different interest groups which is ordered in a particular way and has had a particular history.[17]

Nonetheless, it is basic to any conception of justice that an interest is referred to a community that is ultimately universal. Hence the exclusion of specific interests from communication in a situation where those interests are relevant causes the excluded to serve a critical function. Their exclusion shows the norm to be unjust. The excluded may in fact be indexed in communication under the norm, but only as objects (recipients) of communication: the communication is one-way and the norm monological. Distorted socio-political structures which inappropriately exclude some people and their communication can only be tested and redeemed by the self-communication of excluded interest groups who may then take part in the process of democratic will-formation.

The outcast and oppressed have a priority in the works of redemption and political liberation because they constitute the critical criterion of justice in socio-political reality. The oppressed give the lie to the claim that all is right with the present order or will be right under a new norm of interaction. The present can be criticised from the point of view of the oppressed, whose existence establishes priorities for practice and criteria for justice. In their name the claims of the present to absoluteness and totality must be resisted.[18] With regard to the internal boundaries of communication this represents a further important difference between the liberal conception of democracy and that with which I am operating here. For liberalism permanently excludes minority interests from effective participation, so long as they remain minority, by subsuming them into the 'will of the majority': everyone is taken to consent to majority will, and what most people want becomes the sole determinant of justice.[19] In the conception of democracy which I am putting forward here, minority interests which despite being particular are generalisable and therefore just are secured a constitutive function for democratic will-formation. They must be included in the extended dialogue which constitutes a political community.

Institutional iconoclasm

A democracy structured by dialogue has an open texture about it. It extends participation rights to all within the community who have interests in particular or general socio-political mechanisms or decisions. It also refers its own socio-political norms, through which specific interests are pursued, to the interests of the universal community, of humanity as such. Democratic structures are open not only to wider participation, but to transformation as the requirements of participation in a particular situation change – as the situation itself changes. 'Democracy is not an ideal and not a state of affairs; it is the continual, open and incompletable process of the democratisation of political objectives.'[20]

Investing an institution, norm or interest with absolute, universal and unchanging validity is an act of idolatry which substitutes a principle for the genuine norm of communication in God's image: Christ. Communication is distorted by excluding competing interests in the false claim to an already achieved absolute inclusivity. Clearly, the institutionalisation of dialogue in socio-political structures necessarily imposes a certain rigidity on to societal relations. That in itself, however, is not idolatrous (see below, Chapter 9); institutions become idolatrous through claims to be absolute which exclude their normative base for questioning in dialogue. Idolatrous institutionalisation is isolationist rather than ex-centric, monological rather than dialogical, and is resistant to explication because it is self-legitimating. It cannot, therefore, subject itself to the criteria of a transcendent standpoint, whether it be that of excluded groups or of God's creative–redemptive communication, of which the former may be a mediation.

The norm of undistorted communication in God's creative–redemptive activity (the vertical image and its future) requires institutionalisation so that relations may be semi-stable and ordered through fairly rigid structures of co-intention, expectation and understanding. It is, however, simultaneously transcendent and iconoclastic. Structural rigidity and dependability are required by the ideal, dialogical norm, but they are not norms themselves. For what is also required of institutions under this norm is a structural openness to justifiable claims or, as it might be put, to new and/or different interests, understandings and expectations. As these might place the normative basis of the institution in question, the present norm may have to be rejected and/or the institution changed or dismantled.[21] Between fall and eschatological kingdom, the humanisation of relations and the democratisation of the polity are a process of anticipation rather than full realisation, which may therefore never be fully laid to rest. For this reason, as well as the changing historical circumstances which create new possibilities and therefore different claims, a society's communication codes and norms must be institutionally iconoclastic.

Transcendent and determinate commitments

But here there is an immediate problem. For meaningful, iconoclastic communication has to be determinate (limited, particular and concrete) rather than universal. It has to assume a negativity towards certain aspects of the present, whilst imbuing certain critical forces and possibilities of that same present with positive content. The difficulty lies in preserving the transcendence of theology and faith over their present positive socio-political commitment. For that commitment can only be penultimate, and therefore questionable. A positive political commitment is what is deemed necessary to achieve a *greater* justice in the present, rather than the *full* achievement of truth, freedom and justice – the conditions of universal, undistorted communication. But this answer makes it sound too much as if the mind of faith has a direct intuition of the kingdom alongside a complete understanding of the determination and distortions of the present. If this were so, then it would undermine the way in which the situation is determinate for the cognition of faith itself.

What has to be retained is the sense in which any consensus, even that within the Church and that which is situation-critical in some way, is still determinate. The social form informs consciousness. It must therefore be true in some sense to say that the understanding of a transcendent point from where present social norms of interaction may be judged has itself only a determinate social form. But then the appearance of the transcendent as transcendent becomes severely problematic. We have come full circle to the problem of the universal's presence in the particular. Or, rather, there seems to be a choice between two apparent alternatives. On the one hand, there is a faith which is determinate but which then seems unable to claim a privileged, undistorted insight a priori. On the other, there is a transcendent faith which appears irrelevant and uninterested in the determinate situation and unable, in any case, to incarnate itself in or commit itself to it. By building upon my previous comments in this respect, I hope to show that faith and faithful commitment may be both determinate and transcendent. It is important to note that this is a possibility open only to faith as a logically prior coordination of transcendent and determinate: a coordination achieved, of course, not by the power of the determinate and finite alone.

The point at issue is how, if the distorted intersubjectivity of the determinate situation is somehow determinative of consciousness, persons may criticise it from a more enlightened standpoint which they claim to be undistorted and to know a priori. The dialectical nature of theological commitment places an eschatological reserve against the distortions of the present as well as its own commitment. This principle of iconoclasm prevents the Church's political commitment from slipping into idolatrous and ideological forms. As such, this requires only an apprehension of the *form* of the kingdom as transcendent ideal. This rather abstract cognition would not be problematic in a determinate situation, but only because, having no positive content itself, it could not yield a positive content for present political commitment. The problem really arises with the positive content of theological commitment which claims to represent a transcendent norm of intersubjectivity in the determinate situation. This is problematic in that it claims to enjoin radical newness with the determinate situation. It represents a problem of explication as well as cognition. For a new norm has been apprehended as an a priori by members of a determinate situation and is then, in the determinate dialogical moment, referred for confirmation to those who might have no access to its cognitive base.

How, in its reference in cognition and explication to the particular situation, can the proposed recodification of relations fail to be distorted by the predetermined and socially normative coordination of needs, etc. which characterises the determinate situation? If, in the present encoding of relations – the current communication code – the cognitive content of common good and human needs is distorted by imbalanced power relations, how is an alternative cognition possible within this code, and how may a radical departure from it be communicated within it?

In theological terms this is the problem of revelation; however, the difficulty raised by an apparent claim to know, a priori, the nature and demands of the 'good and true life' is shared by all social criticism which comprehends the distortion and 'false consciousness' of the present which it claims it does not share. The problem of legitimating socially critical sociopolitical commitment with socially transcendent criteria can only be satisfactorily resolved if it is recognised as a religious question. This is not only because the 'transcendent' is the normal concern of religion as such (that would merely confer a quasi-religious status on to otherwise secular ideologies), but because religion is the only sphere within which a critique of the present – a (partial) legitimation of critical political commitment – together with a critique of that same political commitment is possible. Religious transcendence refers not only to this but to all presents, to the pre- and post-revolutionary situations and to the revolution itself.[22] The Church as redeemed communication community and its communication (and hence political commitment) as concrete anticipations of the kingdom are essential referents for a solution to this problem. For both already implicitly contain the claim to incarnate the transcendent in the determinate.

Those in the Church do not become socially critical through a purely internal and private political and religious apprehension, but through membership of a redeemed communication community (the apprehension which occurs through redeemed intersubjectivity is, of course, personal in that it is idiosyncratically transformed). As I suggested in Chapter 7, the Church, whilst determinate, cannot be reduced to a part of its social context, but exists alongside it. As a community with a distinct form of intersubjectivity (in determinate form), the Church has a unique (though still determinate) cognitive form. This not only yields new and different insights into the common cognitive content of its determinate social situation, but yields cognitive content unique (yet in determinate form) to the redeemed community as well. In the Church there may be both an understanding of the present situation which conflicts with that present's self-understanding and an 'apprehension' unavailable, or apparently nonsensical, except within the Church. These two 'a prioris' tend to coincide and be mutually informative.

The Church represents, then, an intersubjectivity which, whilst situation determinate, is situation critical. The structures of recognition within the Church intend all human beings as persons, and therefore as partners in the divine image and as joint members of God's kingdom of truth, freedom and justice. Whatever inequalities presently exist and appear to be determinative, the Church is able to 'recognise' the equality of all by 'recognising' all within an alternative and enduring communication context, the history of God's communication in creation–redemption. This recognition obviously takes determinate form when the Church commits itself to justice on behalf of the 'other' or the 'outcast' of a particular situation. That is to say that the demands of the kingdom are translated into concrete claims within the determinate situation. The kingdom is apprehended as a transcendent ideal, but only through its potential redemption of the present, and only therefore as it makes contact with and is meaningful in the present – although its meaning and reality are also understood to overrun this point of contact.

The unique intersubjectivity and co-intending of the Church is a response to God, a possibility opened only through the creativity of the Father, the empowering of the Spirit and the open structuring of the Word. It is the body of Christ, a human response to the Father. Its intersubjective form, determinate structures and external commitments are anticipations of the kingdom in response to God's communication, which has revealed its approximate form and content. The Church's internal and external communication are anticipatory in a distinctive way, for the kingdom (universal ideal of communication) is future and transcendent in a distinctive way. Its future and transcendence are those of God; it is not a human future in the normal sense of an as yet unrealised human possibility towards which human commitment moves. This future is anticipated through proleptic communication enlivened by the Spirit, structured by the Word, creatively called by the Father. It is not a case of the present moving steadily closer to an evolutionary future, but of God opening up the present and drawing it into the future of the kingdom. It is not a future which can be fully present through human effort, but only anticipatorily present in responding human community. Its mode of presence cannot therefore be complete or uniform, but determinate, partial and anticipatory. The continuity of the present with the eschatological future comes from the future, from God, and is not created by human activity as such and in itself.

Determinate cognition of the kingdom brings something radically new into the situation which could not otherwise be present. It is available in this form only to the community which responds to God within the determinate situation. It is not necessary to have a full and unbounded knowledge of the kingdom's content in order to anticipate it in practice, for a determinate cognition may reveal the impulse of the kingdom and the pattern of commitment appropriate to its anticipation in the here and now. But just because the determinate nature of this cognition and commitment is understood, there is an inbuilt question mark over them. They remain human responses, fallen anticipations, which may be mistaken but which, in any case, must always be referred to the transcendent horizon and context of God's relation with us through the community's internal structures of communication (e.g. worship, scriptural study, preaching, praying) and the continual need for forgiveness.

The problem presented earlier is 'solved' when the sort of claim properly made for Christian political commitment is understood. The distinctive intersubjectivity of the Church provides cognitive content unavailable elsewhere in its situation and therefore, to all intents and purposes, a priori. Yet this a priori cognition is also bound up with its situation and is therefore communicable and practically relevant. But this determinate cognitive content is limited and partial, claiming only an anticipatory form of identity between itself and the transcendent norm of interaction it anticipates. The Church remains faithful, therefore, to the difference between political liberation and redemption. The truth of the proposed codification lies in its anticipative form: not, that is, in its status as a universal, but as a universal in a particular, the (anticipatory) redemption of particular, determinate relations. The truth makes persons free politically, not in some absolute, abstract and indeterminate sense, but in relation to the political and technical possibilities of the present.

Personal freedom

My overarching intention in this book has been intrinsically to relate the unique individuality of personal existence to the existence of others, steering something of a mid-course between collectivism and individualism. The role I have given to personal autonomy in relation to social structures and groupings would, I think, appear unacceptably naive to the collectivist, for whom persons are social atoms determined (strong sense) by higher levels of social organisation. The individualist, on the other hand, for whom persons are not socially determined in any sense (social structures being combinations of individual wills), being intrinsically related only to themselves, would be profoundly suspicious of my understanding of the social determinacy of persons and of their constitution through ex-centric orientation. Clearly the differences between my own and these other positions revolve around the issue of freedom. I do not intend to set out a full and detailed explication of my position regarding all aspects of personal freedom (as this has been a more or less explicit theme running through the work, that would be to labour the point), but to show briefly that there is a place for freedom within the democratic socio-political structures I have described. To talk of freedom within political structures is already implicitly to opt for a position which is neither individualist nor collectivist. In speaking of *personal* freedom as opposed to sub-units or atoms of the social structure, the collectivist position is denied; and in speaking of freedom *within* rather than *from* structures, the individualist position is also denied.

In this chapter I have argued that the socio-political process is, ideally, one of democratic will-formation into which individuals are incorporated as unique and irreducible subjects, but through which both persons and socio-political structures might be transformed by new information. Persons, who are always more than mere individuals, will, in a genuine democratic community, concretely orientate themselves on one another in order to come to an undistorted consensus or genuine mutuality of understanding in conformity to Christ. This process of concrete mutuality, through which persons are transformingly orientated on others, is not a denial of their personal identity; it rather constitutes identity as formed by Christ's presence. Socio-political structures are sedimentations of personal communication and persons are, in turn, sedimented forms of response to a significant history of communication which inevitably includes structural forms and media of intersubjectivity. Free societies presuppose the communicative autonomy of persons within their structures and, in this presupposition, make socio-political freedom possible and nurture other, more personal, forms of freedom.

The rational determination of justice limits (though it may also extend them in certain directions in particular circumstances) the legitimate interests and claims of persons by subjecting them to public scrutiny and criteria of generalisability. I have tried to show, however, that such limitation is, in the democratic process, a self-limitation according to an understood code of interaction. It involves a subjective moment because subjectivity has a determinate, intersubjective content. It is not 'pure', but is intrinsically linked to the existence of others and to the means of relating to them. In redeemed form both consciousness and communication are informed by a unique co-intention of oneself with, for and 'in' others as mutually orientated and limiting. Socio-political emancipation in the image of salvation frees people from being too tightly bound either to themselves or to others, so they may be ex-centrically structured; that is, orientated on God and others from a personal centre. In this ex-centric movement a person is properly constituted as free.

Fundamentally, this freedom is from a binding to the self and the idolatrous pursuit of self-interest by subjecting oneself to generalisable rational criteria of justice. Through reason a person is consciously self-directed towards others. Rationality, communicatively understood, is the centredness of personal autonomy externally directed in responding to the call of God and others, the ex-centric structure of personal being.[23] Reason, informed by creation–redemption, is the subjective moment in which membership of a universal community structured by formally reciprocal co-intending is intended. It has an expansive and generalisable logic; it is not limited to the pure internality of idiosyncratic interest or to the particular location of specific individuals, but intends all others as autonomous subjects of communication alongside oneself.

In the following chapter I will describe socio-political structures as safeguarding and nurturing autonomy. This view must immediately be distinguished from those theories of political order which are based upon the individual pursuit of private self-interest. The consensual nature of democratic will-formation and of the personal freedom which is engaged in the process as I have described them must not be confused with the notions of democracy and freedom in liberal contract theory. In the latter, individuals create a state by consenting to a contract. The contract is not entered into out of a recognition of others as claims and limits, but out of fear that one's own claims and interests may be restrained by another's pursuit of self-interest. The structure of co-intending is of the other as competitor; there is no community as such, but a collectivity of individuals (who remain essentially asocial) who, guided by enlightened self-interest, realise the interest of each in limiting the potential claims of others. So the limitation of self-interest in the contract actually affirms, entrenches and furthers it.[24]

The consensus which occurs through democratic will-formation, by contrast, is constituted neither by self-interest nor by interests which are private, but in an orientation towards the generalisable (just) interests of others. In contract theories one is joined to others through the exercise of a self-enclosed will alone. In contrast, the theory developed here supposes a link between persons in the very structure of personhood. In this theory human society remains a formation of the will, and therefore engages personal autonomy, but the will, along with the consciousness which directs it, is informed by the wills and interests of others in a formally reciprocal structure of co-willing and co-intending.[25] The structures of meaning here will be communal and not purely private. (Indeed, ultimately, this meaning is humanly, not merely individually, transcendent.) Meaning is related to a network of relations larger than the individual. Justice and rightness as generalisable signify a valuation of claims and interests with a more extensive reference than the 'self' and self-interest.[26] It replaces a monological conception of validity and meaning with a dialogical process within which meaning and just interest are formed and identified. The freedom of the person is a self-direction towards God and others rather than an individualised act of 'liberty' (freedom from); it is the will to be incorporated into community with God and others. The understanding involved in rationality is not a moulding of the world into conformity with one's own interests but a self-transcending, comprehensive comprehending of external relations and interests. It is an expansion of the self which, as ex-centric, is not an expansion of individualistic liberty but of freedom for God and others.

Genuine democratic structures are based on mutual understanding and free recognition, the participation of all in the formation of the common will. In this context, personal freedom is a form of identity sedimented through a history of relations, significant both personally and structurally, in which appeals to personal understanding replace coercion and repression. This form of socio-political order and freedom integrates the uniqe structure of personal centredness (self-realisation) with the universal structure of rational self-determination. The subjectivity of self-understanding is linked to the universalised pattern of redeemed intersubjectivity where there is formally reciprocal co-intending. The particularity of one's identity emerges within a socio-political structure and through socialisation processes in which the pattern of intersubjectivity continually refers to and upholds it as a unique and individual location for dialogue. In dialogue a person is addressed in the network of communication as a unique and irreducible personal location, yielding a sense of the uniqueness of personal identity and centredness in the structures of public communication.

In redeemed community persons are ex-centrically structured and intend themselves and others as autonomous subjects of communication. It is therefore right, as it is more than a private self-interest, to pursue the requirements of self-centredness, because this is a condition of one's ability to be for others. But the interest in the maintenance of centred personal identity and autonomy is not an absolute. It exists for others and must therefore be referred to the requirements of others before its validity may be established. The demands of self-centredness are balanced by the universal referent in the redeemed forms of community. This establishes criteria of generalisability and justice for the pursuit of individual self-realisation. This does not cancel the particularity of the requirements for each individual's self-realisation, but relates them to a rationale which transcends the individual concerned: namely, the needs and interests of others. The individual is therefore to become self-critical and open to the conflicting understandings of others. The needs and interests of others are not unrelated to the self-realisation of the individual but incorporate the universal interest, in the process of democratic will-formation, in the expansive presence of uniqueness and full realisation of individual identity under the conditions of dialogue. Differences are not suppressed, but freely enter the democratic process which mediates the particular and universal. Undistorted identity and community (intersubjectivity) are coincident.

The just pursuance of autonomy and identity may mean claiming rights to be met and honoured by others. These rights, however, are not libertarian but communicative. That is, they are not individualising as such (though there may be a legitimate claim to privacy), but are primarily interpersonal, held for others as much as for oneself. This means both that rights which may justifiably be claimed instantiate a generalisable norm, and that the unique personal identity which may legitimately be developed is an identity for others (see Chapter 6). Personal rights are held within an overarching structure of interpersonal responsibility and accountability, such that

> the freedom of consciousness [is conceived] to be oriented toward other persons from the outset, so that it is not unrestricted liberty of action, but mutual confirmation, that marks one as morally autonomous.[27]

There are rights to self-determination but, understood as a dialogical and therefore ex-centric process, this already involves the orientation of others towards one in communication through intersubjective structures of co-intention. Others do not constitute a limit to self-determination and personal freedom so much as their necessary coordinates and constituents. In the democratic process (as in personal ethics) the identities, needs and interests of others, as well as their intention of one in communication, inform personal identity, consciousness, autonomy and self-realisation.

The 'inner nature' which one is trying to realise in autonomous acts of self-realisation is constituted through intersubjective processes, and is therefore intimately linked to the reality of others. One's identity and intention of oneself is tied to those of others. The internal content and nature of a person is a sedimentation of interpersonal communication. Each person is, however, unique and therefore has a unique conglomeration of needs to be satisfied in the pursuit of self-fulfilment and realisation. Yet what we regard as our needs are never purely private. Each culture and society has a specific interpretation of what counts as a need (as opposed to, say, a luxury) which is appropriated by individuals through the same socialisation processes through which they receive their specific identities. The socially relative interpretation of need therefore enters the very structure of personal identity and consciousness to become one's own. The processes of public communication mediate to us the identities and need interpretations of others in ossified form (of a generalised other, it could be said). A personal need, identity or act of autonomous self-realisation is rational only if it is capable of validation (can be shown to be generalisable) through expli-cation in a dialogue with others in this public realm. Personal identity and acts of autonomy and self-realisation therefore have to re-enter this public domain, which is structured by the reality, co-intentions and need interpretations of others. Duty and obligation to others therefore enter into the very structure of personal autonomy. A person does not therefore become free by realising some relationally pure inner essence (for there is no such thing), but by being a subject – and therefore autonomously engaged – in those processes in which one's own and others' needs are interpreted and formed.[28] Personal freedom is consequently inseparable from the political conditions which regulate the public processes of communication.

The rights of the person therefore have to be formulated in terms of rights to communication. In the following chapter I shall suggest that access to public communication depends on the provision of equal opportunity (through educational strategies and/or the provision of appropriate mediating forms which keep the complexity differential between persons and social structures within critical limits) and the securing of institutional openness. Freedom is the right to ex-centric communication, to be orientated on oneself through others and on others through self-centring, to participate in the democratic process. Crucial to such participation is the internal moment of reflection (see Chapter 4) in which others' communication is critically reflected upon (Chapter 6) and otherwise processed (matched with existing information) and, as a result, one's understanding, interpretation of need, etc. may be transformed. In this passive moment of communication there is a critical reflection on one's own and others' communication, the result of which may be a transformation in one's own and/or – as a result of subsequent self-communication – others' understanding. The socio-political structures which enable and mediate public questioning must also respect and preserve the free space–time necessary for reflection free from coercion. There is consequently a proper place for privacy which is to be protected from invalid incursions by others and by the state.

Moreover, the right to privacy clearly has a material aspect. The uniqueness of a personal identity is, in part, derived from the physical nature of personal existence – being a body, a bounded physical space. To be sure, this space is a punctuation between 'self' and world and not an asocial, incommunicative sphere, but it is none the less always *this* person's space. Despite its ex-centric openness to and for others, it never ceases to be the space of a particular person to, for, with and 'in' others. It is not a private space, in the sense that others are deprived of its content and meaning, but a personal space, the informative content of which may be shared with others in communication and exchange and which is only personally lived in and occupied by one person. Access is restricted by its nature as personal, centred and thereby structured space, which is the basis of its sharing.

There is consequently a limitation on forms of communication which intend a complete externalisation of the personal centre so the person becomes a part of an institution or the bearer of another's desires. The particular interest of people in their own bodies and bounded personal space is retained in dialogue, not as an exclusive right of proprietorship but as the autonomous need of a uniquely personal lived space.

This right does extend to the holding of private property, although not to an unrestricted extent. Physical, personal space is centred on the body but need not be exclusively bodily. Personal living necessarily extends itself so that certain external objects become an intrinsic part of a lived personal identity which may, on the basis of this living relationship, be claimed to have a particular interest and significance for a person. This relationship and interest must, of course, be rationally justified with reference to the interests of others, so it is unlikely that full-scale consumerism and patterns of exclusive possession could be justified. What I am thinking of is the sort of living relationship which one person has with the material means of meaningful, secure and sustainable personal life with others: such things as an artificial limb, tools used to exercise a social role or to earn a just living wage, the possession of sufficient food or food sources, and adequate shelter and clothing. There is no justification here of the exclusive use of these personal possessions or of exclusivity of their use for personal benefit, but a recognition of a particular personal source of special interest in objects and their use within a justifiable personal life-style. Freedom is not a simple function of property, but neither is it entirely unrelated to the maintenance of special living relations with material objects and spaces.

The form and extent of personal property and of special relations with material objects is dependent upon socially institutionalised recognition, modes of distribution, etc. The suggestion I am making here is that the social recognition of autonomy requires the provision of some space (both physical and social) and time for the pursuit of personal life in an autonomous manner, protected from invalid incursion. Such independence and exclusivity are never complete, however, and are always to be limited by rational criteria of justice and the wider interests in the community.

9

Institutions

The necessity of stable social structures

The discussion in the preceding chapters concerning relations in the socio-political sphere led me to argue that the mark of a true society is openness. If the social codes of a society are genuinely open, then no person and no possible subject of discussion will be excluded from communication on arbitrary or non-rational grounds. As I have already indicated, however, such openness can never be total. To speak of a 'code' is already, in fact, to speak of structure and regulation, and therefore of some measure of closure; total openness, on the other hand, would imply a situation of complete indeterminacy, randomness and chaos. The fact that sustainable social life requires structures and institutions to carry the social code further implies that what is required is not so much an unlimited and unrestrained openness, but open institutions or – to phrase it another way – institutionalised openness. The institutions of a true society are to be open in two ways. First, they are to ensure the widest participation of all – both inside and outside the society – in so far as they genuinely have an interest in it. This, of course, happens in a changing historical situation in which what counts as a justifiable claim and interest – and therefore the matrix of persons relevant to the discussion of what is good, true, and right in particular cases – will also be constantly changing; second, the institutions are to keep the society open to a radically new future in the perspective of which some aspects, or even the whole, of the society and its institutions may be found questionable and judged to be a negation of the liberation promised in this future. In both these senses, then, the openness required of institutions is towards their own transformation. Institutionalisation, however, involves a certain rigidity in relations – closure rather than openness – and may be considered the societal equivalent of the structured (and therefore partial) openness which was the mark of an enduring, undistorted personal identity.

When institutions over-rigidify (usually by becoming procedurally bureaucratic), they limit participation and freedom by reproducing themselves, by enforcing stereotypical interactions or by encoding some kind of particular power relationship and the dominance of certain interests over others. This represents a distortion of the proper function and orientation of institutions as they become self-legitimating and idolatrous. This tendency is so frequently realised, however, that there is now a deep-rooted suspicion that it is inevitable and a part of the very nature of institutions. In this view institutions seem to contain the exact antinomy to the requirements of openness in interaction and of the needs of the individual for freedom. The suggestion that institutions, openness and autonomous individuals may somehow coincide seems, on the face of it, to be political naivety. For institutions seem, from this perspective, to be either necessary evils or symbols of the inevitable order which chains personal freedom in society. On the contrary, I will argue that institutions are necessary for the social order of life within which legitimate claims are to be met and in which an autonomous personal identity may be lived.

Institutions are ossifications of recurring relations, socially routinised patterns of intercommunication. Even in a one-to-one relation a third term is introduced, independent of either of the partners, as a centre of their relation which endures through time and enables a certain routinisation to occur. This routinisation does not represent an inauthenticity for the partners in the relation, but a previously achieved mutuality of understanding which becomes a background norm for further interaction as the 'objective (or objectified) spirit' of their communication.[1] These people do not have to establish the codification of their relationship prior to each and every contact: this may be assumed on the basis of their history together (though this does not exclude the possibility of future recodification), and this history, as well as determining (weak sense) future relation, may itself be what draws them into further contact. One important effect of institutionalisation of a relation is that it effectively expands the social space and time within it. This present relation may, for instance, deepen on the basis of a (for now) secure routine basis and background. Or, if this is a relation of a more routine type (say, customer and shopkeeper), then instant institutionalisation makes it possible to conduct a plurality of such interactions in a short compass of time, since time is not wasted in explicitly establishing a mutuality of understanding by going through all the procedures for establishing each party's expectations from scratch and then testing them through explication. Institutionalisation simultaneously facilitates the achievement of depth in a relation and breadth in the number of relations conducted within a given period of time. These two aspects are, of course, linked. The complete routinisation of some of our relations and the partial routinisation of our more significant ones give us more space and time for a further expansion of relations, either in quantity or quality.

Furthermore, a mutuality of understanding and, in particular, the formal reciprocity of an undistorted relationship are sustainable only when the reciprocally expected expectations and understood understandings become institutionalised. And it is only in so far as the relation becomes institutionalised in this way that the partners may find it, and so also find one another, dependable. As I have already indicated in Chapter 4, a genuine relation requires and generates a 'law' of interaction which structures the expectations the partners have of themselves, the relation and each other. In other words, the relation achieves an institutional form, which restricts the range of possibilities of communication, relation and identity in appropriate ways. This constraining of the openness of the relation within a structure does not restrict but actually facilitates (structures) dialogue by reducing the infinite complexity which would occur with *total* openness. But if this institution or law is to remain dialogical, it cannot become a closed and permanent norm of interaction and may not be pressed on to other relations inappropriately. If it is to remain a means for structuring dialogue, then it has to remain open to resistance, to the incorporation of new interests and interested parties, and so to its own transformation if necessary. In addition to the particular institutionalisation which may occur between two partners, there are also the codes regulating communication and relation in the wider social context which help determine expectations and understanding and restrict the range of valid possibilities of communication and relation.

The partial routinisation of relations which lends them an element of predictability is the reciprocal requirement for the living of stable and dependable personal identities. For it is only through an intersubjective code of, for the time being, fixed and previously coordinated meanings and cognitive contents that a (partially) unique and autonomous subject, or person, may live.

Just as persons are sedimented from a significant history of relations, the institutionalised and habitualised aspects of which are decisive, institutions are themselves the ossifications of persons' communication. A personal identity is maintained and structured through the 'memory' of a history of being addressed by and responding to significant others. This represents, for the person, a certain institutionalisation of self-communication into a stable structure – his or her spirit of communication or personal identity.[2] Similarly, a social structure represents the ossification and institutionalisation of a shared history of communication into a stable form. Social structures (organised networks of institutions or institutionalised communication) contain institutionalised means, substructures, in which a communal 'memory' of its interpreted past, its meaning and its identity is embedded and through which the way people behave within its ambit is regulated and routinised (e.g. through ritual, written formulae such as rules and regulations, less formal conceptions of professional conduct, or narrative). Through these 'memory' structures, the particular organisation achieves an 'objective' and enduring form in social life. In both personal and communal institutionalisation, the contents of experience are 'objectified' in formularised codes. This turns the original experiences into a generalised 'memory'. This allows two things to happen. First, the person who or community which had the original experience may employ the code in diverse situations removed from the original one. Second, the code may be extended to incorporate and be used by others. In other words, institutions traditionalise communication and so make its codification pattern transmittable in social space–time – to other people and to other situations.[3] This is true of individuals as well as of societies for, on the basis of a significant communication history, a person's communication becomes traditionalised, and this enables a personal identity to endure through different communication contexts – for one's individual spirit to achieve a structured form.

The incorporation of persons into social institutions which regulate meaning and value must be understood as a necessary condition for meaningful communication; it does not, then, run counter to personal freedom or subjectivity in communication. For institutions are intersubjective co-intendings in stable structure. They link the consciousness of individuals together via networks of intersubjectively valid (i.e. 'objective') meaning. As meaning tends toward a universal consistency there is also a tendency of social institutions to interlock, so producing a more or less continuous universe of meaning: a social 'world'.[4] Life in such a determinate social 'world' depends upon an extended mutuality of understanding in which the norms or codes of interaction which regulate public meaning and value are commonly held. Subjective meaning is always personal, but it can never be completely private. Meaning is not entirely particular to an individual, but shared; it therefore requires institutional form. We can interpret our own experience (and therefore, in a real sense, only have the experience), communicate with others and interpret their communication only on the basis of a shared communication code, or meaning-structure. Institutions of this kind, which legislate and regulate public meaning and value, are essential, then, to personal life – which in turn requires the movement beyond oneself to the reality of others as one adapts oneself to their reality in the process of seeking a mutuality of understanding (which may or may not be distorted).[5]

Institutions provide an 'objective' (intersubjective) framework of co-intention which yields socially binding norms for communication. It is institutions which legislate what counts as a legitimate need and which therefore also regulate the chances of having it satisfied and where, when and how it will count as valid as they coordinate interests within a given society. They also legislate where, when and how it is valid for people to occupy social space–time. Institutions enter individual consciousness as structures of meaning which define and encode the contents of consciousness and cognition. This internalisation of socially valid norms and codes facilitates social interaction, which may only take place around such norms and codes. On the other hand, institutions do not simply facilitate interaction around public norms for, considered from another aspect, they may be considered ossifications of communication which originally generated such a norm. It is impossible to say whether norm or institution came first – they are reciprocally determining realities. Institutions are a fact and a necessity of personal and social existence, having both, on the one hand, conservative and coercive elements and, on the other, open, responsive and adaptable ones. They have an inbuilt tendency to resist 'deviant' communication in the interests of normative continuity whilst, at the same time, being open to historical transformation. In particular, they exist in the tension between personal and communal interests. All that is to say that institutions are necessary but insufficient and problematic conditions for the stabilisation of undistorted communication.

Institutional openness
I have so far tried to establish the necessity of institutions for personal existence by arguing that they are the stabilised reciprocity and public form of life upon which the autonomy of personhood depends.

Personhood is not served by any old reciprocity, however, but only by its undistorted variety; therefore persons' interest in institutionalisation will not be equally served by just any institution at any time. Personhood requires open institutions or, to be more precise, institutions which are not entirely closed. Absolute or total institutions cease to be facilitators of dialogue; they become idolatrous barriers to it, facilitating an extended monologue in which reciprocity and co-intention are structured in distorted ways (i.e. there is an absence of *formal* reciprocity).

Closure

In the language of communication, sin should be understood in terms of the absence of genuine communication. As I previously indicated in the discussion of interpersonal relations, this might either involve over- or underexpansion. Since the latter is usually coerced by and reflects the former, I shall concentrate my attention on overexpansion. In personal terms, overexpansion denotes the absolutising of an individual's space, time and value so that meaning and value are found only in relation or with reference to him or herself. This represents an individual's attempt to be a universal, to locate faith, hope and meaning entirely in the 'self'. Properly understood, however, the structure and identity of a person is limited, particular and open. We are blessed in the limitation and particularity of our individual natures and identities but, since personal being is ex-centric, we can only find real security by opening ourselves to God and others. Paradoxically, we lose ourselves if we try to bury our love, trust and hope and find meaning in ourselves alone – if we close ourselves off from God and others. Conversely, we acquire a sense of security when our unique beings and identities are trusted, loved, and so sustained, from afar – when God and others have faith in us. We can neither find meaning nor the right order of our being and identity on our own, but only through dialogue with God and others. For individual persons and human being as such are incomplete and insecure in themselves. The basis of their reality is found only through their open movement towards God and others. The basic sin is to lay our search for meaning to rest prematurely; to refer the finite only to itself and idolise it as infinite. 'Nurtured in insecurity, sin's motivation is to secure, to anchor human being in a cosmos projected by itself, a creation of its own act of meaning or intentionality.'[6]

Sin, for an individual, is a distorted way of intending oneself, others and the world in communication which imbues one's own limited being, one's personal space and time, with universal meaning. Absolutising one's individual life closes one off from others – at least in their otherness – and so closes down any possibility of dialogue. Precisely the same distortion may occur corporately in a communal structure of intention when space and time, as they are patterned in a particular institution or network of institutions, are absolutised. Clearly, if there is no space or time available apart from the regulation of space and time in this particular institutional network, then meaning can only be found in or with reference to it.

It is doubtful whether this could ever be achieved in any complete way, but the attempt can be observed in the operation of all totalitarian (again, the totalitarianism rarely has no gaps) societies in which a political order attempts to suppress all voluntary associations which are not directly controlled by the state. The danger is that these associations pattern the distribution of communication in a different way and thereby institutional-ise alternative meaning and value which might threaten the security of state institutions. In a totalitarian society, people are totally subject to the state institutions which contain the meaning of their existence; personal identity is then reducible to membership of and location in them – the role, meaning and value one is ascribed by them. Similarly, anything or anyone who is outside the sphere of their influence, determination and regulation will be regarded either as meaningless or as posing the threat of disorder (for instance the official attitude to religion in the Soviet Union). So the recognition of those outside the sphere of an absolute social structure – either those outside the society altogether or those 'outcast' within it – is severely restricted. This makes their admittance to and participation in the normal processes of communication problematic. Both external and internal communication are restricted where they might contain alterna-tive information and social codes which might have socially critical implications. This is, then, the closed communication context of a society turned in upon itself. The institutionalised 'memory' of the society will be structured according to the needs of the state to maintain itself. The past history of this particular means of ordering social life will be recalled, glorified and maintained. For the future must repeat the past and present, since anything else is perceived as threatening the loss of meaning and order.

Totalitarian societies also make absolute demands on the personal fidelity of their members and tend to equate personal with institutional meaning. In other words, there is a tendency not to recognise anything truly personal. Autonomy and heteronomy then become indistinguishable as personal meaning is completely externalised and objectified in static institutional structures, effectively emptying the personal of any independent meaning, space or time. Institutions are necessary for the manufacture of personal, subjective meaning which, as I have previously argued, always has a public referent and is intersubjectively secured (and so attains a measure of 'objectivity'). In totalitarian institutions, however, subjective meaning is overrun and squeezed out by objectivity: only what is public, and therefore already coordinated, is recognised as valid. Because the personal, private and subjective are squeezed out of public life, the 'objective', social 'world' ceases really to be a process of intersubjectivity. Since members of a totalitarian society are restrained from manufacturing and communicating information derived from their unique identities, social location and conglomeration of interests, they are unable to inform social processes and structures. They therefore become 'subjects' of an objective, imposed process of life; or, rather, they become subject to this form of life, and so are merely points of reception of an objective social process, social objects subject to the manipulation of an extended monologue. They therefore cease to be subjects in any meaningful sense of the term, since autonomy in communication has been lost.

Liberalism rightly opposes the heteronomy and totalitarian drift of institutions with the rights of the individual – or, rather, with the rights of individuals banded together to make or undo institutions. In conceiving of individuals as isolated and as, in principle, socially abstract (i.e. ontologically and logically prior to institutions), however, liberalism fails to comprehend the true nature either of persons or institutions. In a rather odd way, given its commitment against counter-individual structures, it is incapacitated from taking totalitarian institutions seriously enough because it fails to see them as essential and informative aspects of personal being.[7] It is only by comprehending the formative coincidence of persons and institutions that the threat of distorted, closed institutions for personal being can be adequately gauged. Essential to this view is an understanding of institutions as properly open and of their closure as distortion.

Openness in time and space

A preliminary approximation to such an understanding can be derived from the necessity of social, no less than biological, structures to adapt to environmental changes. If a society seeks to maintain itself through static and monological institutions, it threatens the basis of institutionalised social structure as well as that of personal being. Total institutions and a totalitarian state represent a distortion of both personhood and institutional form in which the endurance of both is put at risk.

The person's endurance is immediately at risk because vital elements of communicative autonomy are lacking where the centre of 'personal' life is in institutions rather than in persons themselves. The stabilised structure of co-intending in this instance makes endurance possible only as a social atom and not as a person. The endurance of the social form, on the other hand, is put at risk since it is so rigid that it will be unable to respond to changes in its internal or external communication contexts which push it beyond critical limits. Changes in historical circumstance which threaten the mode of social reproduction (e.g. technological innovation, actual or threatened invasion, pollution, population explosion, unforeseen effects of policy) can only be met with resistance or collapse if they require a different quality in the encoding of relations or value-structure. Because the structure is geared to its own reduplication into the future, it is unable to adapt itself to a different future, to endure through evolutionary innovation. The deployment of totalitarian institutions therefore places the survival of the society, as well as the survival of personal life and being, at risk.

Institutions may therefore be said to have an interest in their own adaptation and transformation, since that may be necessary to ensure their survival. So, paradoxically, institutions actually endure through a certain openness to change. That which is enduring in and distinctive of a social form is not some static essence, but that which functions as a vehicle for adaptation and innovation in the light of changed conditions of internal or external communication. That which gives continuity, identity and stability is also that which enables transformation, adaptation and change, which keeps the institution open and fluid enough to accommodate itself to changed circumstances.[8] The key social codes of an open society may endure as new forms of transmitting it are adopted through adapted or new institutions. Through an adaptation to new conditions, a new or newly understood determinate situation, the code may itself undergo transform-ation. Attempts will be made to predict the implications of adaptive innovation and thereby to select an appropriate future, on the basis of the understood meaning of the corporate past. This process of selectivity and transformation will itself have institutional form appropriate to prevailing social codification. This is where social continuity is evident: in the structure of meaning, 'remembering' and interpreting the significant past and selecting or expecting a future. It is possible, on this basis, to co-intend the past and innovative present, along with new expectations of the future, within an historically continuous framework of meaning. The innovative present then appears to be a more gentle, natural evolution under the same social code.[9]

What is necessary to meet crises in the current mode of social reproduction is clearly an openness in time. Social innovation or transformation, by definition, represents the incorporation of new information into social codes, structures and institutions – that is, communication content which has not previously been stabilised in social institutions. It would therefore also seem to involve some openness with regard to social space as well as time, since a prime source for such information will be those previously excluded from communication under institutionalised norms (either *in toto* – e.g. members of other societies – or in particular spheres – e.g. socially excluded groups within a society) which may now be extended to them. New and innovative communication content can only be thematised through dialogue, facilitated by institutions open to the perception of new content – that is, to what is other. That which was previously, at the most, only latently available in institutionalised communication structures now becomes informative for them as it transforms these institutions. What this requires is an institutional framework through which dialogue may take place and the innovative potential of excluded persons and groups tapped.[10]

There is an implicit link here between the freedom of communication (and therefore of persons) within a society and the transformative potential of a social form. This is another way of expressing the reciprocal determinacy of institutionalised intersubjectivity and subjectivity. Social codes and institutions which regulate relations also codify the consciousness and communication of persons, determining both their form and content. On the other hand, institutions are ossifications of interpersonal communication and are therefore liable to transformation through the exercise of freedom by persons in communication. Institutions, except in limited cases of internal revolution and deviance, will coincide with appropriate patterns of concrete intersubjectivity. Both are structured around the same code or meaning-structure and share a common spirit, the one 'objective', the other 'subjective'. This 'common spirit' is something like a third term, an ideal above its concrete incarnations in social life-forms (persons and institutions). This provides something like a universal nexus of meaning against which both the concrete social forms and their transformations may be legitimated.

Institutions as anticipatory

This third term is at a higher level than the social code patterning personal and institutionalised social life in any determinate situation. The determinate social code approximates to this third term, which functions something like an ideal regulating the formation and transformation of determinate codes. This idealised form of social life will be known more in its effects than as an explicit, conceptualisable entity. It makes sense to regard the transformation of a determinate social code as guided by an idealised understanding of the inner meaning of the code – and it is this 'inner meaning' which (though differently conceived and incarnated) is understood to endure through successive transformations and which gives a society a sense of its own evolution and continuity. The suggestion is that, in periods of crisis when the need for transformation is understood, the determinate code will be scrutinised as an approximation to a higher ideal of intersubjectivity so that elements which might hinder successful adaptation may be identified and omitted in the future.

Institutions may be open to transformation only if they are understood to have no *permanent* validity in their present, concrete form; to be approximations to some higher ideal of social life rather than an absolute and eternally valid realisation of it. This being so, it is not changes in the social context which press them towards transformation, but this acknowledgement of the distance between ideal and reality itself – although this is undoubtedly more common when social crises make people aware of the limitations of present institutions. The proper function of institutions is to be partially open to transformation by the ideal which they incarnate. The meaning of an institution is to be found by looking beyond its present actuality and referring it to its legitimating ground: an ideal of social life which functions as a quasi-religious basis both for the present form of the institution and for any subsequent transformation. Institutions may become idolatrous but, in doing so, they distort their function for maintaining their quasi-religious basis. The problem of idolatry does not disappear, of course, but is rather compounded with the appearance of quasi-religious universals which may themselves incorporate a claim to be absolute and universal in a strict sense, to be the supreme repository of all meaning. In fact, these 'ideals' of social life may be distorted – in which case they will inform distorted structures of individual and corporate life – and in so far as they claim universal validity, they become idols.

The Church and anticipatory institutions
Openness to God and the kingdom

The theological position I have adopted throughout this book has been primarily informed by the understanding that Christian faith is a new way of being with and responsible to God and others. Individually, this issues in a transformed spirit of communication and structure of personal being; communally, it issues in transformed corporate structures and institutions of intersubjectivity. It issues, in other words, in transformed ways of corporately sharing and reciprocating the intention of one another as co-subjects. The institutions of this transformed community (Church) in any particular time and place will be a determinate incarnation of the community's regulative ideal for social life – the kingdom of God and the presence of Christ. The full realisation of these realities is understood to be eschatological, and therefore always beyond the limits of human agency alone. Christian commitment and identity, including that of the Church, will therefore be iconoclastic – permanently resistant to the idolisation of any and all social realities. This includes, in the final analysis, the kingdom itself. For it is God and not the kingdom who is the supreme and absolute value; the kingdom's value is derived from God's presence in and rule over it.

So the Church does not seek to transform only the concretely institutionalised forms of its own regulative ideal, but those of the wider community too (this commitment does not involve an imperialistic attitude if it is practised dialogically), and to do so not just from time to time but permanently. Furthermore, the distinctive aspect of all of this is that the Church recognises that its ideal – in itself and not just its present understanding of it – is not absolute and ultimate, but something which, even under the conditions of its full realisation, remains a creaturely reality which is therefore limited and directed and orientated above and beyond itself. The distinctive feature of the Church is not so much that its regulative ideal is claimed to have 'objective' reality, but that this claim is made in such a way as to imply the existence of a reality higher than this ideal, which is therefore subject to it. This ideal is itself open to question, on the basis not of yet another higher ideal as such, but of the fallibility of human understanding of any ideal and, ultimately, on the basis of God's existence above and beyond both human conception and the reality of the kingdom.

The determinate institutionalised forms which the Church has taken, and the socio-political institutions it has considered appropriate, have varied immensely with time and place and with the social location of particular churches and their members. These variations clearly represent changes in the Church's determinate social code. But they also indicate changes, differences and disagreements in the understanding of the kingdom in response to changes in the social, political, economic, cultural and intellectual situation or the perception of further direct revelation.

The distinctive feature of the Church, then, is that it is structured through a vertical openness to God's Word through the organisational energies of the Holy Spirit. Through this open orientation on God it is secondarily orientated on a future which it understands to involve the transformation (full redemption) of all reality, including its presently functioning 'ideal'. That is to say that it is aware of its own sin, both in its determinate institutions and in the form of its self-understanding ('ideal' code) to which it seeks institutional approximation. In short, the Church comprehends both its present, concrete reality, and its formative idealised understanding of itself, as anticipatory and approximate – as not yet fully realised – and therefore as requiring further information and transformation; and, in addition, it comprehends all creaturely existence as being under the primary and prevenient reality of God.

This means that to judge the legitimacy of ecclesiastical or socio-political institutions, or their proposed transformation, against the criteria set by Christian faith is to refer them to an ultimate form of social life, the code of which is not yet known except in anticipatory form (as well as referring all to the reality of God above and beyond even the actuality of this form of life). It therefore always remains possible that the coded form of that anticipation may be transformed itself. This may be the result either of changes in the determinate situation which restructure consciousness, or of new information yielded through God's communication. In affirming a really transcendent referent for meaning and value there is an inbuilt basis for both transformation and for deciding what is legitimate. Because, for example, a structure of personhood is not ultimately grounded in a determinate social code, its specific institutions or even its transcendent 'ideal' (at best a human approximation to the kingdom code), but in a reality transcending all of these, there are personal needs and rights which are not reducible to the specific reality of the situation and which must therefore be met in it if its institutional structures are to be judged legitimate.[11] It is only by breaking the closed circle of self-reference, by referring the social realities of a situation and its ideals to something really other, that the meaning and value of personal and social existence may be understood as enduring and universal, independent of the determinate form they take here and now. Ultimately, this is possible only by referring these realities to the being and reality of God.

The institutions of the Church are radically open – to God and the eschatological kingdom and to the realities of the determining situation (so redemption and the social situation co-determine the Church). But this openness to transformation – on account both of its own institutional structure and that of the wider social context – does not mean that these present realities are meaningless and valueless. Present reality may – indeed, must – be affirmed in its integrity as both meaningful and valuable, but not in an unrestricted, ultimate or absolute way. Present ecclesial and social realities are to be considered in the perspective of God and the coming kingdom and thereby found meaningful, valuable and legitimate in so far as they anticipate the kingdom and are open to the reality of God. The determinate is affirmed in the presence of God – and so is affirmed in a limited way. We may take the present realities of Church and society seriously as *pen*ultimate because they are treated this way in God's redemptive dialogue with creation. It is a requirement of human life under the impact of redemption that it takes embodied (corporate) form as appropriate, necessary and possible in a particular, concrete situation. The Church is to take determinate form not just because nothing more is possible, but because that is the only way in which the Church can meaningfully communicate its unique information and work towards the redemption of the society within which it finds itself. The determinacy of the Church is the prime means by which redemption is made available to and Christ made present in a particular situation. The Church can only assist the transformation of the world if it is also informed and determined by it. This double determinacy is necessary, given that redemption is a process which takes the independent reality of creation seriously – which takes dialogical form.

The appropriateness of ecclesial institutions to an anticipation of the kingdom in the here and now gives the different forms of the Church continuity with each other and allows Church as such to endure across different times and places and in different social locations. The redeemed form of intersubjectivity will additionally seek expansion into the wider situation as the impact of redemption informs the socio-political commitment of the Church.

Institutions of redemptive community

Institutions structure a society or community and so give it an identity and carry this across different times, places and social locations. Through the community's institutions, therefore, it may endure and have continuity through changing circumstances.

The form of endurance appropriate to the Church depends, in particular, upon the institutionalised mode of 'remembering' its past and especially its founding, originating events surrounding the person of Christ. Christ universalised redemption by making its actuality independent of the space and time bounded by the social, racial and national reality of Israel. In other words, with Christ redemption becomes unrestricted as to time, place, society, nation or race. The practice of remembering, interpreting and perpetuating Christ, in appropriate ways, as a norm for and in Christian community ossifies into institutionalised forms of life which may make Christ, and therefore the redeemed pattern of intersubjectivity, present anywhere and at any time.[12] Interpretation, perpetuation and remembrance require a communication code appropriate to their content. For the Church that code is *kerygma* and its content Gospel, the two being mutually determining. As appropriate linguistic carriers of Christ's reality and presence they have a normative status for the Church. They do not simply encode the events of Christ's life and ministry (as well as other revelatory and salvific events) as historical facts, of course, but do so alongside the meaning which this story is perceived to have in the light of the community's experience of salvation as that is understood in the present.[13]

Given my argument up to this point concerning the social determinacy of cognition and consciousness – the way in which a determinate social code regulates and structures meaning and value, and therefore also public recognition and exchange – it should be clear that the institutions, codes, interpretation and understanding of the realities of God, Christ, kingdom and Church will take determinate form. The Church's ultimate orientation is towards God and the reality of human life united with God in the kingdom (a community in which the conditions of dialogue are fully met and universally distributed). It therefore has to take its bearings from this future, eschatological, divine reality as it is made present within the institutional structures of the Church. But the mode of this making present in the institutionalised structure and communication of the Church will be socially determinate.

Church, however, is a community which in any time, place or social location apprehends both itself and its social context as set within a more ultimate communication context: interaction with God. That does not annihilate the value, significance, meaning and reality of the determinate social 'world' in which the Church finds itself; but it does relativise it, and also bring to it cognitive content and communication content which would otherwise be unavailable. The latter are made available here and now only in determinate form, of course, but they may thus attain publicly recognisable meaning. The Church cannot step out of its time and place into a space which is solely determined by its relation with, or the pure presence of, God, for the simple reason that no such place exists: God's interaction with and presence in the world are mediated through determinate forms of social life. Neither can the Church pretend to be determined only by the kingdom, since that remains a permanently future reality. Indeed, the task of the Church is to bring its situation into closer approximation to and anticipation of the kingdom; to discern the concrete ways in which this society may be drawn towards a future with God, to see how the kingdom may become *this* society's future. The future will therefore be a *transformation*, rather than an annihilation of present social conditions. In transformation something of the original form is retained, and its reality makes some difference to the resulting transform.

It is in this externally directed and eschatologically orientated mission towards the redemption of its situation that the Church achieves its identity. If, however, the Church is to aid the emancipation of present conditions in anticipation of the kingdom, then it clearly has to maintain a specific identity as a community which can generate and recognise 'new' information. As 'new', the information is not a property of the general situation which could have been known and understood in this way without this specific community which is gathered around its corporate recognition, institutionally secured. As information, however, the Church's communication and understanding will have to take a determinate form. In fact, for communication to be informative it really requires both properties: to be 'new', in the sense of previously uncoordinated or unrecognised and simultaneously recognisable, meaningful, and so on so that it may now enter structures of public or personal meaning and be encoded and coordinated with previous contents.

In order for the presence of Christ and the reality of God's creative–redemptive activity to be a co-determinant of the Church's communication and structure and of its understanding of itself, its situation and the future – in order, in other words, for the Church to have resources for its own and society's transformation – it will have to find institutional means of re-presenting the reality of Christ and redemption. An indispensable means for achieving this will be the institutionally secured attending to scripture and Christian tradition – primary resources of the Christian story around which the community gathers – along with their institutionalised means for their reinterpretation (all taking determinate form). The point of this is not simply to secure institutionally the internal structure of the Church, but to make available information which has the potential to transform the empirical Church and its wider social 'world'. In other words, it is the re-presentation of God's redemptive communication both to the Church and to society as a whole. It therefore involves not only internal, but external, communication. This is the first of three types of communication which must be institutionally secured in the Church, and may be termed proclamation.[14] This is primarily an interpretative activity involving the communication of information derived from an apprehension of God's communication in and of the codification of relations under the conditions of redemption. It is, then, cognitive content derived from the context of communication with God. New understandings of Church and world which are derived from anticipatory incorporation into the kingdom (i.e. perceiving the realities of Church and society in the context of redemption) may also be re-presented and reinterpreted through symbolic enactment and communication – usually termed sacrament. Clearly, if the Church is to assist in the transformation of individuals and social structures towards their redemption, then this commitment to the emancipation of personal and social conditions which distort communication, identity, community and relation requires its engagement in a practice towards this end. That means engaging in therapeutic activity which opens hardened and closed structures of relation and identity – having, in other words, pastoral, ethical, social and political commitments and objectives within the present situation.

Christ's presence, and God's redemptive communication more generally, structures relations anew. Church is a unique form of intersubjectivity which takes determinate form through institutional means of re-presenting Christ's reality in history and revisioning the future redemption of life which is promised and hoped for in Him. The institutions which stabilise the means for re-presenting Christ and the form of social life which takes place under the impact of His redemptive presence must be appropriate not only to the structure of redemptive community but to the situation – they must enable an effective social and material incarnation of redemption, the embodiment of Christ. For that reason they are co-determined by the presence of Christ and the activity of the Holy Spirit on the one hand, and the social and material realities of the situation on the other. Further, because Church is the social structure which embodies Christ's presence, there is an internal pressure in its own institutions towards the future (as well as to a movement beyond its own borders in order to universalise the redeemed form of intersubjectivity), since Christ's rule (the codification of relations in conformity to Him), and therefore His full reality, lie in the future reality of the kingdom. His presence in the Church is therefore promissory, pointing towards a future fulfilment.

All Church institutions and institutionalised ways of being the Church are questionable, given both their determinacy and their orientation towards a future which is eschatological (and which therefore overreaches any possible achievement this side of the eschaton) and universal. The Church is orientated towards a universalisation of the conditions of genuine communication and community (unrestricted truth, freedom and justice). Its mission is therefore to spread these conditions through space (both physical and social) and time; a task which, undertaken in openness to God, requires the transformation of all social structures, including its own. The transformation of the Church will be necessary in all this, not least in the light of the ways in which its own institutions inhibit the universal extension of genuine communication and community.

For all these reasons, it is intrinsic to the nature of the Church to resist the permanent and static stabilisation and over-rigidification of its institutions. Given that this is part of what Church means, this permanent iconoclasm must achieve institutionalised form. At the very least, this must mean, first, the institutionalisation of self-criticism, which will require internal openness in communication so that alternative interpretations, applications and explorations of Christ's presence may be taken up and discussed. Second, it will require an external openness to the validity of other, possibly critical, modes of personal and social life.

In the socio-political sphere the Church will be committed to that same institutionalised openness which it attempts to achieve within its own structures. Taking up the position I came to in the previous chapter, this means securing universal participation in the processes of democratic will-formation. It means, in other words, the institutionalisation of structures of general rationality so that the norms of political interaction are orientated towards an undistorted mutuality of understanding (conformation to Christ) among those potentially affected (which, in the purview of the kingdom, is all human persons). To put it more simply, it means an orientation towards freedom and justice in socio-political structures. Clearly this requires institutionalised means whereby anyone may question any norm of interaction – including the institutions which facilitate such questioning themselves. For, in view of the eschatological and universal nature of the kingdom, openness must be unrestricted. That must be the case, since any constraints on participation in the formation and questioning of norms, objectives and institutions will restrain the distribution of full communication rights from being universal. That restriction will ensure that at some points the mutuality of understanding will be unfree, less than complete, and so distorted.

What is necessary in the present, so far as the Church's socio-political commitment is concerned, is that the form of community or co-intention proper to redemption – and, in particular, the reciprocally held expectation that norms and interests will be capable of justification and validation through explication – be stabilised and secured in institutional structures appropriate to (i.e. within the limits of) the determinate situation (the development and mode of productive forces, level of technology and knowledge, limitations due to other political priorities, etc.).

Law and Gospel

I have been arguing that Christian faith requires institutions, that the redemption of communication refers, at least in part, to the transform-ation of stable structures. Very close to the heart of Christian tradition, however, there seems to be a deep suspicion of stabilised, routinised communication or, as the tradition itself calls it, law. This has sometimes been interpreted in terms of an inherent opposition between the freedom of the Gospel and the bondage of laws (strict codes, norms or institutions) of interaction in which neither subjectivity (personal faith) nor intersubjectiv-ity (community of faith) may be authentic. The question therefore arises whether I have obscured the difference between Gospel and law by subsuming the former under legalistic categories. The answer to this charge is already implicit in the argument above but, because the combination of law and Gospel is a crucial issue for Christian faith and commitment, it deserves explicit answer. Furthermore, the general apprehension concern-ing institutions and, in particular, political commitment is informed from an individualistic misunderstanding of faith and redemption just as much as it is by the reservation proper to faith concerning law. The question therefore runs very much to the heart of my concerns, and for that reason alone should have some sort of answer.

I will not repeat here the arguments throughout the work which show human life in creation and redemption to be fundamentally social; neither would it be appropriate or possible to present the history of the debate over the proper relation of law and faith. Instead, I shall explicate my position regarding institutions arrived at above as it is relevant to this particular question.

First, however, it is necessary to clarify that traditional Christian condemnation or suspicion is directed towards legalism rather than towards law as such. Legalism represents a distortion of law through over-rigidification and closure (compare the discussion of institutional closure above) such that persons come to exist for the demands of the law (Mark 2:27f.), instead of the law incarnating a socially valid, stable structure of co-intentions through which a (relatively) undistorted person may be called into being and communication. Redemption may transform the content of law as currently institutionalised but, more importantly than that, it transforms the mode of having and using law, of being in institutions. The problem with law is not merely the spirit which it encodes but the spirit through which it is appropriated, the two tending to be reciprocally related. The legalistic closure, or idolisation, of institutionalised means of interaction is a distortion of law's proper spirit which leads automatically to distorted codification of relations – both with God and others.

When fulfilment of the letter of the law (i.e. complete conformity to the institutionalised code: as in, say, complete identification with a social role and the value and meaning afforded one by the institution) is understood as the sole means and requirement of redemption, there is a change in self-understanding towards either guilt or self-righteousness, both of which tend to isolate one from change and others. In both cases, there is an idolisation of the particular law involved in which the proper distance between the person and the institution is breached. The individual externalises, objectifies and alienates value, meaning and responsibility, accepting only that which is encoded within a particular institution or network of institutions. This may also enable the person to hide behind the requirements of the 'law' in whatever spheres of life it regulates, so abdicating personal responsibility in them.

In the case of guilt, the inability to meet the demands of the law (to behave in the set way, conforming to institutionalised norms) is internalised, becoming incapacitating and restricting through self-blame or the blame of others. The law isolates the guilt-ridden with their own insufficient potentialities, from any meaningful hope and from the possibility of external assistance from God or others – since this is irrelevant for the individualising task of obedience to the law. Legalistic frameworks of interaction mark the 'guilty' as unfit for decent society. In the transforming cognitions of the Gospel, however, the 'guilty' are actually in a better position than the self-righteous. Conscious of their own sin and incapacity, they are less resistant to the call to faith, for they have less to lose by abandoning all securities to rest on grace and faith alone. They already understand their inability to go it alone.

The self-righteous, by contrast, are conscious only of the ways in which they fulfil the law and not of their imperfections. They are resistant to becoming conscious of their need of grace, for their self-consciousness must first become that of sinners. Self-righteousness represents a belief in themselves and their own power (as well as in the absolute validity of the law, the demands of which they meet) – a belief, that is, in themselves rather than God. But the idol which functions as a religious substitute for God is not so much their belief in themselves as the medium of this belief, the law, legalistically understood. Legalism is the belief in the absolute validity of a law or network of laws, from whence comes the belief that satisfaction of the letter of the law will lead to justification before God and others. Self-righteousness is the belief that this condition is being met by oneself. It attempts to establish a claim on God by demanding justice on the basis of obedience, one's just deserts.

The paradigm of law in Christian tradition is the Torah. In the case of the Torah (and probably in the case of any comprehensive social and religious code), however, constant obedience to the letter of the law is humanly impossible, so the demand to fulfil its every requirement can only lead to retribution. God's hands are tied from delivering mercy and forgiveness in the face of an obstinate infatuation with one's own works as the contractual basis of justification.[15] The distortion of the relation with God undergoes a social refraction as the personality is entirely orientated upon a project of individual salvation in its own power, an orientation upon the contract with God in law rather than upon the needs of the neighbour. Such an orientation also tends to contrast one's own achievements with others' shortcomings in order to seek justification, and perhaps, too, in order to excuse one's own failure to fulfil the letter of the law which almost comes to consciousness.

The Gospel is the good news that liberates from the dead letter of legalism with the enlivening spirit of faith, hope and love. It relativises law by proclaiming salvation as the gracious forgiveness of sinners in its call to repent and believe. Justification is proclaimed by fidelity to God rather than to a code or to oneself as capable of fulfilling it. But this faith can be directed towards God *through* law; by liberating *from* law the Gospel also liberates *for* law, just as by being liberated from oneself one is freed and opened for God and others. The code of redeemed communication and subjectivity is a new way of being in the same world, primarily a new way of being in the world in, through, and with others – more properly described as a form of intersubjectivity or community which, as such, requires structure, and therefore institutionalised form.

Love and justice: personal and political codes

Under the impact of redemption, communal and societal life become properly structures of intersubjectivity – that is, they institutionally secure a communal pattern whereby all members of the community intend themselves, other members and everyone else as full subjects of communication: dialogue-partners in God's image. The spirit in which relations are organised in a dialogical manner, which seeks, intends and is committed to others as free, equal partners, as co-subjects, is usually called love in interpersonal contexts and justice in socio-political contexts. It is, however, the one spirit of faith, hope and love which structures and encodes love and justice in relationships. This makes the intention and recognition of all others as subjects of communication, whether in personal or socio-political contexts, a matter of routine. Both love and justice are concerned with meeting others' needs. Love tends to function through personal contact, whilst justice tends to operate through socio-political structures and to deal with people in greater numbers and/or with people who are distanced from our own contexts of interaction. Both, however, employ law in the sense of a communication code, a semi-stable structure of expectations and understanding which informs all dealings with others. This structure legislates how persons should be recognised – and therefore what we understand their needs and rights to be – in the practice of communication and interrelation. It therefore also enables us to discern how to react to this person or group in that context, especially considering other claims which might be registered within it.

Law is a rational device (i.e. capable of general, undistorted consensus) through which the justice of claims, of opposing interests and rights may be calculated. As a rational instrument law is subject to open, public discussion and is therefore a living process of dialogical will-formation which may itself be transformed through explication.[16] Claims invariably invoke a complex network of relations, even if they do so only implicitly. This is true even for an 'ecstatic' one-to-one relation – for the partners are never bare subjectivities, but *persons* sedimented from a history of relations within a determinate society.

In situations of complexity, either as to quality or quantity, it is necessary to stabilise or standardise relations through a code abstract from any particular relation. That is, it is necessary to subject the claims within a particular relation to generalised and abstract conceptions of a just encoding of relations. A law of relations can also produce as well as scrutinise claims, and so may also generate an understanding of obligation towards others who are not presently registering such claims. The law standardises and fixes principles of personal and political interaction according to the perceived needs of personal being, so that the calculation of conflicting interests, needs or claims need not be made anew every time and in every place.[17] The abstract character of law also makes it possible to understand and thence judge claims *rationally* – i.e. as generalisable and capable of achieving consensus within community, and so with an intersubjective referent – rather than doing so purely subjectively – through private and individual modes of apprehension, ranging from the particularity of feelings (through pity, affection, grief, etc.) to the prejudice of self-interest, which might be entirely particular to one person.[18]

This is why law is no less important in love than in justice. For it is only through law and with reference to a wider community that we may act *rationally*. It is only therefore through law that love may be a reality which really joins people together in a reality which encompasses more than (though certainly not excluding them) the idiosyncrasies and irrationalities of either the partners or their relation. Love for particular others also joins one to a wider (and ultimately universal) community in which rational means for understanding others and their needs are institutionally secured.

If love is understood in purely personal and subjective terms, its reference will be restricted to the time and space of a particular relation. Love would then be momentary and non-abiding, because its intention of the other was entirely dependent upon direct contact and personal proximity. The redeemed spirit of communication, whether personal or communal, however, is universal, applying to *all* personal locations in social space–time. The intention of others which upholds them in their integrity as persons is not restricted to those we happen to meet or to the time when we happen to meet them. Instead, our commitment to those we have met follows them when they depart from us and move into other immediate contexts of communication; and, moreover, our commitment also extends to those whom we have never met. Commitment to others is not therefore based on and restricted to personal proximity; it extends to all persons, whoever and wherever they are, who are or may be affected by communication from our particular location. I am not only referring here to the communication we are undertaking anyway, but to the whole range of communication we *could* make. That means that we need a very general sensitivity to the possible ways in which our lives could potentially impinge on those of others. Furthermore, this is not just an argument that we should be wary of treading on others' toes. For it also means that we must attend to the positive ways in which we *could*, say, intercede or intervene for or be with others in their situations; and this means that we cannot abdicate responsibility for others simply because they are not presently in relation with us or because we are wary of intruding into personal or social spaces not connected with us. Even silence is a communication, and the most sinful intention of others is to remain silent over their suffering when we might have done something to help.

Since the new spirit of communication is universal in its intention, recognition and commitment, it cannot be restricted to the proximity and intimacy of personal or small-scale relations. For that very reason it requires impersonal abstraction into coded form and, ultimately, into socio-political structures. The personal and subjective (moral) element is necessary if law is not to become divorced from its spirit and so turned into an idolatrous form of commitment; but in separation from the communal and the structural (socio-political), a code of personal behaviour not only remains entirely subjective, but becomes sentimental and ineffectual. Moral qualities lose their moral sense if they are independent of or in substitution for the demands of justice in socio-political life. Moreover, a completely subjective and personal code (if it is possible to refer to such arbitrariness as a code) of response to others which admits no external information idolises the exercise of autonomy. The impact of redemption so structures intersubjectivity that there is a co-inherence of personal (moral) autonomy with the heteronomy of an 'objective' law (conditions of intersubjectivity which are actually or potentially capable of public agreement).[19]

There is a productive tension between law and Gospel, but no absolute antipathy or separation. Redemption introduces a certain lightness or freedom from the law, but this is to be understood as an inculcation in the law's spirit which may therefore free one from obedience to its letter. Hence, law is relativised and so becomes a medium for a spirit of communication which transcends it. This relativisation transforms obedience to the law from a dead letter into a living spirit which, far from doing away with it, may transform law by fulfilling and exceeding its demands, albeit in sometimes extraordinary ways.[20] In this transformed spirit, structures are not done away with, but transformed and enlivened.

The stabilisation of dialogue in laws of interaction (be they moral or social codes or socio-political institutions) is a necessary but insufficient condition for the enactment of undistorted relations and personal identities. External works of the law need to be undertaken in a personal spirit of commitment and fidelity,[21] the intention of which corresponds to the communal intention which is held in semi-stable structure in the code. The redeemed spirit of communication maintains the orientation of the law upon God and others without falling into an ethical or political formalism. Lawlike justice is something like a minimum requirement for right relations. Without the subjective moment of personal commitment to others and God *through* law, however, it is worse than useless, since it is an attempt to maintain oneself (by refusing to go beyond the demands of the law and so put oneself out or to transgress them and so open oneself to blame, ridicule and guilt) or the law in isolation from others. This diverts attention from the needs, rights and interests of others and on to oneself and one's own needs or obligations in respect, not of the other, but of the law. The subjective, internal moment of commitment to others through the institutional mediation of law may sometimes require, then, that one exceed or lay aside its obligations and demands.

In the spirit of dialogue one is orientated on God and others and not primarily oneself (rather, one is orientated on oneself through self-transcending movement towards God and others) or on a law of interaction, no matter how undistorted that law might be. This means that, in this spirit, there is an internal prohibition on dealing with others *solely* on the basis of law; but there is also a prohibition on dealing with them apart from the minimum requirements of justice – reciprocity and generalisability – which exclude acting on purely particular interest or subjective caprice, etc. The minimum requirements of dialogue and personhood make individual and social existence mutually formative and limiting conditions. Just as communal life presents limits of justice and generalisability to individual expansion and claims, so the autonomy proper to personhood establishes critical limits to the demands and expansion of law and social institutions.

The scale of relations

It should be clear by now that in the position I am adopting, the large scale and consequently 'impersonal' lawlikeness of relations are not in themselves destructive of genuine personhood and genuine relation. At several points I have tried to show that 'impersonal' stabilised structures and institutionalised communication codes are necessary to reduce complexity – either in terms of quality and/or quantity – of relations and in order to maintain consistency and continuity in integrity, commitment and fidelity. This complexity-reduction is necessary not only in interaction designed to attain some goal (strategic communication), but for all meaningful interaction. By meaningful, I mean interaction which is understood by the subject and which is open therefore to interpretation by others (since meaning has intersubjective reference) and potentially also to the personal involvement of others in dialogue.

Communication structures – whether personal or social – do, however, tend to ossify into forms of closure which inhibit genuine personal communication. Instead of being restricted *by* the demands of personhood, they become restrictive *of* personhood. Structures of communication are sedimented (in the case of persons) or ossified (in the case of social structures) from a history of interaction. Closure seems to result where this process of sedimentation or ossification stops at a previously coordinated position. Any further development will therefore exclude any new or different information, and thus any really personal communication free from the constraints of the structure. Since further inter*personal* communication is excluded, the further development of the structure can only be a further solidification of the institutional, 'impersonal' aspect alone. In which case, no matter what was previously the case, Christ cannot be presently structuring these forms of personal and social life.

So far as social structures are concerned, the problem with institutionalised communication is not its scale, so much as its consequent tendency towards a solidified exclusion of personal communication. As I have suggested already, however, institutions are set limits by the requirements of dialogue and personhood. In particular, this limiting requirement may be described as the need for communication which may be found meaningful and which therefore structures social space–time in such a way that facilitates subjectivity, autonomy, and so also participation in the structure.

The importance of proximity and of one-to-one relations

Whilst necessary, social structure and its law of large-scale interaction cannot become a substitute for smaller-scale, personal interactions – no matter how undistorted and open they may be. Personal identity is a sedimentation of a significant history of relations which will have had both a societal and an interpersonal aspect. A *personal* identity derived *only* from non-proximate and large-scale relations institutionalised at the societal level is as unthinkable as a secure and stable identity *without* involvement in societal institutions. Despite the importance for personal being of socio-political structures, the fact remains that it is from inter*personal* relations of a much smaller scale that we draw our understanding of ourselves as *persons*. It is intersubjectivity at this level which is absolutely indispensable to personhood. The socio-political structures and processes do not have this primacy in and of themselves; as indispensable means for securing dialogue in small-scale interactions, they too are essential for personhood, but their importance is secondary. They therefore have to be judged according to the quality of small-scale relations which they directly or otherwise facilitate. For the basic paradigm of humanity is one-to-one relations: dialogue. It is only possible to retain a sense of the personal by keeping the requirements of interpersonal dialogue sharply in focus. Notwithstanding that, however, the focus of our attention and concern cannot lie exclusively with the interpersonal if we are to keep sight of the structural, institutional and socio-political aspects of personal being; if the understanding of personhood is not to dissolve into unreserved and unrestrained forms of personalism.

> We describe humanity as a being of the one man with the other.
> Fundamentally we speak on both sides in the singular and not in the
> plural. We are not thinking here in terms of individualism. But the
> basic form of humanity, the determination of humanity, according to
> its creation, in the light of the humanity of Jesus ... is a being of the
> one man with the other. And where one is with many, or many with
> one, or many with many, the humanity consists in the fact that in
> truth, in the basic form of the occurrence, one is always with another,
> and this basic form persists. Humanity is not in isolation, and it is
> in pluralities only when these are constituted by genuine duality, by
> the singular on both sides.
>
> The singular, not alone but in this duality, is the presupposition
> without which there can be no humanity in the plural.

> In its basic form humanity is fellow-humanity. Everything else which
> is to be described as human nature and essence stands under this sign
> to the extent that it is human. If it is not fellow-human, if it is not in
> some way an approximation to being in the encounter of I and Thou,
> it is not human.[22]

I hope that readers will understand that none of this is intended to imply or to advocate a sole commitment to smallest-scale relations. I am suggesting neither that they are ontologically or logically prior to sociality or polity, nor that they are of more intrinsic value as such than larger scales of relation. I merely mean that they are indispensable to personal identity and being, that the humanity of relations may only be retained where one-to-one interaction is possible, where the conditions for dialogue and intimacy are met. Larger-scale relations and structures are neither inhuman nor anti-personal by virtue of their size. Whether they are so can be judged only by examining the extent to which they facilitate inter-personal dialogue and participation in their structures. This will show whether, in fact, participation rights are afforded those within them; whether people can be subjects of the intercommunication they structure, or only passive recipients of an objective process. To put the question another way: Do they approximate to the dialogical ideal of smallest-scale personal encounter?[23] It is only through the involvement with proximate Thous that we come to understand ourselves as Is. Proximate and small-scale relations are therefore of fundamental importance.

Further, the identity of the individual person is, in a sense, more profoundly shown in proximate and small-scale interaction. There is nothing inauthentic about seeking justice for non-proximate persons through institutionalised forms of response to their needs. There is, however, a sense in which the authenticity of our commitment to others (and therefore our personal identity) is ultimately testable only in proximate relations. In dialogue we are orientated upon others, not in the abstract but in their concrete identities – as our real neighbours. Love of neighbour (the proximate Thou) is the acid-test of love of God and of the genuineness of our non-proximate human commitments.[24] The importance of our orientation on our neighbours means both that our orientation on others must have proximate content (we cannot only love those we never meet!), and that non-proximate relations are to conform to the dialogical reciprocity and co-intention implied by the commitment to love our neighbours as ourselves.

Complexity and meaning

A person is a *subject* of communication. That means that she or he may interact autonomously (in a centred and controlled way) in a variety of contexts and may independently find and communicate meaning. Whilst that meaning will be personal, and therefore partly idiosyncratic, it none the less draws upon intersubjective structures and codes of public meaning and interaction. We learn to become persons, subjects of communication, within a determinate social world by internalising these public structures of meaning and value. In particular, this happens by internalising the meaning and value which are attached to our public presence in communication – the ways in which we are intended, expected and recognised as subjects by others and by institutions. Becoming a person, then, depends on the provision of social space–time for our autonomous communication in the relationships and structures most significant to us. It also depends on the socially derived ability to find the world meaningful. For only if we can understand and interpret the world according to a rational code can we understand the way it impinges on us and make sense of the way it reacts to us and our communication. For if we are unable to perceive or to understand (decode) the communication which is directed towards us from our environment (this becomes more difficult in larger-scale environments – and especially in bureaucratic institutions – since environmental response is often delayed and may take unexpected form), we will be unable to internalise and then deploy an appropriate communication code, and hence be unable to centre our experiences and act autonomously in the world. Personhood and the ability to find and manufacture personal meaning are therefore intimately related.

Combining these points with my comments above concerning the importance of proximity suggests that personhood depends upon meaningful interaction within the proximate contexts of communication – that is, localised and/or relatively small-scale networks of interpersonal relations (the following are possible examples: close family, place of work, a street; but not all potentially indentifiable relatives – and probably not all those actually known to one – not all members of the multi-national corporation and not the population of the whole city). That is to say that personhood is dependent upon the existence or creation of space-time for autonomy in the proximate communication context. Personhood also requires from this context the provision of sufficient feedback loops for the effects of one's communication to be perceived and understood. For one must be able to 'feel' the response to one's communication if one is a subject engaged in a process of intersubjectivity.[25] It is therefore a requirement for personal being that proximate contexts are responsive to our presence and communication: only if this is so can we be clear that we are being addressed, heard and responded to. In so far as institutional structures constitute a part of these proximate contexts they will be bound, on this principle, to incorporate and respond to the personally held and communicated understanding of those within their frame. This means that institutions cannot be centred in their own structures but must be decentralised in order to incorporate the meaningful participation and autonomy of persons.

As I argued above, the tendency of institutions to develop a logic of their own instead of operating and developing according to the logic of dialogue is not in itself a problem of scale. It is, however, linked with scale. The difficulties of safeguarding personal communication within social structures seem to be proportionate to the scale of interaction they institutionalise. Overcomplexity, whilst usually connected with scale, is not, however, directly reducible to it.[26] One of the major factors which turns the scale of very large, institutionalised networks of interaction and contexts of communication into depersonalising processes is the accompanying increase in the level of complexity and the raising of the ceiling of interaction. This may (but, again, need not) mean that people enter the institution at a level of complexity which they have not yet acquired the means to deal with, but can find no intermediary. They then end up faced with too much information and communication to cope with, or find that the structures are set up to deal with so many people (usually on the basis of a stereotyped person) that it is hard to discern what, if any, information is directed or relevant to them. As institutions grow in size, they may also grow away from the possibilities of personal interaction: the places where accountability is located, for instance, may be out of the reach of some or all persons. And if that is the case, then there can be no possibility of helping steer the institution, and there will be a much decreased chance that it will continue to incorporate the interests of these people.

What is crucially at issue here is where the institutions are centred and what kind of participation they allow – whether there are localised possibilities of meaningful incorporation into the life regulated by the institution, or whether the structure is so centralised that this has become impossible. One example of this might be the centralisation of an education system so that the crucial decisions are no longer taken in the neighbourhood school, or even in town or county hall, but in central government. The practicalities of gaining access to the decision-makers of central government may well be quite different from those at the local level, and the chances of doing so and then of being heard, of having one's interests entered into the decision-making process, and of securing effective response, will usually be much decreased. The chances of making the right decisions for a particular neighbourhood school, taking all the local circumstances into account, also decrease with the removal of decision-making and information gathering from the local level. This need not accompany centralisation, but it will tend to do so unless local structures mediating communication between neighbourhood and central government are in place.

In situations of overcomplexity there is likely to be either too much or too little response for the non-competent person or community to find meaningful. An overcomplex environment therefore decreases the possibilities of making rational response (i.e. of acting responsibly) for two reasons. First, it provides insufficient information which people may understand and so destroys their basis for meaningful and rational communication. The effects of this might range from a general lack of stimulus to apathy or to eventual atrophy in this particular relational context (and possibly also in others). Second, the overcomplex environment might present a person with a massive overload of information which can only be partially understood because there will be too much (because of sheer volume or because of how complicated and difficult it is to comprehend) to sort and decode, and therefore to find meaningful, in the time. Information overload will create stress and may lead to an eventual breakdown. The amount of information directed towards one in this context is beyond what is, in present circumstances, personally manageable, and there is a consequent loss of meaning within that context.

Similarly, an undercomplex environment might prove understimulative because information presented in it would either already be understood, and would therefore cease to be informative, or else it would be so infrequent that it could hardly constitute a constant and reliable context of communication. In either case, it is unlikely to hold one's attention. Overcomplexity, on the other hand, refers to an environment in which some people are unable to interpret all the communication directed towards them and therefore to relate it to their present understanding. There is thus a latency of meaning and significance in the communication such that it cannot be directly informative for these people here, now and like this.[27] This is directly attributable to a mismatch between personal and environmental complexity.

A communication context which outgrows the present possibilities of meaningful and therefore autonomous personal communication will tend to be monological. That is, it may continue to be crucial and determinative for social life and therefore for personal being, but fail to facilitate, recognise and incorporate personal responses. If this is the case, then the communication will be one way. What this represents is the removal of significant institutionalised aspects of social life from the scope of personal interaction. As I have suggested, this creates a mismatch between the meaning which persons might expect, perceive and interpret within this context and that which is actually encoded and stabilised in it. It is therefore difficult to communicate effectively, if at all, since the meaning and effect one expects one's communication to have will be difficult to gauge. They could turn out to be more, less or quite different from that expected. That is what makes control and therefore subjective engagement so difficult. The fact that there could be more or different meaning lying latent in the social code than one is aware of means that there could be an overrun of meaning and implication of one's own communication quite beyond personal control. This is a situation of incomplete competence in the communication code, which may be generalised throughout the society or localised to particular classes, castes or individuals in it. This incompetence may only apply when relations reach a certain structural scale or intensity which makes it impossible to encode or decode information, to be a subject capable of understanding and centring one's life.

The problem of environmental overexpansion or overcomplexity may have to be solved by shrinking social structures and institutions to a more manageable scale or intensity. Alternatively, smaller-scale structures may be set in place to perform a mediating function. Clearly, if more structures are deployed then, in one sense, it becomes a *more* complex society, but one which is (it is hoped) no longer *over*complex, because these extra structures have helped reduce the different levels of complexity in social and personal organisation. Overcomplexity does not refer to a fixed level of organisation, but to a relationship between the social and the personal. It is not therefore measurable in absolute, but only in contextual and relative terms.

Since, however, a situation of overcomplexity might indicate the underexpansion of some persons or groups (especially where the incompetence is unevenly distributed), it might be more appropriate to expand their capacity for effective communication. This may mean, for example, the extension of education or the alteration of social codes which restrict the access of some to particular contexts of communication – such as females to home and family and lower social classes to interpersonal, as opposed to structural, interactions.[28] The strategy here would be to increase personal complexity and/or the complexity of smaller interpersonal structures and contexts of communication which might mediate between the personal and societal. In this way more effective (i.e. understandable, meaningful, response-finding and responding) communication becomes possible in widening horizons of communication, so that the codes regulating communication in these larger contexts might gradually be 'learned'.

'Learning' a code means acquiring competence in it so that we may control communication because we understand the range of possible effects and meanings it could have. For learning to take place we will have to receive feedback which allows us to check what effect the communication had and what meaning was given to it by others. In regard to overcomplex structures, this requires reducing the difference in complexity between ourselves and social structures. (Essentially, this is the mediating function parents perform when they step in between their children and complex spheres of interaction, either interceding or providing interpretations for, or else explaining things to, their children.) This might happen either by reducing the complexity of the structure and/or by increasing personal complexity relative to it. It is not so much the level or scale of social structures which determines the possibilities of communicative autonomy (in this case freedom within structure) as the extent of the relative difference in complexity between personal and social structures of communication.

In order to act autonomously as a subject in communication, it is necessary to centre one's experience and action. As I have previously argued, this capacity is socially acquired and it is, indeed, the history of interaction which has taken place around one's particular social location which sediments a unique personal identity – which gives this personal centre a specific character and means of organisation. All this happens as one internalises the way in which one is intended, expected and recognised by significant others and in the wider structures of society more generally. When information is centred within a person who is a unique social location and who has a unique identity sedimented from previous interaction, it is also transformed in an idiosyncratic way and incorporated into a meaning-structure which is personally unique (though having intersubjective reference). Personal centres are structures which 'hold' information which may then be used in the organisation of personal being and communication. But the way in which we hold it, as much as what we actually hold, will be unique to us. For when we receive new information, we have to process it before we can understand, hold or use it; that is, we understand it and find it meaningful by combining it with previously coordinated understanding and internal structures of meaning. The possibility of finding information meaningful, of being informed by it, is therefore directly related to the already existing organisational structure of the person and its complexity. The information previously sedimented from communication is held in the form of a specific personal identity and structures of 'memory' which will be of a given complexity. This determines the critical levels of complexity within which new communication must fall if it is to be understandable and meaningful and therefore to hold possibilities for the exercise of autonomy. The person will not be able to cope with new information which is *vastly* more complex than that held in the present structure of personal identity.

Information which falls within the present critical limits of complexity without falling below the critical levels of interest may then be internalised by the person concerned. In other words, it can be brought into interaction with presently sedimented information and the meaning-structure of personal identity. The information will be transformed by this combination with a unique meaning-structure (or, to put it another way, by its appearance in a different context), but so, potentially, may the person. For there is always the chance that this communication may significantly inform the person. Information must present sufficient variety (complexity and newness) for it to be recognised as new and therefore as worthy of incorporation into the personal centre, and possibly as requiring a transformation in identity – a new way of initiating and responding to communication. The information must not, however, contain so much complex variety that understanding and meaningful response are impossible. Because information is, by definition, new, it always invokes personal, idiosyncratic, and therefore autonomous reflection (processing and transforming), in order for an understanding to be consciously coordinated and a response to be decided upon. The consciousness (or internal, cognitive complexity) of persons, and therefore their autonomy in communication, expands or is 'learned' through interactions with successively complex communication contexts (again, the development of children presents a good example). For the present complexity of persons which determines the levels of social complexity they can deal with is directly related to the complexity of previous contexts of interaction in which they have related and communicated in a meaningful way, relations and information from which will have entered the sedimented structures of identity and 'memory'.

Increasing environmental complexity which remains within the limits necessary for nurturing autonomy is actually necessary for its further expansion and development. There is likely to be a point at which further interaction within contexts of the *same* complexity (i.e. no context of interaction increases in complexity) furnishes no new information and therefore little stimulation for the meaningful exercise of autonomy. What is required in these contexts is entirely understood and has become so much a matter of routine that it does not have to be thought about any more, and so communication is not so much autonomous as that of an automaton:

routine, mechanical response to stimulus. We may be able to survive as persons if it is only one context of interaction which remains exactly the same (think of most production-line jobs). However, if it is most or all of them, then our personhood will be increasingly difficult to sustain (imagine someone who is kept in childhood contexts of interaction into adult life by her or his parents and the effect this is likely to have on the development of personhood, the ability to act as a subject in a range of contexts), unless we can sustain increasingly complex fantasy worlds – and there are dangers in that too. An increase in complexity, on the other hand, requires the exercise of autonomy in order to effect a development in understanding, and possibly in personal identity too. In this case the increase in contextual complexity, because it remains within critical limits, invites a corresponding increase in the complexity of the personal centre and internal structures necessary for the processing of its complex content. It must therefore be the case that, within critical and changing limits, the organisational complexity of social structures may actually contribute to personal autonomy rather than inhibiting it.

> Hence whereas relatively simple systems become cogs in the superordinate system, complex systems with learning-capacities retain and even evolve their autonomy. They do become more determinate in a highly structured situation, in the sense that their randomness is reduced and their purposiveness increased. But this form of determination involves the decision-making capacity of the system, and thus it *contributes* to their freedom rather than restricting it.[29]

The more complex the internal information structure (and therefore the more complex the significant history of relation from which it is sedimented), the greater the capacity for self-determination in increasingly complex (and, if the complexity refers to quantity rather than quality, possibly also more distant) environments. Personal understanding and autonomy may expand in complex social structures which challenge present structures of identity without overrunning them. Of course, as personal complexity increases, it is likely that the complexity of context will have to do so too in order to nurture further advances in autonomy. There is therefore no necessary or intrinsic opposition between personal autonomy and the complexity and scale of social institutions and structures – provided, that is, that these are referred to the requirements of the personal being and life of real people here and now (which might translate into demands for intermediate institutions, structures or technologies, education, training, or institutional change).

*

This conclusion may be considered an advance on my discussion of personal freedom at the end of the last chapter. There I argued that personal freedom can only occur within structures, since it requires a stabilised background of reciprocity. Further, where reciprocity is properly structured, it becomes a dialogical process for the mutual formation of personal wills, identities, understanding, expectations, and so on. In the case of socio-political structures, they become processes of democratic will-formation. This has two chief implications. The first is that individual identities and wills are formed and orientated on one another through the mediation of democratic institutions and structures which enter into, inform and structure consciousness. The second is that these institutions and structures respond to and incorporate the personal and interpersonal exercise of will and the decisions made at these levels concerning what is right, just and true. Both these conditions require that the complexity differential between persons and socio-political institutions and structures be kept within the limits which make this dual responsiveness – of persons to the institutions and of institutions to persons – possible.

In the previous chapter the conception of persons as *subjects* of communication in a determinate social 'world' translated into the democratic principle of *participation* in socio-political structures. The impact of redemption on a particular society requires as universal an extension of participation as is possible within present conditions. It therefore requires that, wherever there is incapacity to participate, structural initiatives be taken to facilitate, nurture, encourage and extend subjectivity in communication. Silence is to be taken as a criticism of the present encoding and structuring of relations, and such silence is a communication demanding a structural response. But ensuring an ever-widening personal participation in society will mean increasing the complexity of the socio-political structure. For if complexity is not to lead to alienation, stress, breakdown or servitude, there will have to be mediating structures of a human/personal scale which make what goes on at, and what reaches one from, higher levels meaningful. It is only if meaning can be found that autonomous and centred interaction, and so the steering of one's own life and contributing to the steering of that of the institution, become possible – indeed, are nurtured. Furthermore, there must be a permanent need to increase complexity, since the possibilities of autonomy are unlikely to be maximised and strictly universal participation will not be achieved until the realisation of the kingdom.

*

I am sure that my argument in this part of the book would worry many of those who take personal freedom and individuality with utmost seriousness and who regard all institutions and structures with an eye of suspicion. Perhaps there may even be some sense of betrayal that a book which set out not only to reconceive but to protect individuality and personhood has ended by emphasising the role of social structures and institutions; and not only that, but talking positively about increased social complexity and using the language of social determinacy in the process. However, my discussion in this last part of the book, where I have been chiefly concerned to discern the form of institution and socio-political structure required by the understanding of the person advanced earlier, can hardly have come as a surprise given my desire to explore personhood and individuality in terms of relation. It has been an integral part of the argument from the beginning of the book that persons and their relations do not occur in a vacuum, but within a social context. This context is structured and provides order; it regulates, encodes and structures relations and persons themselves. It has also been a basic contention throughout the book that social structures are neither non-essential nor are they necessary evils, but that they are absolutely necessary for personhood and for personal relation – principally because subjectivity is socially acquired from stabilised and repeatable processes of intersubjectivity. This move towards the importance of structures and institutions is made already, at least implicitly, as soon as one decides to move away from individualism.

It is with one eye looking back over my shoulder at the reservations of those suspicious of any and all institutions and structures that I have developed my position regarding the socio-political sphere. That is why the main discussion about the form institutions and structures should take sometimes breaks off into arguments parallel to the main one which try to establish, in a variety of ways, that institution and structure are not counter-personal. Because these reservations do not simply reflect certain Western cultural values and assumptions but are actually realistic assessments of social organisation as it too often takes place in the real world, I felt continually forced to justify my contention that any failure was not intrinsic to institution and structure. So, for instance, having argued that institutions should be open and free, I felt it necessary to anticipate the criticism that the social organisation of personal freedom was a contradiction in terms by further elaborating freedom in communication terms to show how it depends on structures and institutions. In so far as these are

reservations concerning the empirical operation of structures and institutions as many people know them, I share them. But the problem, as I see
it, is not structures and institutions in themselves, but the ones we have.

I hope that it has remained clear that the focus of my concerns,
even in this final part, remains on the person. But, since I understand the
person in terms of communication and relation, that focus cannot lie
exclusively here but must expand outwards and upwards – to other people,
social structures and to God. Further, to think of redemption – the perfection
of everything in creation – in terms of a *kingdom*, and especially as a
kingdom of universal truth, freedom and justice, is hardly to conceive of it in
individual terms! The Christian vision of God's kingdom is of a *society* under
the rule of Christ, who orders and structures identities and relations in a
dialogical manner, and in the power of the Spirit, who is the organisational
energy of openness. It does therefore contain a vision of individual well-
being and fulfilment, but only as communally understood.

An important part of my argument has been that meaning is only
secured in community: it is not manufactured in an isolated subject, but
through processes of intersubjectivity. Just as the meaning of information is
idiosyncratically transformed when it enters individual consciousness, so it
is similarly transformed by the structures of meaning and intersubjectivity
prevailing in different communities. This has implications for the language
of my argument. If meaning changes within different communities, then
surely I cannot expect the language of a specific community, the Church, to
carry the same meaning outside it; should I not, then, expect the specifically
Christian and theological aspects of my argument either to have quite
different meaning or be quite meaningless outside the ambit of Church or
theological discussion? I think the answer is 'no' for three reasons.

First, although the Church is a specific community, it is also a
determinate one. It is part of its social world (although not completely
bounded by it) and makes sense of itself through the more widely available
structures of meaning and processes of common life as well as those which
might be specific to it (which will, of course, be socially determinate).
Because of the social determinacy of the Church, it should be the case that
not *all* Christian talk of redemption will be meaningless. Second, that talk
not only arises out of but is directed towards the determinate situation,
along with acts of practical commitment towards the redemption of this
social situation. The Church directs its communication towards its situation in an attempt to comprehend it in the wider horizon of God's
creative–redemptive activity. This comprehensive comprehending is practical. It means trying to transform the situation, to relate the possibilities of

redemption to its particularity: it means seeking emancipation from those conditions here and now which most bind the present from the future liberation of the kingdom. Third, the *full* meaning of Christian terminology is not accessible to any present community, even the Church, since it refers to an eschatological reality. Christian faith is ultimately concerned with the conditions of perfect community and dialogue: the kingdom of God. And it is only in that perfectly structured community that Christian talk about the reality of community, love, justice, solidarity, about the world more generally, and about God, will attain their full meaning and be fully understood.

From a Christian point of view, the transformation of people and societies towards the conditions of free personhood and true community do not only draw the present into closer anticipation and approximation of the kingdom; such transformation also increases the meaningfulness of Christian language of redemption. The reverse, of course, is also true. The destruction of the values of community and of community itself, whether in Church or society, makes Christian faith less meaningful. As individuals or communities close in upon themselves, as they try to carve out and secure their future in opposition to others and to other communities, as universal value is placed upon the pursuit of self-interest above all else, then community is lost. For community is based upon dialogue, upon the open recognition and seeking of the other without restraint; it is a binding of oneself to others which ossifies into structures of interdependence. All this is destroyed by talk of independence over against others and independence from common structures of life, by talk of society and relationships as merely the coming together of people seeking their own, independent interests. All this obscures the fact that something independent comes into being between people in their interrelationships which binds them together and really adds something to them which they could not otherwise have or be. Then talk of openness, of love and justice, of regard for the other before oneself, of values transcending one's own reality, and of commitment and fidelity beyond one's own borders: all this seems quite meaningless and senseless.

The destruction of community therefore also diminishes the possibilities of responding to the Christian vision of the common future of all humankind in a community of perfect truth, freedom and justice. God's intention of humankind as dialogue-partners and of human being itself as an extended dialogue are primarily retained in the pattern of intersubjectivity proper to Church (though, of course, subject to the conditions of social determinacy and the fall). But the further both Church and society fall away from God's intention of dialogue, the more remote become the possibilities of making an adequate response to God's communication and offer of it. Given that so much of our present social and political situation can be described as a reversal of the values of true community, our situation is one of immense seriousness and urgency. Christian faith, however, speaks not only of human incapacity, but of divine empowerment in these things. The Christian language of community and of redemption can only achieve its full meaning in the kingdom – the community where the true meaning of communal and personal life will be perfected and lived out in structures of intersubjectivity and formally reciprocal co-intention. This vision of community and Christian talk about it comes from the future, as does God's creative–redemptive activity which calls us towards it. We may therefore be empowered by this future as it is made available to us primarily (but only primarily) through God's communication re-presented and mediated to us through the institutions of Church. But appropriate response on our part remains necessary and, because the intention is of a dialogue partnership, whatever empowerment we may receive in the spirit of the future cannot take away our personal and collective responsibility for and towards it. All that I have written of in these pages is therefore a matter not only of love, justice or good will, but primarily of faith and hope.

Epilogue

Having engaged in some fairly abstract, systematic thinking throughout the book, I should now like to indicate a route back to matters of
more direct, practical concern. My purpose in this is to invite readers who
have engaged and put up with the abstraction of my argument thus far to
do two things. First, to step further into the conceptuality I have been
developing by exploring some of the ways in which it might be brought to
bear on practical situations. Second, to find their own ways out of this
theoretical interlude back into their own practical situations and continue
their dialogue with this way of conceiving person and community there.

I have not found it at all easy, however, to decide how best to do
this. The first difficulty is to select appropriate situations which might serve
as illustrations or examples. The immediate problem here is that any way of
conceiving personhood, community and society has infinite applications
and implications in practice, and this makes it difficult to be precise about
what it might mean in any particular case and to select an instance which
exhibits something approaching the full range of potential required of an
example. Furthermore, because the implications are pretty well infinite,
whatever examples are chosen must avoid giving the implication that they
define the range and extent of application. There are not just a few major
problems which this way of thinking might be applied to, for the theme of
the book is how we live the whole of our lives as persons in community.

There are, in addition, difficulties peculiar to my own argument
and some of the positions basic to it; in particular, the concern for dialogue
and the particularity of context. Both these concerns restrain me from
offering set principles or a formula which can be applied to each and every
situation. Quite basic to my position is the idea that what is true, right and
good cannot be known in advance, but can only be established through an

extended dialogue in which all those with interests in a situation speak and define their own interests for themselves. People and the situations they find themselves in cannot be fully understood without some means for attending to their specific reality. In so far as they are problematic in some way, they cannot be 'solved' from outside by the imposition of solutions, principles or priorities generated elsewhere without reference to the specificity of the situation and the self-communication and understanding of those in it. The attempt to impose solutions in this way can hardly be called a dialogue, since there is an effective silencing of other voices. Of course, ultimately policies can only be imposed by backing them up with sufficient force to deter or counter any resistance, and this is the inevitable result of a continual failure to attend to the situation and to those in it. Instead of this kind of imposition of solutions formulated in advance and from outside as applying to any and all situations, sensitivity to the particularity of different contexts is needed which can allow them a certain degree of freedom.

Dialogue has not only been a concern of the content of the argument; it has also been my intention and hope that readers will engage with and question the text from a number of different perspectives. I have therefore, perhaps not always successfully, tried to set out my own views in a way which allows readers to make their own response, to enter into a dialogue. It would therefore be inimical to my intentions in the rest of the book if I were now to spell out its practical implications in such a precise, complete, dogmatic and fixed way that readers would be left observers at this point. I do not think that my argument supplies any pat answers or total solutions, and would be most disturbed if it could be shown to do so. What I hope it does is offer something rather more than a bare conceptuality: what is perhaps best termed a sensibility to the nature of personhood and community in different situations – a way of perceiving or reading them. It is this rather imprecise thing which I hope readers will take up in their own ways in the various contexts which make up their lives. That, of course, means that I have left readers with the hardest work to do: to work out for themselves what all this might mean in their own situations.

What I am aiming to do here, then, is merely to indicate the kind of questions which might be raised by this sort of sensibility in regard to one particular context, education, which I hope might serve as a living example rather than some complete and final conceptualisation. I have chosen this field because educational institutions are multi-levelled organisations which claim to meet the needs both of individual persons and of the wider community. Alongside much that is good or well intended in it there is also a good deal of distortion in communication, much of it quite subtle. Some of the most relevant questions to ask about educational provision from the perspective of the book might be as follows:

Does education foster a sense of being a responsible subject in a community, or does it regard students as passive recipients or consumers of information? Is pupils' autonomy engaged in the processes of learning and in membership of the school community more generally?

To what extent does the educational process approximate to a dialogue and to what extent does it take the form of monologue (inculcation)? Is there scope for open-ended questioning and for independent exploration, manufacture and communication of meaning?

What sort of subjects are people called to be through formal education; what form of communication processes and which communities are children being equipped to be part of, and in what ways? Are they, for example, pressed to be subjects or objects of economic processes of communication and exchange, or do they learn socially appropriate yet fluid ways of centring and finding meaning in their own lives and the world?

What sort of language are children given for understanding, perceiving, analysing and speaking about their situations and relationships?

Are children learning to relate to and be incorporated in ever-widening or relatively restricted contexts of interaction as subjects? Are they enabled to take and accept responsibility in this widening context?

How much interest is and can be taken in the particular needs and identities of pupils and of the needs of the local community?

Is what education offers universally and equally distributed, or are there differences according to class, ethnicity, locality, gender, intellectual or physical ability, parental background and interest, etc.? In what ways and on what basis do differences occur in the way pupils are intended, recognised, expected and valued within the institution?

What kind of communication exists between the different levels of the structure and within each school? How is the communication within the institution structured?

To what extent are those within the educational structure, whether parents, pupils, governors, teachers, cleaners, cooks, local education committees, or whatever, and all those who have a genuine interest in education – potentially every member of society – able to participate meaningfully and appropriately in it? Who participates in and steers the structure at any level, and to what extent?

What kind of communication has been ossified in this institution?

Can and do people deal with one another on a rational basis within the institution? Are the interests steering and secured in the institution rational?

I do not pretend to know the answers to all these questions, and much less to know how to resolve the problems which some of the answers may show up. There are other questions which could have been raised from the same perspective and also other, equally valid, perspectives which would yield other important questions.

Raising this sort of question is more akin to artistry and wisdom than to strategic planning which, whilst undoubtedly necessary, tends to make absolute and universal claims for its administrative programme, goals and objectives. What I am trying to indicate, however, is more respectful of the particularities of context and of the irresolvable complexities of personal situations. It is as indefinite and indefinable as a *feeling* for certain values and nuances in the *particular*. To recapitulate on the points I made above: I have not been trying to formulate a programme of fixed and definite solutions which can be applied in and to each and every situation, but to indicate the kind of questions which might be raised by this sensitivity in a particular institutional context. What I hope this book provides is a vision and understanding of persons, relations and community which in turn offers a way of looking at and understanding situations which illumines some important features relating to personhood and community. I hope that it does so in a way that does not lead to the totalitarian imposition of absolute and universal solutions in the misconception that people are problems to be solved by efficient administration, but which rather contributes to the permanent dialogue concerning what is true, right, good and just, and how we are to achieve these things together in community.

Notes

1 The creation of individuality in God's image: Trinity, persons, gender and dialogue

1 There is therefore a continuity between creation and redemption. Creation is not simply a one-off act of origination, but a continual engagement by God with the world which is necessary for the continual securing and sustenance of its reality. One of the major conditions of creation which God sustains is its freedom and integrity. Out of respect for creation and the freedom and integrity proper to it, God's communication with it is fundamentally non-coercive in character. Instead of forcing the fulfilment of the divine intention for creation on it, God elected to operate in a much more open and dialogical way. God's redemptive communication seeks this fulfilment of creation by involving creation in the process so redemption is not simply a renewal of or return to original conditions, but God's eternal intention that those conditions should be fulfilled through the right use of freedom. Redemption is not a consequence of the fall, but of creation itself. The use of the conjunction creation–redemption indicates that this is a continuum which ought not to be separated out.

2 Dialogue is a relationship in which the mutual orientation of the partners is based on their personal uniqueness and discreteness (independence from one another and their relation). It is therefore a bipolar interaction involving both distance and relation. Because it is based upon the unique identities of each and because these must remain unknowable in any final and complete sense by the other, each partner must make her or his own independent contribution to the relation (i.e. be a subject and originator of communication and communicate herself or himself) and give space and time for the other to do the same. So each partner will be passive and active, the subject (I) and object (Thou) of communication.

3 Cf. Karl Barth, *Church Dogmatics* (Edinburgh, T. & T. Clark, 1936–61), III/1, pp. 182ff.

4 Emil Brunner, *Man in Revolt*, p. 98 (quoted in David Cairns, *The Image of God in Man* (London, Collins, 1973), p. 155).

5 Barth, *Church Dogmatics*, III/2, p. 166.

6 Cf. Barth, *Church Dogmatics*, III/2, pp. 168, 193ff.

7 Jürgen Moltmann, *God in Creation* (London, SCM Press, 1985), p. 202.

8 The modern forms of this modalism, which similarly secure an exclusive, individual subject, are intrinsically linked to the Idealist conception of subjectivity as the circular movement of self-distinction and recollection. Through the process of self-distinction God repeats Godself in different revelatory modes, becoming the subject, object and predicate of revelation. It might be possible to arrive at some derivative sense of individuality for the Son in this way, as an eternally generated self-giving (recollection of the Father), but the subjectivity of the Spirit is clearly destroyed. The Spirit becomes the common bond of love between Father and Son but, as this is already given in their relationship, She is a relational form rather than a personal centre of subjective activity. In this revised modalism, the Father is the one absolute subject from whom all personal activity proceeds; the Son is the self-differentiation of the Father in whom He contemplates, recollects and manifests Himself, who cannot have any really individual centre of personhood in Himself, but only in the Father to whom He is to return in the Father's act of self-recollection. Cf. Jürgen Moltmann's criticism of Barth in *The Trinity and the Kingdom of God* (London, SCM Press, 1981), pp. 141ff.

9 This, for example, is the role often given to self-consciousness, the possession of the external, 'objective' world, including the reality of other persons, by its reduction to phenomena appearing within subjective consciousness. Clearly the epistemological individualism which is implied here represents a radicalisation of Kantian Idealism such that the objective world is not merely reduced to universal categories of a universal, abstract individual subjectivity, but to a reflection of the knowing self. If knowledge is essentially a subjective, private, process, then the knowing individual within whom it occurs has to be posited as its source (this was the position of, e.g. Locke, Berkeley and Mill which was extended in the psychological atomism of Hartley and the tradition stemming from Locke). This view is so pervasive that even Teilhard is able to attribute to self-consciousness a similar function as a centring through which 'the ego only persists by becoming ever more itself, in the measure in which it makes everything else itself' (*The Phenomenon of Man* (London, Collins, 1959), pp. 191f.; cf. p. 183). Paul Tillich understands the essence of the problem and the practical consequence of a knowledge based on the internalisation (or external manipulation) of difference and otherness which subsumes them under indifferent and self-confirmatory categories. This is knowledge based on reduction of difference rather than on participation in difference without reduction (*Systematic Theology* (London, SCM Press, 1978), vol. I, p. 177).

10 Thus this issue is linked with the 'doctrine of the internality of relations', clearly set out in David L. Norton, *Personal Destinies* (Princeton, NJ, Princeton University Press, 1976), p. 60: 'The doctrine of the internality of all relations introduces contradiction only on condition that the foreign terms of the relation appear within each other as foreign. If *B* is substantially different in kind from *A* and by relationship to *A* appears within *A* as *B*, then indeed *A* stands in self-contradiction as being both itself and what it is not. But if *B* appears within *A* under an aspect that is determined by the principle of *A*, then no contradiction is involved.' Norton thinks he safeguards the independence and otherness of each element by positing each individual as a 'universal-particular', by which he intends to indicate the inclusion of all human possibilities within each individual as at least potentially realisable. Therefore that aspect of *A* into which *B* is incorporated is actually *B*! (See pp. 60f., 243ff., 248, 252.) This bears comparison with Sartre's notion that what appears *in* consciousness appears *as* consciousness. Even Hegel takes a somewhat similar position in describing objectivity's truth as being ultimately alienated self-consciousness which must be recaptured by it.

11 This leads, in the first case, to forms of anthropocentrism which bind the existence of God to specific human interests and, in the second, to an individualisation of this anthropocentrism such that God's purpose is exclusively orientated towards and concerned with individuals. Both errors are grist for Feuerbach's mill, who criticised religion for validating belief in God by a preordinate and determinating belief in oneself and one's individual salvation. See especially *The Essence of Christianity* (New York, Harper and Brothers, 1957), pp. 173f. Cf. Barth's critique of eighteenth-century theology for subsuming God to forms of self-affirmation in *Protestant Theology in the Nineteenth Century* (London, SCM Press, 1972), p. 76, 113f., and A. Roy Eckardt, *The Surge of Piety in America* (New York, Association Press, 1958), pp. 85f.

12 Moltmann, *The Trinity and the Kingdom of God*, pp. 171f.

13 Ibid., pp. 172ff.

14 Ibid., pp. 173f.; Jürgen Moltmann and Elisabeth Moltmann-Wendel, *Humanity in God* (London, SCM Press, 1983), p. 98.

15 This is a recurring theme in John. See especially John 14: 10, 11, 'I am in the Father and the Father is in me.' Also: 1: 8, 5: 19ff., 17: 25f. A theory of the relational identity of the Persons of the Trinity might lead to an interpretation of John's earlier formulation, 'no one comes to the Father except by me. If you knew me you would know my Father too' (14:6ff. (NEB)), in non-exclusive terms. For the identity of God as (personal rather than universal) Father, as a relational identity, can only be revealed through His Son. But that need not imply that ignorance of the Son made knowledge of God per se absolutely impossible. It is a distinctively Christian understanding that the Fatherhood of God refers primarily to an internal relationship (i.e. trinitarian relation) within God and only subsequently, and on that

basis, to His external relations with creation or humanity. In Christian tradition God as Father is the Father of Jesus Christ and does not primarily denote a universal relationship to humankind or creation as a whole.

16 For the foregoing, see Moltmann, *The Trinity and the Kingdom of God*, pp. 111–14.

17 Other forms of differentiation (e.g. wealth, health, class, race) are neither structural nor essential to human nature, as is evidenced by the lack of such distinctions from some human communities. Sexual difference, however, appears within every human community and every other form of differentiation (so there are men and women who are both poor and rich, well and ill, with high and low status, black, white and oriental). See Barth, *Church Dogmatics*, III/1, pp. 186, 312f., III/2, pp. 286, 288, 292f., III/4, pp. 117f., 150. The gender-distinct/ gender-related structure is an inescapable and irreducible aspect of human existence (ibid., III/2, pp. 286, 289, 311f.).

18 For other references to solitariness being an unfortunate condition see Eccles. 4:9–12; Jer. 16:1–9.

19 Barth, *Church Dogmatics*, III/1, p. 290.

20 Westermann, *Genesis 1–11* (London, SPCK, 1984), p. 232.

21 Barth, *Church Dogmatics*, III/4, p. 163.

22 Ibid., III/2, p. 286 (*Die Kirchliche Dogmatik*, p. 344).

23 Cf. ibid., III/4, p. 167.

24 The modern feminist movement began by trying to assert women's identity with men, largely because arguments for their subordination rested on the attribution of difference. More recently there has been an emphasis on women's difference. This has been a development generated by a switch from understanding difference in itself as a sign of subordination. This accompanied the move of feminism away from liberalism and its understanding of equality – a move which was necessary before difference, suppression and oppression, especially in the private sphere, could be explicitly thematised. (See, e.g., the essays in Anne Phillips (ed.), *Feminism and Equality* (Oxford, Basil Blackwell, 1987).) Amongst other things, this has enabled women to find their own dignity apart from men and from male definitions of female reality and needs. Women's liberation is then seen to begin with their complete reassessment of themselves, the finding of new possibilities not defined by the preconditions of men. See, e.g., Germaine Greer, *The Female Eunuch* (St Albans, Herts., Granada, 1981), pp. 19f., and Dale Spender, *Man Made Language* (London, Routledge & Kegan Paul, 1980), pp. 54–78.

25 Paul K. Jewett, *Man as Male and Female* (Grand Rapids, MI, Wm B. Eerdmans, 1975), p. 125. If derivation were in itself an indication of subordination, then the man's creation 'of dust from the ground' would imply his subordination to it! Further, value may not be attributed here on the basis of temporal precedence. Quite apart from the modern

notion that developmental complexity accrues through time, on this basis Adam would have to be subordinated to the whole of pre-existent creation just for the sake of subordinating Eve to him! Barth, however, does take derivation to be a sign of subordination. Despite all his protestation to the contrary, and his placing this subordination only in the context of their joint subordination to God, this order does become for him a sexist one of value (an evaluative hierarchy). Barth denies that the pattern of super- and subordination is evaluative by resting it on an analogy with the covenant relation (*Church Dogmatics*, III/3, p. 301). He thereby in this instance subordinates creation to covenant, whereas his great insight elsewhere is that a non-sexist theology demands the centrality of the creation narratives. Barth makes the order of human relations a strict transform of the vertical image which in turn is a transform of the relations of super- and subordination he identifies in the Trinity. He hardens the *analogia relationis* into an *analogia entis* by universally prescribing a definite order so as to secure their difference and likeness without overextension either into separation or interchangeability (III/1, pp. 310f.; III/4, pp. 168f.). The immediate switch from talking about the need for living in one's own gender whilst confronted with the other to this order of domination is a *non sequitur*. All that is really demanded is the repetition of the command to live as male *or* female, male *and* female. To be sure, this needs to be concretely instantiated in socially specific relational patterns, but there is no need to make such universal prescription here.

26 Barth seems to assume a direct encounter with the universal form of the command at *Church Dogmatics*, III/4, p. 153 (cf. p. 156). 'Thus it is the command of God himself which tells them what they have to guard faithfully as such. As the divine command is itself free from the systematisation by which man and woman seek to order and clarify their thoughts about their differentiation, so, in requiring fidelity, it frees man and woman from the self-imposed compulsion of such systematisation. To what male or female nature must they be true? Precisely that to which they are summoned and engaged by the divine command – to that which it imposes upon them as it confronts them with its here-and-now requirement. As this encounters them their particular sexual nature will not be hidden from them. And in this way the divine command permits man and woman continually and particularly to discover their specific sexual nature and to be faithful to it in this form which is true before God, without being enslaved to any preconceived opinions.' Openness to the command constitutes for Barth a sort of hot-line not only free from any preconceptions, but apparently non-systematising in character and free from social determinacy. So, although law is an acknowledged necessity, it is saved from being confused with the command itself by the direct encounter with the Gospel, against which it may be checked. The

implication is that the command requires systematisation only at the extended interpersonal level (does Barth include the Church here?). For Barth seems to be suggesting that the command can encounter a man and a woman directly, and that they may have a direct line of communication which yields certainty in both what the Gospel is as such and the form in which it should gain expression in the present. Whilst Barth is adamant throughout his work that the command can only be heard in the Church, this injunction would, in any meaningful sense, seem to be abandoned here in order to protect the command (and, it would also seem, smallest-scale personal relations) from social determination.

27 Barth, *Church Dogmatics*, III/4, p. 131, speaking specifically of coitus; cf. pp. 130, 191.
28 So Westermann, *Genesis 1–11*, pp. 232f.
29 Moltmann and Moltmann-Wendel, *Humanity in God*, p. 101.
30 Barth, *Church Dogmatics*, III/4, p. 163.
31 Ibid., III/1, p. 195.
32 Cf. ibid., IV/1, pp. 434ff.
33 Cf. Dietrich Bonhoeffer in *Creation and Fall* (London, SCM Press, 1959), pp. 61, 63, 79.
34 Moltmann understands the image as open for and directed towards the incarnation in *God in Creation*, p. 218.
35 See Bonhoeffer, *Creation and Fall*, pp. 68, 70, 74.
36 J. Bettis, 'Political Theology and Social Ethics: the Socialist Humanism of Karl Barth', *Scottish Journal of Theology*, 27 (1974), 297.

2 The re-creation of individuality: the call of Christ

1 'Context' in this sense is a communications term signifying the system of relationships which forms the environment for particular persons, relations and communications. None of these terms may be isolated from the concrete communication context in which they occur. If the currents of ecological thought and the criticism of European theology by liberation theologians have taught us anything, it is the ideological nature of claims to purity or abstraction from context. In this chapter context usually refers to the proximate systems of relations in which a person finds him or herself. But this very localised context also has its wider context of time and place, which will largely be the concern of the next chapter. Everything has its context, and the context always makes a difference. That is to say that everything is related, that these relations are not purely arbitrary but occur within larger systems of relations which constitute the way in which the world is 'given' to us (but that does not mean that the context is unalterable).

2 The original meaning of the word individual indicated indivisibility, the strength of internal self-bonding relative to external bonds. (See Raymond Williams, *Keywords* (London, Fontana, 1983), pp. 161–5).) An individual is a spatio-temporal location whose internal

organisational structure establishes a demarcation between self and external environment. The physical and psychical bonding at the level of the individual constitutes his or her existence as structurally centred. That is, this 'whole' is neither directly reducible to its constituent parts, which are only analytically separable as subunits (e.g. organs, etc.), nor is it itself a mere subunit of a higher level of environmental organisation. If this were not so then the individual would be indistinguishable from either the next highest level of organisation, or else the next lowest would appear to consist of separately centred individual existences. It is the relative strength of internal, indivisible bonds which makes the individual visible, for the individual rather than constituent organs to be seen, for individuals to stand out in relief from their environment (physical or social) as (partly) independent, centred beings.

3 Matt. 10:34–7/Luke 12:49–53, 14:26.
4 This seems to be part of Bonhoeffer's rather confused picture in *The Cost of Discipleship* (London, SCM Press, 1959), p. 84.
5 *Saint Mark* (Harmondsworth, Middlesex, Penguin, 1969), p. 71. Italics in original.
6 Ibid.
7 Mark 2:13–17/Matt. 9:9–13/Luke 5:27–32.
8 Cf. Eduard Schweizer, *Lordship and Discipleship* (London, SCM Press, 1960), p. 13.
9 Cf. Karl Barth's comments concerning election in *Church Dogmatics* (Edinburgh, T. & T. Clark, 1936–61), II/2, p. 321.
10 This is emphasised by the use of *proskaleō*. See, e.g., Mark 1:30, 3:13; Acts 2:39, 13:2.
11 This is Bonhoeffer's view in *The Cost of Discipleship*, pp. 54f.
12 The transformation of redemptive existence by the determinate situation and its contingencies is discussed in Chapter 7.
13 Bonhoeffer, *The Cost of Discipleship*, p. 56.
14 Matt. 16:24f./Mark 8:34f./Luke 9:23f.; cf. John 12:25f.
15 Matt. 19:16–22/Mark 10:17–22/Luke 18:18–23.
16 Bonhoeffer, *The Cost of Discipleship*, p. 62.
17 John 1:38. The meaning of the words is derived from their more specific use at 5:44, 7:18 and elsewhere.
18 T. W. Manson, *The Sayings of Jesus* (London, SCM Press, 1957), p. 73.
19 Bonhoeffer, *The Cost of Discipleship*, p. 56; cf. p. 74. Schweizer notes, in *Lordship and Discipleship*, p. 15(n.), that the use of the aorist signifies that the severing of ties is a one-off event, whilst the use of the perfect shows that following is a continuing activity. This further implies that the act of decontextualisation cannot be understood apart from the continuing following of Jesus towards which it is directed.
20 Cf. Bonhoeffer, *The Cost of Discipleship*, p. 64. This happens primarily through moral procrastination: see, e.g., Luke 9:57–62/Matt. 8:18–22.

21 Acts 1:4–8.

22 John V. Taylor, *The Go-Between God* (London, SCM Press, 1976), pp. 3f. See also John 20:21f.; Acts 1:2.

23 Luke 4:18. This is also the implication of 12:49. See Manson, *The Sayings of Jesus*, pp. 120f.

24 See, e.g., Matt. 13:45f.; Matt, 22:1–8/Luke 14:16–21; Luke 14:33.

25 Matt. 19:14/Mark 10:15/Luke 18:17.

26 E.g., Mark 5:18–20/Luke 8:39. Legion is instructed to publish the Good News in his home environment despite his own wish to be with Jesus. Lazarus may also have been a sedentary follower of Jesus (see John 11:1, 11). It must certainly be said that membership of the band of disciples physically following Jesus was not a condition of salvation. Jesus' effect was much wider than this small group. Many more believed and 'followed' in their own way. See Hans Küng, *On Being a Christian* (Glasgow, Collins, 1978), pp. 280f.

27 Contrast this with Bultmann's position concerning the dehistoricisation of people before God's judgment in Jesus' proclamation. See *Theology of the New Testament* (London, SCM Press, 1952), vol. i, pp. 25f.

28 This does not only indicate the linguistic mediation of the call in recognisable forms of human speech, but the symbolic context which a social meaning-frame or communication code creates. Acts such as the choosing of the twelve, feasting with outcasts, footwashing, etc. can only be understood with reference to this socially relative communication context. The priority of the mission to Israel (see, e.g., Matt. 15:21–8/Mark 7:24–30) may be interpreted as the determinacy of Jesus' and his followers' ministry to their specific situation.

29 Because personal redemption is a subjective form of intending other subjects and relating to them, it is properly understood as a form of intersubjectivity. The redemption of individuals brings them into a new form of intersubjectivity (Church) which is not the product of individual intentions but the socially encoded community within which such intentions and subjectivity have meaning. In fact the subjective and intersubjective are reciprocally and mutually determining. The Church can only exist through the existences of redeemed individuals whose redemption is, in turn, dependent upon the co-intentionalities, or intersubjective form, of the Church. The basis of this view should become clearer in the next and subsequent chapters. See also Edward Farley, *Ecclesial Reflection* (Philadelphia, Fortress Press, 1982), pp. 230–4.

30 Küng, *On Being a Christian*, p. 281.

31 Barth, *Church Dogmatics*, ii/2, p. 444.

32 In Matt. 27:55/Mark 15:41, *akolouthein* is interpreted as *diakonein* – so Schweizer, *Lordship and Discipleship*, p. 13(n.).

33 Cf. E. Feil's discussion of abstraction and concretion in Bonhoeffer in his *The Theology of Dietrich Bonhoeffer* (Philadelphia, Fortress Press, 1985), pp. 36, 39–43.

34 Cf. Bonhoeffer, *Ethics* (London, SCM Press, 1955), pp. 23ff.
35 See Feil's precise and careful presentation in *The Theology of Dietrich Bonhoeffer*, pp. 59–95.
36 Bonhoeffer, *The Cost of Discipleship*, p. 88.
37 Cf. 1 Cor. 12:12f.; Eph. 2:11–22.
38 I am implicitly adopting an interpretation of sacrament, akin to the Lutheran tradition, as intrinsically communal, an activity of the congregation. The Word becomes concrete only in spiritual and material community.
39 Cf. Bonhoeffer, *Christology* (London, Collins, 1978), p. 50.
40 Ibid., p. 60.
41 Cf. Bonhoeffer, *Act and Being* (London, Collins, 1962), pp. 126f.; Barth, *Church Dogmatics*, III/4, pp. 335, 386f.
42 Cf. Barth, *Church Dogmatics*, I/2, pp. 696f.; II/1, pp. 25f., 31f.; III/4, p. 73. This is not a principle of concretion in Barth's theology as it is in Bonhoeffer's. Bonhoeffer equates concretion with specificity and therefore holds that God's Word becomes concrete only in specific acts of obedient human response. For Barth, however, the Word is concrete already by virtue of the preordinate activity of God. It may receive specific application in human response, but this can only be an analogy, symbol or even playful repetition of what is already concrete, Real and complete.
43 See, e.g., Fritjof Capra, *The Turning Point* (London, Fontana, 1983); Ilya Prigogine and Isabelle Stengers, *Order out of Chaos* (London, Fontana, 1985) and Anthony Wilden, *System and Structure* (London, Tavistock, 1980).
44 The Spirit's operation in nature is dialogical because partly closed systems communicate and exchange with one another and 'listen' to each other through a system of feedback loops. The system's present form of communication is the product of sedimented past exchanges which are present to it through some form of 'memory' device, such as instinctual behaviour and evolutionary processes. The system's future selection of advantageous forms of communication is subject to future change by way of adaptation to changed relations within its proximal environment. It is hence also diachronic or dialectical because present relations produce new 'syntheses'. To refer to this as dialogue is to speak analogically. Dialogue is a phenomenon of the social, rather than the biophysical, world. The process whereby persons seek understanding is not identical to the simple adaptations or more complex symbioses which occur in the biophysical world. The requirements for life in each sphere are the bipolar processes of integration and individuation. The organisational and life-giving energies of the Spirit are directed towards maintaining proper structures of communicational openness. In the natural order, however, it may not be possible to speak of distorted structures of communication except at the extremes of complete openness or

closure which lead immediately to death as an integrated and centred existence. And even here it is not possible to derive an ethical norm from the structure of communication necessary for life. There can, indeed, be no such thing as a natural morality in that sense. Communication is necessary for life and must take place within certain critical limits if that life is to be sustained. The cosmos is structured in such a way, however, that disintegration is one of its necessary and natural features. The activity of the Spirit cannot therefore be tied to the eternal sustenance of each and every individual life. That would be a reversal of the true situation, for it is individual lives which are tied to the activity of the Spirit, not the Spirit which is bound to respect the integrity of individuated and centred existences. The system of exchange structured by the Spirit includes physical death. Natural life is based on subsumption which, in the social sphere, would represent a distortion of relations. Every living being feeds from the decomposition of others. Life is recycled in an eternal circulation of life-energies.

45 Moltman has tended to do this and too easily to equate the Spirit's operation in the natural and social worlds. For instance, he makes the unsubstantiated and extraordinary claim that everything 'exists, lives and moves not only with and "in", but also *for* one another' (*God in Creation* (London, SCM Press, 1985), p. 11. My italics). He explicitly confounds language appropriate only to the social community with that of the biological interconnectedness of creation.

3 The social formation of persons

1 In non-theological terms, this seems to be Habermas' problem and the principal reason for his recent revision of his claims for the 'ideal speech situation' which his 'universal pragmatics' generates. He tries to show that the structures of undistorted communication are present even in distorted speech which is parasitic on them, but this observation, even if it were unproblematic, is insufficient to ground his preference for the former over the latter. The transcendental conditions of communication cannot be adequately grounded within a closed reference to actual practice. The door is therefore left open for Habermas' theory to be developed in a theological direction which would ground the ideal conditions of communication in properly transcendental realities – God, creation–redemption, and eschatology, for instance – which should, of course, be properly rooted also in the practicalities of the given situation which is a co-determinant of cognition and of the possibilities of action.

2 Dietrich Bonhoeffer, *Sanctorum communio* (London, Collins, 1963), pp. 30f. The implication of Bonhoeffer's argument at this point is that the primacy of ethics in epistemology requires a distinctive understanding of space and time – a demand I try to meet in what follows.

3 I have given relation an historical priority over individuals because it is by, in, and through antecedent networks of relations that individuals are born and formed. As bipolarities of a single process, however, individual and relation must be considered ontologically coincident. My position is therefore to be distinguished from that of Harold H. Oliver in *A Relational Metaphysic* (The Hague, Martinus Nijhoff, 1981), who, by affording relation an ontological priority, destroys individuality as anything but a 'turn' in a particular relation. See especially pp. 151f., 154f.

4 Rom Harré, *Personal Being* (Oxford, Basil Blackwell, 1983).

5 See Harré's consideration, ibid., pp. 206–9.

6 The recognition of the dynamic relation between body and personal identity is crucial for a theology of the incarnation. God's human embodiment is understood, in Christian tradition, to be the prime locus of the revelation of his personal identity. But that identity cannot be exhaustively identified with the body of Jesus because, apart from other philosophical problems associated with such an identification, God would then be exclusively bound to this bodily presence, unable to communicate and be communicated with apart from its physical presence. Cf. Arthur A. Vogel, *Body Theology* (New York, Harper & Row, 1973), p. ix.

7 Harré, *Personal Being*, p. 60.

8 Ibid., p. 61.

9 Ibid., pp. 59f., 211; cf. Vogel, *Body Theology*, p. 15.

10 Harré, *Personal Being*, p. 81. Harré seems to overstate his case because of an overconcentration on first-person pronouns. He states: 'since the indexicals in the pronoun system are used by speakers in the first person, then the indexical system cannot function to refer to possible persons'. By this he presumably means that all indexical pronoun use must index actual 'speakers of the moment'. Silent people may be taken to be passive contributors to communication who may therefore be indexed alongside their contributions. But it is also possible to imaginatively index potential persons and their potential contributions to communication as if they were personally present. Examples of this might include: imaginatively constructing a conversation between ourselves and representatives of a future generation in order to understand their interests in the present and our responsibilities towards them; or imagining what potential third parties might contribute to a particular situation. We could index the potential partners to an imaginative discourse by indexical use of second-person pronouns.

11 Anthony Wilden, *System and Structure* (London, Tavistock Publications, 1980), pp. 221f.; cf. 225 (n).

12 Harré, *Personal Being*, p. 212; cf. p. 161. Cf. Thomas McCarthy, *The Critical Theory of Jürgen Habermas* (Cambridge, Polity Press, 1984), pp. 295–7, where he describes Habermas' view that the necessary

conditions for experience are derived from communicative activity within a given framework of public meaning. Also cf. Wilden, *System and Structure*, p. 222, who urges that 'I' be understood as a locus in a social system of communication rather than as an entity.

13 See Wilden, *System and Structure*, pp. 221f. The implication of this is that individuals do not merely change the roles they play when context changes but, at least in some sense and to some degree, their identities too. This is one of Erving Goffman's basic premises in *Relations in Public* (Harmondsworth, Middlesex, Penguin, 1972), pp. 23ff.

14 I am indebted to Peter Scott for pointing this out to me and for suggesting this illustration.

15 Cf. Harré, *Personal Being*, p. 65: 'Conversation is to be thought of as creating a social world just as causality generates a physical one.' Despite his terminology, he does not understand interpersonal communication to be limited to speech, operating – as he does – with a notion of Austinian speech-acts. The distinction made by Habermas (in 'On Systematically Distorted Communication', *Inquiry*, 13 (1970), 212) between causality and substantiality as applied either to objects in the world or to the linguistically constituted world shows that he has an identical understanding at this point; i.e. that communicative activity creates persons in a way analogous to the fashioning of objects through causality. Neither of them suggests more than an analogical correspondence between physical causality and the social processes through which persons are formed.

16 Harré, *Personal Being*, p. 65.

17 Human beings are open systems in continuous interaction with their environment. This openness, whilst a permanent, ontologically necessary feature, need be neither conscious nor undistorted. It may be manipulative or manipulable. See R. Felix Geyer, *Alienation Theories* (Oxford, Pergamon, 1980), pp. xviif.

18 Cf. Vogel, *Body Theology*, pp. 12, 22f.

19 Jürgen Moltmann, *God in Creation* (London, SCM Press, 1985), p. 144. Karl Rahner, in a discussion of power (*Theological Investigations*, IV (London, Darton, Longman & Todd, 1966), p. 396), notices that, because the realm of human freedom is interpersonal, 'no one can act freely without impinging on the sphere of another's freedom'. For the space between the subjects and objects of communication is not a void or a vacuum, but is inhabited. Communication is bound, therefore, to have consequences for others. Hence the entrance of this public space is an ethical project.

20 Harré, *Personal Being*, p. 76.

21 Ibid., p. 85.

22 See ibid., pp. 92f., 104ff.

23 This is borne out by the wide range of psychopathologies which rest on a distorted self-identity (e.g. anorexia and bulimia nervosa) which

tend to be resistant to treatment except through forms of family therapy. This suggests that the pathological identity is sedimented from the structures and processes of communication in the family.

24 Harré, *Personal Being*, p. 104: 'Self-consciousness ... is not a new kind of consciousness but rather a new way of partitioning that of which one is aware by reference to a theory, one's theory of oneself.' The position unfolding here is very similar to that Bonhoeffer saw as required by much the same issues in *Sanctorum communio*, p. 45: 'Material spirituality [organised bodily communication] in each person is bound up with self-consciousness [point of experience] and self-determination [point of action] as the authentication of structural unity, and these can be formally defined as the principles of receptivity and activity. These acts are only conceivable as resting on man's sociality, arising from it and also with it and in it.'

25 Cf. L. Feuerbach, *The Essence of Christianity* (New York, Harper and Brothers, 1957), pp. 82f.: 'The *ego* first steels its glance in the eye of a *thou* before it endures the contemplation of a being which does not reflect its own image. My fellow-man is the bond between me and the world. I am, and I feel myself, dependent on the world, because I first feel myself dependent on other men. If I did not need man, I should not need the world. I reconcile myself with the world only through my fellow-man. Without other men, the world would be for me not only dead and empty, but meaningless. Only through his fellow does man become clear to himself and self-conscious; but only when I am clear to myself does the world become clear to me. A man existing absolutely alone would lose himself without any sense of his individuality in the ocean of Nature; he would neither comprehend himself as man nor Nature as Nature... That man is, he has to thank Nature; that he is as man, he has to thank man; spiritually as well as physically he can achieve nothing without his fellow-man.' On my reading of him, this conflicts with W. Pannenberg's view in *Anthropology in Theological Perspective* (Edinburgh, T.& T. Clark, 1985), pp. 407ff. He correctly asserts that consciousness of others is linked to the perception of the object-world – i.e. that others are discrete, physical objects and that the corresponding awareness of them as such indicates a more diffuse awareness of an object-world. He is, I think, wrong then to suggest that this object-awareness is primary (as well as ontogenetically prior) for subject-consciousness (i.e. consciousness of oneself and/or others as subjects). Object-consciousness is not linked to subject-consciousness because it is a direct mediation of the latter, but because both arise out of a public, intersubjective framework. I would not wish to deny that 'our knowledge of others is mediated through our object perception as such' but would add that consciously centred and controlled (subjective) interaction with either 'world' can only be the result of sedimentations within the intersubjective sphere.

26 See Harré, *Personal Being*, p. 22; and the view of Habermas in *Zur Logik der Sozialwissenschaften*, p. 147, quoted in McCarthy, *The Critical Theory of Jürgen Habermas*, p. 147. See also McCarthy's account of Habermas' critique of behaviourism, p. 151.

27 For the foregoing see Edward Farley, *Ecclesial Man* (Philadelphia, Fortress Press, 1975), pp. 116, 192f., 203–5, 207f.

28 Habermas' notion of communicative competence is therefore to be preferred to Chomsky's of linguistic competence, as the latter presupposes the existence of socially transcendent (i.e. monological) linguistic capacities. The acquisition of competence is therefore, for him, a matter of biological maturation, albeit mediated through language games. According to Habermas, it is a process of social maturation in which a particular language is acquired. See Habermas, 'Towards a Theory of Communicative Competence', *Inquiry*, vol. 13, part 4 (1970), 360–75; Noam Chomsky, *Aspects of the Theory of Syntax* (Cambridge, MA, MIT Press, 1965).

29 Harré, *Personal Being*, p. 87.

30 Ibid., p. 86.

31 Ibid., p. 161 (italics in original).

32 Ibid., p. 145.

33 I am grateful to Professor D. W. Hardy for the suggestion of this example.

34 There must, then, be the supposition of some internal process through which particular moments of the sedimented past are accessible to the perceived communication requirements of the present. This indicates a mechanism whereby 'a future output [is programmed] on the basis of a [*sic*] open feedback loop between the present situation of the subject ... and the present memory of a past relationship...' (Wilden, *System and Structure*, p. 97). Through such processes a person may reinterpret the fact and meaning of his or her past by maintaining a continuing relation with it: by carrying it into present relations. There is therefore a diachronic and dialectical relation between past relationships as presently sedimented and structuring identity and communication, and the present relationship which might require sedimented past and identity to be reinterpreted and re-presented. Such reinterpretation is the task of emancipatory reconstructions of history, whether of a group or an individual, and is what occurs through redemption. Communication is information. Individuality is information sedimented from a unique transactional history which can be subject to different forms of decoding or encoding in the future. Wilden (p. 97) makes an interesting comparison with Sartre's personal *projet* (*pour-soi*: present situation; *en-soi*: present memory of past relations) and Freud's *Nachträglichkeit* (and the three-fold structure of the ego). Edward Farley argues that societies endure as continuous identities in a similar way by 'remembering' their past through specific social institutions. See his *Ecclesial Reflection* (Philadelphia, Fortress Press, 1982), pp.

362–5, 368–72. Similar conceptions form the base insights of narrative theology – that Christian identity depends upon the retelling of the Christian narrative in community.

35 James Ogilvy (*Many Dimensional Man* (New York, Oxford University Press, 1977), pp. 100–4) takes a different line in assuming that the traditional domination of the ego is the outcome of an intrapersonal struggle between competing 'personalities' with equal claims. As an alternative he argues for a democratisation of one's diffuse 'personalities' in order to allow greater freedom. His argument is useful in showing the variety of non-identical 'personalities' (communicative self-identities) and self-interpretations available to one, but he fails to show how any transcendent self may exist as a *real*, though not necessarily tyrannical and mono-dimensional, point of unity.

36 This, for instance, is the position adopted by M. Foucault in *The Order of Things* (London, Tavistock Publications, 1970) and elsewhere.

37 This is a problem which has been recognised and partly addressed by Bonhoeffer in *Sanctorum communio* and by Daniel W. Hardy in 'Man the Creature', *Scottish Journal of Theology*, 30 (1977), 111–56.

38 Cf. Geyer, *Alienation Theories*, pp. xviii, 7, 22f.; and Ervin Laszlo, *Introduction to Systems Philosophy* (New York, Harper & Row, 1973), pp. 251f.

39 Cf. the position of Pannenberg, *Anthropology in Theological Perspective*, pp. 225f.

40 As made by C. F. Merton in *Social Theory and Social Structure* (Glencoe, The Free Press, 1949).

41 So Niklas Luhmann, *A Sociological Theory of Law* (London, Routledge & Kegan Paul, 1985), pp. 53f.

42 Harré, *Personal Being*, pp. 282, 284.

43 Habermas, *Knowledge and Human Interests* (London, Heinemann, 1978), p. 155.

44 Cf. Habermas, 'The Public Sphere: an Encyclopaedia Article (1964)', *New German Critique*, 3 (1964), 49.

45 Cf. Wilden, *System and Structure*, p. 491.

46 Cf. Moltmann, *God in Creation*, pp. 267f.; McCarthy, *The Critical Theory of Jürgen Habermas*, pp. 247f.; Farley, *Ecclesial Reflection*, pp. 354f., 358–61.

4 The redemptive transformation of relations: dialogue

1 Clearly, as the call may also bring to consciousness the existence of an oppressive network of relations through which that individuality has been sedimented, it can be socially as well as personally transformative. Jesus' ministry had an essential social component directed at Israel's distortion of the law into forms of legalism which distorted relations and individual identities. In freeing individuals from bondage to the law and from the effects of that bondage, He

incorporated them into a new form of community with God which eventually becomes socially transformative through the distinctive identity and orientation of the Church.

2 It is a very similar understanding of communicative activity inherent in the illocutionary force of performative utterances which yields the basis for Habermas' investigation of language through the reconstruction of the Universal Pragmatics of an ideal speech situation. In other words, to say something is to do something. Communication is, in part, the construction of a certain relationship. See 'Towards a Theory of Communicative Competence', *Inquiry*, vol. 13, part 4 (1970), 367–9. Communication establishes relations between oneself and others, oneself and the world, in which the very structures and orders of material human spirits become sedimented and expressed through call and response. Cf. Martin Buber, *I and Thou* (Edinburgh, T. & T. Clark, 1937), p. 3: 'Primary words do not describe something ... they bring about existence.'

3 Buber, *I and Thou*, p. 3.

4 Buber reaches this conclusion from a different route. For him the I–It relation means seeing the world as totally differentiated and therefore incapable of 'identity' (i.e. relation). One can see the other only as *totally* other and therefore as having no intrinsic claim on one, as an It rather than a Thou. In Buber's depiction there is difference but no identity, whereas for me this form of relation implies identity but no difference. The two positions are in fact different sides of the same process whereby difference is kept at a distance in order to be 'managed'. This distance is epistemic in the sense that it is not perceived by the monological subject, in whose mind there is identity only because differences have been screened out by the perception and feedback processes which are desensitised to them. This way of apprehending the world as identical with oneself, or with one's own designs (i.e. a total utilitarianism) actually fractures it into irreconcilable oppositions which have no point of contact because it is not recognised in its distance. In actual fact, then, I–It is a 'word of separation' because the 'object' is not seen in its independence and therefore relation (non-identity).

5 Habermas makes a distinction in this respect between instrumental action (orientated to success by technical interaction in the objective world), strategic action (orientated to success by manipulation, coercion, influence, etc. in the intersubjective world) and communicative action (orientated towards a mutuality of understanding via rational interaction in the intersubjective world). See *The Theory of Communicative Action*, vol. 1 (London, Heinemann, 1984), pp. 285ff.

6 *Sanctorum communio* (London, Collins, 1963), pp. 33f.

7 Bonhoeffer makes the theological grounding of this position clear in *Act and Being* (London, Collins, 1962), pp. 118, 148ff. Ultimately, no

person or group of persons can place themselves in truth on the basis of an autonomous self-understanding. Truth is a contingent event directed to people 'from outside', i.e. in the movement from God to humanity in Jesus Christ. Faith is therefore bestowed, rather than self-imposed, truth in which a person is directed to God in Christ and, in this movement, is opened to and directed towards the 'from beyond' of others.

8 'Law' has a two-fold structure of generalisation. In the first place, it can be abstracted from the particularity of the expectant person, whose expectations need not be based on personal experience or history, but mediated through public meaning-structures. It is unnecessary to undergo every experiential referent oneself in order to validate, or believe in the validity of, an expectation. Part of the nature of expectation is its abstraction from the particular events or circumstances from which its 'lawlikeness' was first derived, and therefore from the particular individuals experiencing those events. (Cf. Niklas Luhmann, *A Sociological Theory of Law* (London, Routledge & Kegan Paul, 1985), pp. 64f.). In the second place, it can be abstracted from the particularity of the expected person, who can be approached on the basis of the generality of, say, a social role or a biological organism. Though this is generally viewed by personalistic philosophy and theology as an inauthentic objectification of a subject, it is, in fact, a necessary means of dealing with people in the real world where there is neither complete freedom nor randomness nor subjectivity, but a high degree of semi-predictable, lawlike behaviour. See my further comments in this regard in Chapter 9.

9 Ibid., pp. 62, 64.

10 Ibid., pp. 57f. The obligation for continuity of identity in communication could, I think, be read as a theme in the Old Testament. God remains constant to Israel, but they fail to understand fully the nature of their relation in which Yahweh yields ethical space–time for Israel's response in the creative, free expectation of fidelity and is therefore open for the consequences of infidelity too. Israel misunderstands the divine judgment as a withdrawal from the relation because the Israelites understand Yahweh's intention and obligation towards them as contractual and therefore externally binding rather than as an expression of the divine will in self-obligation.

11 Habermas describes the 'double structure' of communication as 'a) The level of intersubjectivity on which speaker and hearer, through illocutionary acts, establish relations that permit them to come to an understanding *with one another*; and b) the level of *experiences and states of affairs* about which they want to reach an understanding in the communicative function determined by a)'. From 'Was heisst Universal Pragmatik?', p. 225, quoted in Thomas McCarthy, *The Critical Theory of Jürgen Habermas* (Cambridge, Polity Press, 1984), p. 282. Italics in original.

12 A positive celebration of difference should be a crucial element in the developing genitive (e.g. black and feminist) theologies and the positive addition and transformation they could represent of other theologies of liberation based more usually on economic class.

13 Daniel W. Hardy and David F. Ford, *Jubilate* (London, Darton, Longman & Todd, 1984), pp. 199f.; cf. pp. 153f. Buber's position, on the face of it, tends towards the extreme in his reservations concerning any and all verbalised responses to the Thou which, he suggests, immediately objectify it. The objectification is, of course, inevitable, but the stronger and more definite our response, the more strongly we bind the Thou and crush its mysterious and numinous quality. He suggests the paradox, presumably as a warning, that in saying, 'Thou', we in fact say, 'It', because, in forming the word, we project our preconceptions which filter Thou's reality. So we don't meet Thou in the relation, but only our ideas about Thou, and therefore only an It. Buber's recommendation is to maintain a silence before Thou to allow for Thou's self-communication in which we say, 'Thou' in an unformed, pre-linguistic (!) way. 'The melancholy of our fate' which haunts Buber's *I and Thou* here appears in its full and startling light. Every response I make to Thou which is not pure silence and which has any kind of structure (even that of a conversational pause) binds Thou to the world of It. See *I and Thou*, pp. 39f. (but cf. his more usually positive view of spirit at pp. 102f.).

14 The passive moment is therefore a means to more adequate self-knowledge as well as knowledge of the other and of the objective and intersubjective worlds. R. Felix Geyer's explication of this passive moment in terms of the off-line functioning of open systems is informative, although for him self-knowledge is 'reality tested' whilst off-line because he thinks the private, internal world is its appropriate communication context (*Alienation Theories* (Oxford, Pergamon, 1980), p. 44). In the passive moment 'information processing' takes place in which new information from external communication contexts may be interpreted and combined with previously coordinated contents of experience and consciousness, a previously sedimented identity. In the process of integration new inputs become coded as information, ascribed a meaning in terms of the combinations and transformations with and of presently stored information. This process therefore represents an information exchange cycle internal to the structure itself. The combination or impact of new input brings new meaning to previously stored information which has now to be recodified as new information, present to consciousness in a transformed way, creating a series of new 'inputs' removed from the original external stimulus for such an exchange. By temporarily (almost) halting communication with the environment so that a transformed self-integration may take place on the basis of this internal information exchange, subsequent

interaction may be improved on the basis of refined self- and other-
understandings. (See ibid., pp. 25, 31–3, 42–5.)

15 Cf. Carl R. Rogers, *On Becoming a Person* (Boston, Houghton Mifflin,
1961), p. 33, on the necessary components of a 'real' relationship: 'I
need to be aware of my own feelings, in so far as possible, rather than
presenting an outward façade of one attitude, while actually holding
another attitude at a deeper or unconscious level.'

16 Rogers, ibid., p. 332, suggests trying this as an experiment. 'Each
person can speak up for himself only *after* he has first restated the
ideas and feelings of the previous speaker accurately, and to that
speaker's satisfaction.' Italics in original.

17 Jürgen Habermas, 'On Systematically Distorted Communication',
Inquiry, vol. 13, part 3 (1970), 210ff.

18 Habermas, 'Towards a Theory of Communicative Competence', 369f.
Cf. W. Pannenberg, *Anthropology in Theological Perspective* (Edinburgh,
T. & T. Clark, 1985), p. 408; and Martin Buber, *Between Man and Man*
(London, Kegan Paul, 1947), p. 29: 'The two who are loyal to the
Eros of dialogue, who love one another, receive the common event
from the other's side as well, that is, they receive it from the two sides,
and thus for the first time understand in a bodily way what an event
is.' See also p. 170: 'In an essential relation ... the barriers of
individual being are in fact breached and a new phenomenon appears
which can appear only in this way: one life open to another... The
other becomes present not merely in the imagination or feeling, but in
the depths of one's substance, so that one experiences the mystery of
the other being in the mystery of one's own. The two participate in
one another's lives in very fact, not psychically, but ontically.'

19 This is the implication of Pannenberg's position in *What is Man?*
(Philadelphia, Fortress Press, 1970), p. 98.

20 Cf. Pannenberg, *Anthropology in Theological Perspective*, pp. 407ff.; and
Luhmann, *A Sociological Theory of Law*, pp. 25f.: 'The possibilities
actualised by other people are also possible for myself; they are my
possibilities too... Possibilities retain concreteness in me through
others, in that I experience what others experience without myself
being in the situation to actualise all their experiences as my own. I
thus attain the opportunity to adopt others' perspectives or to use
them in place of my own, to see with others' eyes, to hear reports and
am thus able to expand my own horizon of experience without loss of
time... To understand and adopt the perspectives of others as my
possible own ones is only possible if I see others as another I.'

21 Luhmann, *A Sociological Theory of Law*, p. 28. For his full position see
especially pp. 26–9.

22 Cf. Matt. 15:11: 'not what goes into the mouth defiles a man, but
what comes out of the mouth, this defiles a man'.

23 This is Barth's phrase, which he uses in his explication of being-in-

encounter in *Church Dogmatics* (Edinburgh, T. & T. Clark, 1936–61), III/2, pp. 250–74.

5 Personal integrity: centredness and orientation on others

1 The implications of this for social work and personal counselling are very rarely put into practice. The very human tendency to interpret all manipulation as *ipso facto* an unwarranted overreaching of the 'client' is widespread and often leads both to a resistance to the manipulation and to a more general resistance to the 'client' (by, e.g., the withdrawal of services).

2 For convenience, I have adopted traditional Christian terminology to discuss the relationship between 'self' and body. The terms 'soul' and 'self', as they are used in this book, are interchangeable in meaning, 'soul' being an understanding of 'self' generated within a religious context.

3 So Karl Barth, *Church Dogmatics* (Edinburgh, T. & T. Clark, 1936–61), IV/2, p. 443: 'Without his fellow-man he cannot be that which he would obviously like to be when he withdraws into himself – he himself in this totality, as the soul of his body. And I cannot and will not be an I without a Thou ... If he will not give himself to this other, he himself withers and perishes. Nor can a preoccupation with causes afford any substitute for that which only his fellow-man can offer him – the acceptance and positing of himself. It can do this only when in it he has a concern for man, and not to be free from man. If it is merely an instrument of this concealment he will not find himself in it; he will lose himself. He will lose both soul and finally body and become a mere vehicle of the cause, a wheel which drives and is itself driven.' He later identifies pursuit of exclusive self-interest and personal projects or 'cares' as the source of social and, consequently, personal fracture. One is isolated with one's own being in a state of anxiety over its dissolution in the future which, as anxiety, is actually brought into the present. This leads directly to the disintegration of soul and body. 'He reacts against it as a soul by that roving flight into better regions which he himself has selected or invented. And his body reacts against it in the form of all kinds of self-assertion, or in the form of renunciation, or in the form of sickness in all its organs' (IV/2, pp. 478f.).

4 See Jürgen Moltmann, *God in Creation* (London, SCM Press, 1985), pp. 17, 98–103, 263.

5 Jürgen Habermas, 'On Systematically Distorted Communication', *Inquiry*, vol. 13, part 3 (1970), 211f. Or, as Barth puts it, 'Man does not exist except in his life-act, and this consists in the fact that he animates himself and is therefore soul, and is animated by himself and is therefore body. His life-act consists in this circular movement, and at every point in it he himself is not only soul or body, but soul and body' (*Church Dogmatics*, III/2, p. 426).

6 Cf. Barth, *Church Dogmatics*, III/2, p. 367: a person 'is (1) there, and has existence, and in this respect is soul; and he is (2) there in a certain manner and has a nature, and in this respect is body'. The dual, hinge-like, aspect of the body is what is characterised in the polarities of *having* a body and of *being* a body. See Erich Fromm, *To Have or to Be?* (London, Sphere, 1979); Gabriel Marcel, *Being and Having* (Westminster, Dacre Press, 1949).

7 Cf. Barth, *Church Dogmatics*, III/2, pp. 396f.

8 Cf. again Barth's position, ibid., III/2, pp. 344, 394f., 419; III/4, p. 133; IV/2, pp. 421f.

9 Jürgen Moltmann, 'Resurrection as Hope', *Harvard Theological Review*, 41 (1968), 143.

10 On this point, see Reinhold Niebuhr, *Man's Nature and his Communities* (New York, Charles Scribner's Sons, 1965), p. 109; Donald Evans, *Struggle and Fulfilment* (London, Collins, 1980), pp. 24ff.; and R. D. Laing, *The Divided Self* (Harmondsworth, Middlesex, Penguin Books, 1982), pp. 39–43.

11 Cf. Bonhoeffer's combination of identity and committed action in his understanding of the sacramental identity of the Church. See E. Feil, *The Theology of Dietrich Bonhoeffer* (Philadelphia, Fortress Press, 1985), pp. 48–52.

12 Cf. Moltmann, *God in Creation*, pp. 261f. and, on the nature of friendship, *The Open Church* (London, SCM Press, 1978), pp. 51f., and *The Church in the Power of the Spirit* (London, SCM Press, 1977), pp. 115f.; also cf. Arthur A. Vogel, *Body Theology* (New York, Harper & Row, 1973), p. 92.

13 Niklas Luhmann, *A Sociological Theory of Law* (London, Routledge & Kegan Paul, 1985), pp. 57f., 66f. See also Habermas, 'What is Universal Pragmatics?', in *Communication and the Evolution of Society* (Boston, Beacon Press, 1979), pp. 61, 64.

14 Cf. Wolfhart Pannenberg, *Anthropology in Theological Perspective* (Edinburgh, T. & T. Clark, 1985), pp. 526f.

15 So Edward Farley, in *Ecclesial Man* (Philadelphia, Fortress Press, 1975), pp. 95–8, 109f., 164f.

16 Barth's view is oversimplistic on this point. In addition to the problems posed by the hierarchical relation he operates between the ruling soul and obedient body, he implies that communication is rational, and that there is a whole presence of soul in body, when that order or command structure is maintained: i.e. where the body carries out the intentions of the soul, or where communication is intentional, deliberate and aimed towards a specific goal. In other words, he equates the whole and genuine presence of the person in undistorted communication with the (in his theology, hierarchical) integration of soul and body (i.e. integrated, rational communication). See *Church Dogmatics*, III/2, p. 419.

17 This is surely *the* guiding principle of Christian ethics. See Lev. 19:18; Matt. 22:39f./Mark 12:31/Luke 10:27; Rom. 13:10; Gal. 5:14; Jas. 2:8.

6 Ethical resistance: testing the validity of disagreements

1 See Paulo Freire, *Pedagogy of the Oppressed* (Harmondsworth, Middlesex, Penguin, 1972), p. 61: 'to say the true word ... is to transform the world, saying that word is not the privilege of some few men, but the right of every man. Consequently, no one can say a true word alone – nor can he say it *for* another, in a prescriptive act which robs others of their words.'

2 Resistance here does not simply indicate a non-compliance (resisting another's will) which could be an acceptable alternative within the same general structure of expectations, but a non-compliance which cannot be immediately integrated into the normative structure of expectations and acceptability which are being operated by the other.

3 See Niklas Luhmann, *A Sociological Theory of Law* (London, Routledge & Kegan Paul, 1985), p. 32: 'It is only with the background of different possibilities that structures [of normative expectation] can become theme and problem.' And also p. 62: 'It is only disturbances which stimulate the (always possible) question of what the other is really experiencing and expecting.'

4 See ibid., p. 43, and also pp. 34, 38, 40, where he presents the option as 'to learn or not to learn' from disappointment.

5 See ibid., pp. 45f.

6 Cf. Daniel W. Hardy and David F. Ford, *Jubilate* (London, Darton, Longman & Todd, 1984), pp. 6f., 158ff.

7 It is sometimes appropriate to say, 'not now' or 'not here' as well as 'not like that'. The justification for this can only be the wider locus of commitments in which one is embedded. It is, in other words, a recognition of the demands placed on one by one's transcendence of that particular relation – e.g. in rushing to summon an ambulance to an accident one is justified in ignoring or brushing aside a friend wanting to engage in conversation. The 'not now' may also apply to age constraints on communication.

8 Jürgen Moltmann, *The Future of Creation* (London, SCM Press, 1979), pp. 122f. For Moltmann's further examination of the divine *pathos* see ibid., pp. 267–74, and 'The Crucified God and Apathetic Man', in *The Experiment Hope* (London, SCM Press, 1975), pp. 69–84.

9 The question of violence is rather more complex than space here allows me to indicate. I am uncertain, on this basis, as to the amount of restraint which may be justifiable, and the use of restrained force it may be necessary to use in more complex relations, especially on behalf of third parties. I cannot see, however, that this position obviously rules out the question of limited force or restraint in certain circumstances. Moltmann's rejection of the position taken here, despite the counter-logic of his argument elsewhere concerning suffering, love and hope, is instructive. He makes a major error in equating non-violence with non-resistance ('Racism and the Right to Resist', in *The Experiment Hope*, pp. 138–40, 143), thereby replacing the question of

violent or non-violent resistance with that of resistance or non-resistance. He therefore allows violent struggle within certain 'humane' limits set by the just aims of the struggle (basically a just war theory for revolution and insurgency – see 'Racism and the Right to Resist', pp. 140f.; 'The Hope of Resurrection and the Practice of Liberation', in *The Future of Creation*, pp. 99f.). Non-violence, however, need not be a principle or an abstract law (as Moltmann fears), but could function in a much more open way as a general norm of interaction with Christ as its formative 'principle'. Moltmann surrenders his all-embracing conception of simultaneous liberation in all dimensions of human life (see *The Church in the Power of the Spirit* (London, SCM Press, 1977), pp. 163–88; *The Crucified God* (London, SCM Press, 1974), pp. 291–338; *The Future of Creation*, pp. 109–14) for the supposedly *realpolitik* of political liberation alone. Precisely at this point Moltmann ignores the interconnectedness of all opposition and violence. This is instructive here because the incompatible direction and content of Moltmann's political and ethical commitment arises by the cross being 'treated as a formal principle in social ethics but not as a material principle. It formally indicates those with whom the Church must identify, but not the material content of that identification. The cross functions on a noetic level by leading to a critical theory, but not to a critical practice' (George Hunsinger, 'The Crucified God and the Political Theology of Violence', *The Heythrop Journal*, 14 (1973), 393f.

10 Habermas, 'What is Universal Pragmatics?', in *Communication and the Evolution of Society* (Boston, MA, Beacon Press, 1979), p. 59.
11 Ibid., p. 61.
12 Ibid., p. 1; Thomas McCarthy, 'A Theory of Communicative Competence', *Phil. Soc. Sci.*, 3 (1973), 139; Thomas McCarthy, *The Critical Theory of Jürgen Habermas* (Cambridge, Polity Press, 1984), pp. 279f.
13 'Zwei Bemerkungen zum praktischen Diskurs', in *Zur Rekonstruktion des historischen Materialismus* (Frankfurt, 1976), pp. 339f., quoted in McCarthy, *The Critical Theory of Jürgen Habermas*, pp. 323f.
14 Habermas, 'What is Universal Pragmatics?', p. 3.
15 See ibid., pp. 63ff.; Habermas, 'Towards a Theory of Communicative Competence', *Inquiry*, vol. 13, part 4 (1970), 370f. Habermas' position, however, is restricted to speech and, it could be argued, to a specific, elitist formulation of it (philosophical discourse or argumentation), via an implicit equation of communication with Austinian speech-acts. His notion of objective content has simply to do with propositional statements about the world ('constatives') in which a claim to truth is expressly made. Behaviour as such implicitly makes claims to truth which might become questionable to others and thereby the subject of dispute. For instance, stopping to pick up a hitch-hiker makes claims about the objective world such as: the car is

travelling in the right direction for the hiker; the place of destination will still be at the same physical location; the road map has been drawn accurately; internal combustion drives a motor car; there is enough room in the car for the hiker plus luggage; the car is capable of making the journey; etc.

16 Cf. Steven Lukes, *Individualism* (Oxford, Basil Blackwell, 1978), p. 73.

17 Habermas, *Theory and Practice* (London, Heinemann, 1974), pp. 150f.

18 Individualism, and Kantianism in particular, do of course draw strict ethical consequences from the spatial separation of individuals, but these really only create 'no go' areas for others in mutual recognition of the identical absoluteness of each as a monological constructor of a separate, though formally identical, world. In securing an identical and exclusive space for self-development and complete self-determination, monological ethics, in denying individuality as a structure of relatedness, destroys that part of the individual which is truly individual. It does this by making personal differences a function of numerical or spatial distance, thereby making the individual as a rational being an abstract and general creature rather than a particular, ethically transcendent person. In this way the moral claims and interests of each are considered formally identical: the pursuit of self-interest through exclusive personal projects. But this apparent identification hides the inherent conflict in such a view. For the personal projects of asocial individuals are exclusive, involving expansion into a social world which is, in fact, shared with others. This generates a conflict model of ethics and society.

19 Habermas, *Legimation Crisis* (London, Heinemann, 1976), p. 89. Genuine individuality therefore depends on proper internalisation of right norms. Cf. Karl Barth's distinction between the internal and external covenant in *Church Dogmatics* (Edinburgh, T. & T. Clark, 1936–61), III/1, pp. 228ff. For Habermas, however, it is only through intersubjectivity or shared autonomy, that right norms come about.

20 Habermas, 'Towards a Theory of Communicative Competence', pp. 371f.

21 Anthony Wilden, *System and Structure* (London, Tavistock Publications, 1980), pp. 432f., points out that total understanding is impossible because of the complexity of code, information and the simultaneous integration of the relation into a variety of relational contexts. He also considers that total understanding 'is not possible because such a situation has no survival value. It would amount to an overload of information and thus to death.' However, it should be noted for clarity that Wilden carefully equates 'full' or 'pure' dialogue with conditions which actually signify monologue.

7 Theology, Church and politics

1 See Wolfhart Pannenburg, *Anthropology in Theological Perspective* (Edinburgh, T. & T. Clark, 1985), pp. 480f.

2 So Edward Farley, *Ecclesial Reflection* (Philadelphia, Fortress Press, 1982), p. 243.

3 Edward Farley, *Ecclesial Man* (Philadelphia, Fortress Press, 1975), pp. 92f.

4 Ibid., p. 103.

5 This is why the kingdom is not, but requires expression in, a particular cosmology and the thought-forms of a particular social context. In using particular cosmologies and thought-forms to express the realities of redemption they are transformed. So Farley, ibid., pp. 103ff., 123f.

6 Ibid., p. 124: 'redemption involves both an incorporation of the [Christian] story and image into the myth [of determinate thought-forms] and the breaking of the myth'. Cf. Moltmann's understanding in this respect (though the issue arises for him with a much more restricted intention) in *The Crucified God* (London, SCM Press, 1974), pp. 324f. He identifies political theology in the bourgeois world as problematic because the Church seems forced to adopt one of two irreconcilable, but equally ineffectual, positions: to become a bourgeois civil religion, and thereby a part of the bourgeois order, or else retain a differentiated identity by remaining on the outskirts of the social world and so be removed from the scope of effective interaction with it. His solution is for the Church to 'make the idols of bourgeois religion superfluous in their own place and destroy them'. His assertion, however, is rather general and lacking in content, raising precisely the same problems as those he intends to address.

8 Political community

1 Because this is a 'creative appeal', grace and faith are not subsumed under independent, rational human categories. God's communication creates the ontological possibility of freedom-in-response which includes the passive moment involved in understanding. The power of the Holy Spirit through which the transformation of faith occurs is not coercive in an heteronomous sense, but imploring, beguiling and perhaps even compulsive – but it is so internally: i.e. it appeals to, transforms, but does not destroy the identity and rationality structure of the person. A sign of this is actually the inherent ambiguity (apparently non-compulsive rationality) of God's communication. It does not take the form of logical, rational propositions but, paradigmatically, the crucifixion of the incarnate which, in appealing to human understanding, actually transforms the understanding contained in human predicates. So God's rule is not despotic because it creatively appeals to human rationality in a way which allows people to participate through their own rational communication in that rule. That is the key issue. It is a difference between the use of power to induce a mechanical response and power in the sense of an authority appealing to understanding. See, for example, Dietrich Bonhoeffer, *Sanctorum communio* (London, Collins, 1963), pp. 58f.

2 See R. W. Lovin, 'Covenantal Relationships and Political Legitimacy', *Journal of Religion*, 60 (1980), 4f.

3 Cf. C. J. Friedrich's view of authority as derived from and/or referred to a consensual community in *Man and his Government* (New York, McGraw-Hill, 1963) and *Tradition and Authority* (London, Pall Mall Press, 1972).

4 Cf. Jürgen Habermas, 'The Public Sphere', *New German Critique*, 3 (1974), 49f.

5 Karl-Otto Apel, *Towards a Transformation of Philosophy* (London, Routledge & Kegan Paul, 1980), p. 278, states that it is the means of coming to true agreement, rather than the agreement as such, which is normative. This is also Habermas' position. See, e.g., 'Moral Development and Ego Identity', in *Communication and the Evolution of Society* (Boston, Beacon Press, 1979), p. 90.

6 Thomas McCarthy, *The Critical Theory of Jürgen Habermas* (Cambridge, Polity Press, 1984), pp. 314f. Luhmann defines potential third parties as those who, realistically, might be in a position to fulfil the same expectations under the norm – i.e. those who are members of a relevant communication community sharing a reciprocity of intentions. He also states the danger of institutionalising reference to participant third parties who would never have to be in the position of fulfilling such expectations themselves. Although he is referring to hierarchical social stratification, the warning would also apply, in principle, to horizontally differentiated persons (members of a different society in which such expectations are meaningless). 'With hierarchical differentiation we note that the ruling group no longer knows the conditions under which the people work and therefore set exaggerated demands. Today we are more aware of the opposite case: namely, that the people no longer know the conditions under which the ruling group works, and therefore set exaggerated demands.' (Niklas Luhmann, *A Sociological Theory of Law* (London, Routledge & Kegan Paul, 1985), p. 56; cf. p. 59). That, however, does not break the requirement that institutionalised expectations are generalised and anonymous in character, applying to those who actually have not so far been involved. Stabilised (institutionalised) expectation has to refer to non-actual but potential and therefore relevant third parties. So Luhmann, ibid., pp. 54f.: 'We now see more clearly why it is not simply a matter of the consensus of expectations of the person addressed when it comes to the social stabilisation of behavioural expectations. It would be too easily reversible and therefore not temporarily stabilisable. The tempting thought occurs that it should be sufficient to motivate appropriately the person whose behaviour is expected – the person who has to sweep the roads, who has to arrange a funeral, who has to hand in his declaration of income. But this is not sufficient. Such a strict specification and social localisation of the required consensus would reduce institutionally underpinned to

factually fluctuating consensus, would lower the communication barriers that surround the institution to a minimum and potentially put the removal of the institution always on the agenda. The "yes" or "no" could thus become dependent upon moods, situation, personalities or "partnership" agreements. A more long-term expectation, learning of expectations and anticipation of expectation in fairly unfamiliar situations, would thus be made impossible or at least made difficult. It is precisely the uncertainty, anonymity, unassessability, inaccessibility to questioning of relevant third parties which guarantees the reliability and homogeneity of institutions. It depends upon the neutralisation of all reference points, which could lead particular third parties to have any concrete expectation of something different. Institutions, therefore, do not depend on actual agreement between determinate expressions of opinion, but on their successful overestimation. Their continuity is guaranteed, as long as more or less everyone presumes that everyone agrees; possibly even when nearly everyone presumes that nearly everyone agrees.'

7 Given the need for autonomous and competent self-communication in what is, however, an unequal political situation, there is a requirement that political discourse should contain institutionalised strategies for refined other-reflection (corresponding to the requirement in personal discourse in Chapter 6).

8 Oppression is silence, an effective disenfranchisement from moral and political community by the absence of the specific experience of the world felt by the oppressed from the communication code. The fact that subjective experience cannot here be named in intersubjectively valid form, however, distorts both subjectivity and its experience. When such subjective contents become recognised by and expressible in community – i.e. become intersubjective contents of a community's experience – the fact that the experience may now be named and shared in a public world actually changes the experience. A topical instance is the recent concern over incest in particular and all forms of child abuse in general. Because their suffering is recognised and is now explicitly publicly nameable, child victims may now experience themselves and their suffering in a quite different way. Most importantly, they can experience themselves as innocent victims, rather than dirty and guilty, as the isolation of their suffering is broken when they realise that they are not alone, but part of a wider corruption of adult/parent–child relations. A similar case is indicated in the feminist slogan 'The personal is political', which declares the suffering and oppression of women in patriarchal domestic situations to be an aspect of the public oppression of women with immense political significance, rather than a result of purely individual identities and private arrangements. In their public repression, women have been refused their own words and the ethical space–time to manufacture their own definitions of themselves and the world. By

coming together and forming women's groups, they enter a
community whose structure of co-intention is radically different from
that of patriarchy. In it women index themselves as full
communicative subjects who may name the world together and
produce for themselves a distinctive version of it, with new contents of
experience, as a result of their now conscious distinct social location
together. Previously private contents of experience, cognition and
interpretation gain intersubjective validity in new community, the
provision of a new social matrix. See, especially, Dale Spender, *Man
Made Language* (London, Routledge & Kegan Paul, 1980), *passim*;
Marielouise Janssen-Jurreit, *Sexism* (London, Pluto Press, 1982),
pp. 290f., 296ff.

9 Cf. Karl Barth's position at *Church Dogmatics* (Edinburgh, T. & T. Clark,
1936–61), III/2, pp. 150ff., that real knowledge (faith) is a relation
between subject and object in which both subject and its thought are
created.

10 See Jürgen Habermas, 'A Postscript to *Knowledge and Human
Interests*', in *Knowledge and Human Interests* (London, Heinemann,
1978), p. 372.

11 See Habermas, *Legitimation Crisis* (London, Heinemann, 1976), p. 89:
'... only communicative ethics guarantees autonomy (in that it carries
on the process of the insertion of drive potentials into a
communicative structure of action – that is, the socialization process –
"with will and consciousness")'.

12 Habermas, *Knowledge and Human Interests*, pp. 312f. For the foregoing
cf. McCarthy, 'A Theory of Communicative Competence', *Phil. Soc. Sci.*,
3 (1973), 144f. and *The Critical Theory of Jürgen Habermas*, p. 317
(drawing on Habermas' *Wahrheitstheorien*); and Apel, *Towards a
Transformation of Philosophy*, p. 298, n. 113.

13 Habermas gives this role to the hermeneutic or cultural sciences:
'Whereas empirical–analytic methods aim at disclosing and
comprehending reality under the transcendental viewpoint of possible
technical control, hermeneutic methods aim at maintaining the
intersubjectivity of mutual understanding in ordinary-language
communication and in action according to common norms. In its very
structure hermeneutic understanding is designed to guarantee, within
cultural traditions, the possible action-orienting self-understanding of
individuals and groups as well as reciprocal understanding between
different individuals and groups. It makes possible the sort of
unconstrained consensus and the type of open intersubjectivity on
which communicative action depends. It bans the dangers of
communication breakdown in both dimensions: the vertical one of
one's own individual life history and the collective tradition to which
one belongs, and the horizontal one of mediating between the
traditions of different individuals, groups, and cultures. When these
communication flows break off and the intersubjectivity of mutual

understanding is either rigidified or falls apart, a condition of survival is disturbed, one that is as elementary as the complementary condition of the success of instrumental action: namely the possibility of unconstrained agreement and non-violent recognition. Because this is the presupposition of practice, *we call the knowledge-constitutive interest of* the cultural sciences "practical". It is distinguished from the technical cognitive interest in that it aims not at the comprehension of an objectified reality but at the maintenance of intersubjectivity of mutual understanding, within whose horizon reality can first appear as something' (*Knowledge and Human Interests*, p. 176 (italics in original)).

14 Cf. Bonhoeffer's comments on the differences between communities being characterised by the direction of their will in *Sanctorum communio*, pp. 53f.

15 Apel, *Towards a Transformation of Philosophy*, p. 277.

16 Ibid., pp. 277f.

17 Habermas, *Knowledge and Human Interests*, pp. 312f., and Apel, *Towards a Transformation of Philosophy*, p. 298, n. 113.

18 Liberation and European political theologies are therefore correct in proposing an identification between the Church's interest in the universal redemption of communication and the interest of oppressed groups. But that is not to say that the claims of such groups are necessarily just and their self-identification unproblematic. It is really too simplistic to propose an identity between the hoped-for different future of the oppressed and that of the Church, as that would imply that the claims of the oppressed constitute the determinate demands of the kingdom as such. On the contrary, such claims must show themselves to be just (i.e. generalisable) in the process of democratic will-formation, in which the claims may actually change. All claims are, in other words, subject to the universal determination of justice in the kingdom in which the just claims of the oppressed do, indeed, occupy a special critical position for the identification of the Church and the determination of justice more generally.

19 Liberalism is based on the contract-view of society – that people consent to government and socio-political order, since the best reliable means of securing their own self-interest and freedom is by limiting the claims, activities and self-interest of all under the law. The coercion of dissenters in any particular case may therefore be established on the basis of their own implied consent to that general form of ordered life. In every particular instance it is therefore only the will of the majority which counts. Through their explicit consent to the contract, individuals consent to their own coercion should they prove recalcitrant when in the minority. This unification of opposing interests so that, when differences arise, the dissenters accept the majority will (or the majority's right to resort to coercion) is possible only because the differences in interest are outweighed by their

supposed coincidence. Locke, for example, was able to equate (abstract, universal) individual with majority consent in the following way. He was keenly aware that differently propertied groups held opposing interests concerning the extent and direction of taxation, but could also see that all held in common an interest in the continuance of private property, facilitated by the order maintained through public taxation, as such. Dissenting minority interest would actually be served by identifying itself with the majority, preserving the greater self-interest – the minority will could then be identified with that of the majority, or rather subsumed by it, even in dissent! (See the discussion in C. B. Macpherson, *The Political Theory of Possessive Individualism* (Oxford, Oxford University Press, 1962), pp. 252ff.) In affording the individual a voice in the determination of society, liberalism makes two initial assumptions: that its recognition of socio-political subjects who are to be included in its franchise is unproblematic; and that individual reason and interest remain pure from social taint, so that all expressions and consequent aggregate majority decisions are unproblematic for all. See also n. 24 below.

20 Jürgen Moltmann, *The Church in the Power of the Spirit* (London, SCM Press, 1977), p. 177. Moltmann refers to W.-D. Marsch, *Christlicher Glauber und democratisches Ethos* (Hamburg, 1958).

21 Cf. Lovin, 'Covenantal Relationships and Political Legitimacy', 15.

22 Habermas' grounding of critical theory in the quasi-transcendental nature of language which provides an a priori apprehension of responsibility and autonomy (*Mündigkeit*) as a universal interest seems to represent a slip into an unjustified form of idealism. It does not admit the possibility that the apprehension and anticipation of ideals are determinate and may themselves be distorted and ideological. He is unable to ground language as a quasi-transcendental bearer of responsibility and autonomy alongside the distortions it inevitably accrues in the present because there is no reference point beyond language itself. Similarly, he is unable to justify adequately his preference for the dialogical form as a universal and not simply a restricted interest against the interest in, say, manipulation. If theology uncritically adopted this position, then it would run into these same difficulties whilst also constructing the sort of natural theology which would run into difficulties of a theological kind too. It is only by grounding responsibility and autonomy primarily in the vertical image and anticipative political activity in a truly transcendental communication context that theology may avoid the difficulties which both Habermas and natural theology run into. (The issue of an adequate notion of transcendence is also one of the points of contention between Moltmann's theology of hope and Bloch's philosophy which it appropriates. (See *The Theology of Hope* (London, SCM Press, 1967), pp. 19f., 221; and *Religion, Revolution and the Future* (New York, Charles Scribner's Sons, 1967), pp. 152f.).

23 This is in direct contrast with the notion of reason which equates its possibilities for centredness and decision-making with an individualised notion of freedom as independence. It is therefore through reason that persons (and groups) free themselves from dependence on natural and social systems and on others to become agents in history. Reason becomes the servant of private self-interest, especially the interest in complete independence. Most notably, this was the position of Hobbes in *Leviathan* (Oxford, Basil Blackwell, 1935), e.g. pp. 82, 117.

24 Every private interest requires the furtherance of the social possibilities of the privatisation of interests as such. In classical contract theories (Hobbes, Locke and Mill (in *On Liberty*, at any rate)), individuals are taken to be social atoms, ontologically independent of each other and logically and ontologically prior to social forms. They therefore have irreconcilable personal rights, interests, projects and destinies (for a modern statement of the notion of individualised projects and destinies see D. L. Norton, *Personal Destinies* (Princeton, NJ, Princeton University Press, 1976)). The state is necessary to prevent the irreconcilable personal projects and interests of these pure individuals from colliding and to protect the 'rights' of all to their irreconcilable interests which, because collision is inevitable in finite public space, must now be limited from impinging on others in order to protect the universally shared, but materially non-identical, interest in self-interest. The loss of autonomy to the social order is balanced by the security such an order achieves in limiting others' claims and exercise of power by agreeing to limit one's own. This sets the foundation for classical liberalism as it contains an explicit recognition of the valid rights and existence of others as other, and of interests which are not coincident with one's own. But the recognition of others is constituted in a way which precludes any real community with them and effectively isolates one with one's own interests, for to assist another in the purely individual act of being is in itself a denial of his or her supreme individuality and otherness (see Norton, *Personal Destinies*, pp. 10, 14, 87ff., 143; J. King-Farlow, *Self-Knowledge and Social Relations* (New York, Science History Publications, 1978), p. 135). The common interest in self-interest is held by individuals alone in an irreducible and often other-conflicting manner. Cooperation only occurs where the terms of cooperation further the interests of the contractors. The state in liberalism exists only in the interstices between individuals as a sort of buffer. Its constitution in this fashion secures individuals from incursions from others and from the state. The key feature of liberal and contract theories of the state is that individuals remain free and completely independent except through the exercise of their wills enclosed by the demands of self-interest. A useful critical orientation on contract and other liberal political theories is provided in C. B. Macpherson, *The Political Theory of Possessive Individualism*. See also n. 19 above.

25 Bonhoeffer rightly holds that community is founded on purposive acts of the will (intending communicative activity), i.e. a structure of co-intention: 'Specifically human community is present only when conscious human spirit is at work, that is, when community is based on purposive acts of the will. Human community does not necessarily arise from such acts of the will but it has its being in them . . . It is characteristic of communal acts of the will that they are not necessarily directed towards an object outside the person, but that they all point in the same way, that is, towards one another. The one man must in some way intend and will the other, and be intended and willed by him . . . "Agreement" which lacks this reciprocal relation is simply parallelism, and this is not overcome by the knowledge that the other will is running the same course. The agreement must have this two-way traffic, and only then can we speak of "unity" of will: it rests upon the separateness of persons. Community is not having something in common – though formally this is found in every community – but it is constituted by reciprocal will. Communities which are founded on merely formal agreement (an audience in a lecture room, etc.) are not communities of will . . . "Unity" of will means that the content which is intended and willed is identical for all' (*Sanctorum communio*, pp. 53f.).

26 Cf. Lovin, 'Covenantal Relationships and Political Legitimacy', pp. 5f., where Lovin, quoting from Jonathan Edwards, argues that the incorporation of the subjective moment of understanding into a covenantal relation with God does not mean that events make sense to *me*, evaluated in terms of my interests and needs, but indicates an incorporation into a more comprehensive view and rationality. The moment of understanding is a comprehensive comprehending.

27 Ibid., p. 11.

28 Habermas, 'Moral Development and Ego Identity', p. 93.

9 Institutions

1 Martin Buber's notion of 'the between' (*der Zwischen*) has this status (see, e.g., *I and Thou* (Edinburgh, T. & T. Clark, 1937), pp. 39, 63; *Between Man and Man* (London, Kegan Paul, 1947), pp. 21, 36, 202ff.), as does Bonhoeffer's use of 'objective spirit' in *Sanctorum communio* (London, Collins, 1963), pp. 65f.

2 The mode in which information is retained is as important as the actual content of the 'memory' as such. Repressed or otherwise subconscious contents are informative for identity in probably inverse proportions to their availability for conscious recollection and reflection.

3 Compare this view with the positions taken by Peter Berger and Thomas Luckmann in *The Social Construction of Reality* (Harmondsworth, Middlesex, Penguin, 1967), pp. 85–9.

4 This is the function Niklas Luhmann gives to law. See *A Sociological Theory of Law* (London, Routledge & Kegan Paul, 1985), pp. 73–82.

5 Cf. W. Pannenberg, *Anthropology in Theological Perspective* (Edinburgh, T. & T. Clark, 1985), p. 412: 'Permanence arises only when to particularism is added the element of mutuality, which motivates individuals to adapt themselves to others. We are dealing here with an aspect of the exocentricity of human behaviour, due to which the relation to the objects of the perceived world is connected to the relation to other human beings [i.e. through an intersubjective code which establishes 'objective meaning'] ... A first condition for the institutional stabilization of human behaviour is that interaction should take the form of reciprocity (correspondence), that is, that the element of mutuality, of adaptation to others, be operative on both sides. Institutionalization is accomplished as soon as a *measure* of correspondence determines the behaviour of human beings toward one another; behaviour then becomes reciprocal' (italics in the original). Also Jürgen Habermas, 'A Postscript to *Knowledge and Human Interests*', in *Knowledge and Human Interests* (London, Heinemann, 1978), p. 365: 'When psychic processes like sensations, needs and feelings enter into the structures of linguistic intersubjectivity, they are transformed from inner states and episodes into intentional contents. Intentions can only be stabilized over time, if they become reflexive, i.e., if they are connected with one another through reciprocal expectations. In this way, sensations, needs and feelings (pleasure/pain) are transformed into perceptions, desires and satisfactions or sufferings. Once transformed in this way, they claim to be objective, or remain merely subjective. Perceptions of objects of experience are always put forth in an objective form, i.e., as *statements*. Desires *can* be put forth in an objective form: If they are, they claim to express generalizable interests which can be justified by referring to norms of action. The same goes for satisfactions. They, too, can be objectivated, if they submit to justification by standards of *evaluation*. Statements (declarative judgements), prescriptions (normative judgements) and evaluations (evaluative judgements) all express an objective "content of experience". The objectivity of perception is guaranteed by the intersubjectively shared structure of objects of possible experience, whereas the objectivity of prescriptions and evaluations is guaranteed by the universal acceptance of norms of action and standards of evaluation, respectively' (italics in the original). Cf. Luhmann, *A Sociological Theory of Law*, p. 30.

6 Edward Farley, *Ecclesial Reflection* (Philadelphia, Fortress Press, 1982), p. 232.

7 In liberalism there is an individualistic conception of personal essence as that which is asocial and indeterminate. The person is a universal social abstraction remaining constant within changing social formations. That which is constant is the inner nature or self, the realm of pure individual freedom which remains a source of autonomy no matter what the character of external circumstances. It is easy to move from this internal sphere of freedom which – free from the taint

of all external relations – always freely constitutes or chooses their meaning and substance, to a position where the private freedom is so divorced from external conditions that it ceases to have any interests in external emancipation or public, socio-political life as such. Where freedom is completely identified with an inalienable, individual attribute, it may co-exist with any form of authoritarianism or oppression which has to be posited as the freely chosen form of external, public life. See, for example, Herbert Marcuse's criticism of Sartre and Calvin (though his comments in this respect do not really apply to Calvin himself) in *From Luther to Popper* (London, Verso Editions, 1972), pp. 51f., 57, 63f., 71, 83f., 172. Cf. B. Gerrish's remarks concerning the implications of the Augsberg confession in *The Old Protestantism and the New* (Edinburgh, T. & T. Clark, 1982), pp. 259f.

8 So Farley, *Ecclesial Reflection*, pp. 345f.: 'No actual human society has an immutable essence that endures, successfuly resisting change by adopting different modes of appearance in altered historical situations. Social duration is itself a process, the structural aspects of which are certain continuities. These continuities enable us to differentiate one global society from another by grasping each one's distinctive structures, which in some sense persist over time. But this persistence itself is an ever-adapting phenomenon and therefore a process . . . such continuities are an abstract cross-section of a larger entity (an actual society or community) which is itself in a constant, even if very slow, state of alteration. Nor should we see structure and process as simply alternative qualities of social entities. The *structural* or continuity aspect of a society must constantly change if it is to continue over time. Thus, without change and adaptation in new historical situations (such as the diaspora), Israel's continuity as a community of the Torah would have been severely threatened if not lost. Thus the vehicles of *continuity* must at the same time function as vehicles of adaptation and *innovation*' (italics in the original).

9 See ibid., pp. 370ff.

10 See Thomas McCarthy, *The Critical Theory of Jürgen Habermas* (Cambridge, Polity Press, 1984), pp. 255f., where he quotes from Habermas, 'Geschichte und Evolution' in *Zur Reconstruktion des historischen Materialismus* (Frankfurt, 1976).

11 Cf. Pannenberg, *Anthropology in Theological Perspective*, pp. 446ff., where he links the independence of individuals from the state with their destiny beyond history and therefore beyond any and all states.

12 I agree with Farley's view that it is the proper mode of the redeemed community's duration which determines the way scripture functions in the Church, rather than an antecedent 'scripture principle' authorising specific forms of duration (*Ecclesial Reflection*, pp. 278f.). He is also correct, in my view, in his suggestion that, because the Church is an ideal in determinate, historical form, uncovering the essential elements of ecclesial duration as such cannot be a

straightforward empirical exercise; for historical incarnations of the Church contain its ideal only in implicit and (though Farley does not say so at this point) in transformed ways. The necessary procedure will uncover 'teleological ideal elements resident in the actual' (pp. 219f.).

13 See ibid., pp. 224f. and Farley, *Ecclesial Man* (Philadelphia., Fortress Press, 1975), pp. 176ff.

14 For this and the following, see Farley, *Ecclesial Reflection*, pp. 252–8 (and cf. the earlier position in *Ecclesial Man*, pp. 178f.).

15 On the impossibility of achieving righteousness within the law and condemnation of the failed attempt so to do, see, e.g., Ps. 143:2; Rom. 3:20, 27–31, 6:23; Gal. 2:16, 3:11; Jas. 2:12f.

16 This may seem a dangerous position with regard to the biblical conception of law as divinely ordained and therefore having a changeless content; however, that law is only known indirectly through determinate forms. Human cognition and application of the one divine law are therefore plural.

17 Cf. Reinhold Niebuhr, *The Nature and Destiny of Man* (London, Nisbet, 1943), vol. II, pp. 257f.; W. Pannenberg, *Christian Spirituality and Sacramental Community* (London, Darton, Longman & Todd, 1984), pp. 65f.; and Luhmann, *A Sociological Theory of Law*, pp. 24f., 31f., 52.

18 Niebuhr, in *The Nature and Destiny of Man*, vol. II, pp. 259f., understands the intersubjective commitment necessary for justice and the meeting of obligation towards others: 'The unemployment benefit which the community pays to those out of work is partly an expression of the sense of obligation of the more privileged members of the community towards those who are less fortunate. They find an advantage in meeting this obligation according to fixed principles instead of relying on their occasional feeling of pity for this or that needy person. They know furthermore that their own knowledge of comparative needs is very inadequate and that they require the more impartial and comprehensive perspective of the total community, functioning through its proper agencies. This function of the principles of unemployment relief presents the most positive relation between specific rules and the sense of brotherhood.' He also realises the social compromise which fixes the level of such benefit: 'The actual schedule of payments upon which the community finally decides represents the conclusion of social, rather than any individual, mind, and is the consequence of a perennial debate upon the subject. It is probably a compromise between conflicting viewpoints and interests. It is certainly not an unconditionedly "just" solution of the social problem involved. The privileged may in fact accept it for no better reason than that they fear the revolt of the poor. This aspect of the situation proves the impossibility of completely separating the concepts of "principles of justice" from the hopes and fears, the pressures and counter-pressures of living communities, expressed below the level of a rational calculation of rights and interests.'

19 In fact, this is what the democratic process in which normative codes of interaction are formed (which is simultaneously the democratic formation of wills), in which all potentially relevant interests are explicated in free communication orientated towards genuine and rational understanding, provides – a narrowing of the gap between political and public legitimacy and the morality of personal life.

20 See, e.g., Matt. 5:17–48; Rom. 6:15–23, 7:4–25, 8:1–4, 13:8–10; I Cor. 9:20f.; Gal. 5:6, 13f., 18.

21 See, e.g., Matt. 6:1–24. Cf. the position of Karl Barth, *Church Dogmatics* (Edinburgh, T. & T. Clark, 1936–61), III/I, pp. 228ff.; and Niebuhr's criticism of Brunner's *The Divine Imperative* in a footnote to *The Nature and Destiny of Man*, vol. II, pp. 260f.

22 Barth, *Church Dogmatics*, III/2, pp. 243f., 286.

23 This does not necessarily mean, however, that institutions need to contain face-to-face or one-to-one relations within their actual structure. A charitable institution committed to justice in the Third World, for instance, which functions on the basis of single contacts between the givers and recipients of aid (as in some child sponsorship schemes, for example) will almost certainly prove counter-productive and wasteful of resources where limited resources are a major problem. It also substitutes the partiality of one-to-one relationships for the structural commitment to justice which is necessary. In a situation of this sort, the principles of dialogue in smaller-scale relations may be secured simply by securing some system of feedback so that the giving–receiving relation attains to some form of reciprocity, at least in the intentions of the givers. A paternalistic monologue is more difficult to sustain where recipients are intended and recognised as full human partners, and so as subjects and potential givers themselves who might be expected to make decisions concerning aid priorities, be able to assist themselves in some ways, and so on. At the very least, it must mean attending to their own self-understanding and definitions of need, even if this can be done only by imaginative empathetic 'indwelling'. A priority in the aid programme is also likely to be the facilitation of autonomy in the receiving community and a determination not to foster vicious cycles of dependence. This kind of feedback in dialogue might lead to a better-informed understanding of the realities of the situation as well as to a sensitivity to the ways in which givers may themselves be partly responsible for it (e.g. through unjust patterns of world trade). There may be scope here for one-to-one relations, but these are likely to be on a representational basis (as in, say, a fieldworker meeting a village leader), but these relations are not constitutive of the organisation and must be subjected to the requirements of the receiving community as may become apparent in their communication.

24 See, e.g., Matt. 5:23ff.; 22:39f. Love is not limited by proximity (Matt. 5:48), Jesus' definition of neighbour being typically expansive –

including anyone to whom one may be of concrete, practical assistance.

25 Cf. Pierre M. Brunetti, 'Health in Ecological Perspective', *Acta Psychiatrica Scandinavica*, 49 (1973), 400f., 403, who – in contrast to the position I adopt below – holds that 'ecological autonomy' requires *direct* participation in the 'proximal ecological sphere'.

26 R. Felix Geyer, *Alienation Theories* (Oxford, Pergamon, 1980), p. 124, states that: 'the trend towards indirect-interpersonal and societal environments, and away from natural and direct-interpersonal ones, implies a *decrease* in environmental observability – which is a correlate of increased environmental complexity' (italics in the original). The natural environment, as relatively stable (i.e. reacts only little as a whole to input) and with individual elements of relatively low internal complexity, is readily observable and understandable. In contrast, the interpersonal environment is more complex and less observable because of the increased internal complexity of its personal elements relative to one's own (the observer). This is heightened where interaction is indirect. The societal environment has a higher degree of internal complexity than the personal observer and is sometimes of a divergent (anti-personal) form. It is difficult to observe and predict because it is hard to reduce its complexity to understandable and predictable laws which would make response to input reliable.

27 Ibid., pp. 18f.

28 On this last point, see ibid., p. 118. The restriction is both subjective (motivational) and a part of the 'objective' social structure (restriction of education, opportunity, etc.). The subjective side might, of course, represent an internalisation of the social expectations attaching to this particular social location. So oppressed groups may not experience the will to enter socially restricted areas of life. This is usually compensated for by an increased motivation to enter and succeed in others (e.g. the disproportionate number of black athletes).

29 Ervin Laszlo, *Introduction to Systems Philosophy* (New York, Harper & Row, 1975), p. 253 (italics in the original).

Glossary

autonomy, communicative
The capacity to enter relations and communicate as a partly
independent and free subject, as someone whose being and
communication are not completely determined by the past, by others,
by context or by the present relation. As autonomous and
independent, one may therefore manufacture and communicate
meaning which is unique to oneself and which could not have been
predicted. Similarly, one may initiate and be the original source of
communication in ways which cannot be completely predicted by
others in advance.

centred
The achievement of organising one's life from an organisational locus
within oneself; the ability to refer the features of the world to oneself
and one's own location, so that the possibilities for action may be
focussed on as they relate to oneself and so be self-ascribed. It is this
which makes it possible to organise one's life and communication in
an autonomous way, to exercise control in communication and over
oneself. It also makes acceptance of responsibility for one's actions
possible, since by being centred one may act intentionally and
deliberately.

co-intention
The intention of one or more partners in a relation or community
which is shared by those in it. *See also* intention.

collectivism
A way of understanding what is human which emphasises large-scale,
societal structures over against the personal and interpersonal, and
which generally regards the latter as determined (strong sense) by the
former.

communication
Any interaction in which there is change and exchange and in which information is transformed and transferred.

communication code
A social 'language': the rules which order and codify relations by regulating the public meaning and exchange value which particular communications, acts, persons, events, and so on may have in particular contexts within a society. The code therefore indicates the social appropriateness and the public meaning of, for example, this person saying this or doing that here and now.

communicative form
(a) The stance a person takes in relation; the form of his or her presence in communication and relation. The communicative form habitually taken corresponds to his or her personal identity.
(b) The type which a communication corresponds to; the way in which it is patterned as either dialogical or monological, undistorted or distorted.

communicative identity
The personal identity derived from and present in one's communication.

community
A form of common life involving reciprocity and sharing which is based upon the difference and independence of the members. All members of the community are admitted as subjects; it is therefore a process of intersubjectivity. *See also* intersubjectivity.

context
The system or network of relations which forms the environment in which particular relations and communications take place and within which particular persons live and act, representing at least one dimension of their lives.

creation–redemption
A compound word expressing the continuity and co-inherence of all God's interaction with the world, and in particular rejecting the notion that God acts sequentially first as creator and then as redeemer.

deep 'self'
A structure of selfhood which is deeply embedded and so at some remove from the immediacy of particular relations and their effects; it generates a series of models (local 'selves') which structure and

organise communication and experience within particular, local contexts. *See also* 'self'.

determinate
Referring to the particular ways in which a particular society, group, relation, communication or person is determined, informed and otherwise influenced by the prevailing network of historical, social, political, interpersonal and other forces.

dialogue
A relation of mutuality and reciprocity which involves the subjective engagement, and therefore autonomy, of two or more partners. In dialogue there is a sharing of the dialogue roles of I and Thou, so that all partners are given space and time for independent communication and are attended to by the others. Because attending to the independent communication and being of others can change one's own understanding of them, oneself or the world (and potentially one's identity as well), dialogue is also a dialectical process and more like a spiral than a circle.

distorted communication
Any communication in which either communicator or recipient is intended as an object of communication. Where this is deliberate, the communication will be orientated towards the misunderstanding and manipulation of the recipient by keeping real intentions and interests guiding the communication private.

ex-centric
Structured by a movement from a personal centre outward towards the personal centres of others. Through dialogue one moves towards (and therefore recognises) the independent realities of others and returns to oneself, becoming centred in oneself by moving beyond oneself.

explication
An ideal form of interaction free from coercion, constraints and all other possible sources of distortion; enjoined in order to establish whether certain norms, interests, understandings, etc. are true, valid or just, by establishing whether they are purely particular or rational (generalisable).

individual
Generally used of a person, although sometimes applying to other entities, who is separated in some way and to some degree from others and from the environment in such a way that she or he may be counted as one. The bonds which hold internal organs and structures

together will be stronger than external ones in at least one dimension of life (e.g. the physical).

individualism
Any form of explanation or understanding which takes individuals as the primary or sole reality; which explains social realities by reducing them to their constituent individual parts in the belief that only individuals really exist. There is also a tendency to attach greater significance to internal states and properties than to external conditions or relations in explaining the nature of personal life.

individuality
The unique identity of an individual; that which makes him or her identifiable as a separate person in social interaction. *See also* personal identity.

information
Any communication content which is ordered and may therefore be ascribed a meaning according to a communication code. Since it may be decoded, it may affect a recipient, provided the information is somehow new. For information to be informative it must also be sufficiently different from the recipient's present states of understanding, knowledge, etc. to make a difference to them.

institution
A semi-stable structure of communication and relation; a stabilised pattern of co-intending through which relations may take on a structured and routine character.

intention
The underlying expectation, assumption, or hope carried in all communication, relating to the forms in which one offers one's own or seeks others' presence in a relation or to the form the relation itself is to take.

intersubjectivity
A process of common life formed through, involving and requiring the interaction of persons as subjects.

'memory'
A metaphorical use of the word to refer to any way in which past interaction, its effects and its interpretation are held by a person in, e.g., structures of understanding and identity, or instinctive behaviour (it therefore refers to more than psychological phenomena or processes). Through the processes and structures of 'memory', past interaction is carried into the present and may inform present and future communication and identity.

mutuality of understanding
An agreement (often implicit) concerning the truth of a communication and the rightness and acceptability of the form of relation between the partners and of their respective identities in it. This is genuine and undistorted where there is an absence of coercion and deception, and where it is based upon the free and formally reciprocal recognition and intention of the partners, and consequently may incorporate their genuine interests.

object of communication
(a) A person who is simply a recipient of communication rather than an originator of or autonomous participant in it.
(b) A person who or entity which is being referred to or named in communication.

other-reflection
This occurs in the passive moment of communication and entails reflection on one's perception of the other's self-understanding and on her or his understanding of oneself and of the world as these are embedded in her or his communication. This is especially important where the other's understanding is unexpected or conflicts with one's own. In other-reflection one tries to explore and comprehend the meaning and possible validity of the other's understanding.

overcomplexity
Refers to a communication context or social structure or institution being so much greater in organisational complexity than that of some or all persons, that meaningful, autonomous and centred interaction becomes impossible for them. Complexity may refer either to the quality or quantity of information.

overdetermination
The coercive and complete determination of an interaction, a person, or a state of affairs which affords no room for independent, responsible existence and which therefore squashes autonomy and subjectivity.

passive communication
The stance of receptivity to another's communication in a relation. This attending to the other should still be considered communication, even though it is not an explicit or active form of engagement, since it is none the less a maintenance of oneself in the relation, and this always contains implicit communication because it has a particular form and structure.

passive moment
A communicative pause which allows space and time for others' independent communication and for self-reflection and other-reflection.

person
An individual who is publicly identifiable as a distinct, continuous and integrated social location from whence communication may originate and to which it may be directed; who has the capacity for autonomous engagement in social communication, and who has a unique identity sedimented from previous interaction.

A person's being and communication are not therefore externally determined, but are generated by this unique identity. This, in turn, is not something purely private, for it has been derived from the history of relations which has taken place around this particular social location and in which this person has participated as a subject. A person is thus not simply 'thrown up' by a process of communication going on around him or her over which he or she has no control, but is born and nurtured through a process which seeks his or her engagement as a subject. It is through the person's own participation in and interpretation of this history or interaction that it takes a particular character, becomes centred on the person in a particular way and builds up an idiosyncratic identity. *See also* sedimentation.

As a unique social location, a person is a unique point of view or experience to which communication may be directed and from which it may be experienced/received in a unique way; and a unique point of action from whence communication may originate. As a unique location, a person may also become the subject or object of communication in ways unique to him or her.

personal identity
The unique way of being and relating of an individual person which is a compounded sedimentation of a significant history of interaction: the form of punctuation operating between oneself and others, the world and God; the way in which one exists 'in', to, for and with others; a dynamic line of continuity which endures (though often in changed form) through changes in context and through time which make one identifiable as, at least in some sense, the same person in different times and places.

primary public structure
The abstract social 'world' consisting of persons and their intercommunication, indicating the universal constituents of personal and social life – such as: physical embodiment, a communication code, etc.

proximate communication context
A local and/or small-scale network of interpersonal relations – e.g. the household, the immediate place of work.

proximate relations
Interaction between those one meets face to face, especially those whom one normally meets in the course of everyday life.

secondary psychological structures
Internalised reflections of the structures of the public, social 'world'
which are acquired through social interaction. They operate as models
or theories of personhood which enable competent interaction in the
social 'world' from which they have been learned by enabling a
person to organise psychical activity (and so communication) in a
socially meaningful way. *See also* 'self'.

secondary social structures
The specific and concrete ways in which the distribution and
organisation of labour and social status (and thereby of material goods
as well) are regulated in particular societies; the specific ways in
which a society is structured.

sediment
The personal identity which has 'settled', been 'deposited' or 'laid
down' through a history of significant relations. It is temporary and
dynamic because it may be transformed through subsequent
interaction, the effects of which may 'fall out' and accumulate around
the personal centre already deposited.

sedimentation
The process whereby a personal identity is accumulated through a
significant history of address and response which has flowed around a
particular point location and gathered around it in a unique way, so
structuring a uniquely centred personal identity.

'self'
A particular theory concerning the nature and structure of the inner
personal core around which a personal identity is structured; a belief
that one has a certain identity-giving internal complex. It is through
the deployment of such a theory that one is able to centre one's
experience, consciousness and communication (and to do so in a
socially appropriate and meaningful way), and so organise one's life as
a subject of communication able to interact with some degree of
control and autonomy. 'Self' should therefore be understood as a means
of organising oneself through a belief about oneself; as an
organisational process rather than a substance or entity.
   The 'self' one takes oneself to be is a portable means of organising
oneself in diverse times and contexts as a unified and continuous
subject of communication – the same person.

self-identity, personal
The understanding one has of one's particular identity; one's own
experience of oneself as a specific 'self'.

self-reflection
Occurs in the passive moment of communication and refers to self-checking procedures whereby one reflects on the honesty, accuracy, efficacy and validity of one's own communication and stance in the relation, and on the reception and interpretation of these by the other. Because it involves attending to the other's interpretation as this is carried in her or his communication, it cannot be considered to be any kind of attempted withdrawal from the relation.

sense of self
A person's own sense or experience of being one and self-same, a single unity of consciousness, experience and action; the sense of being a stable location in interaction.

Spirit, Holy
The third Person of the Trinity; divine, life-giving energy, the social consequence of which is organisation; the organisational energy of communication open to others and to self-transformation. When the Spirit co-inheres with the Word, which gives order and structure, open forms of individual and communal life are formed.

spirit, individual
The interactional dynamism of a person which occurs with the operation of the 'self' or soul which gives a specific form of identity in relationships by organising communication; the energy with which a person organises her or his appearance in communication and relation and the boundary between 'self' and others.

subject of communication
A sender or source of communication capable of self-directed and controlled interaction in various contexts and dimensions of life, who – since he or she is centred – may recognise, 'own' and take responsibility for his or her own communication.

Thou–I
The double-aspect of a person who is simultaneously an I for her or himself and a Thou for others who recognise this fact; simultaneously source and recipient of communication.

undistorted communication
Communication which recognises and intends both oneself and others as autonomous subjects of communication whose realities are to some degree independent of one another and which can only be known through their independent self-communication; the communication is therefore undertaken in recognition of the other's independence and mystery and provides space in the relation for the other's free communication.

Word

The second Person of the Trinity; the divine form-giver and rational structurer of organised life. God's Word gives order and structure, whilst the Holy Spirit is the dynamic energy which opens structures up to change and otherness. Their co-inherence therefore leads to open structures and forms of organisation.

Index